Teaching Industrial Education:
Principles and Practices

Teaching Industrial Education
Principles and Practices

By **ROBERT C. ANDREWS**
Associate Professor of Industrial Education
Keene State College of the University of New Hampshire
Keene, New Hampshire

A revision of TEACHING THE INDUSTRIAL ARTS, *by Emanuel E. Ericson*

Bennett Publishing Company
PEORIA, ILLINOIS 61615

Copyright ©1976

By Maurine E. Ericson
and Robert C. Andrews

Previous edition copyrights 1946, 1956, 1960 by Emanuel E. and
Maurine Ericson under the title TEACHING THE INDUSTRIAL ARTS

All Rights Reserved

81 82 83 84   RRD   5 4 3 2

ISBN 87002-079-X

Library of Congress Catalog No. 75-15361

Printed in the United States of America

Preface

This revision of TEACHING THE INDUSTRIAL ARTS reflects the necessity for updating a fundamental text, yet maintains the intended design of Emanuel E. Ericson, as expressed in his Preface to the first edition. TEACHING THE INDUSTRIAL ARTS discussed the two main activities of the industrial educator: analysis and planning, and the presentation of teaching material.

In maintaining that format, this revision devotes Chapters 2–7 to a discussion of the principles of industrial education. These chapters provide the historical and philosophical foundations necessary for teacher preparation. Chapters 8–14 discuss the practices of teaching in industrial education. These chapters include suggestions for the implementation of teacher-directed instructional activities and student-oriented learning activities. Chapter 1 and Chapter 15 relate directly to the industrial educator and to the teaching profession in general.

The subject matter has been expanded to include both major areas of industrial education: vocational-industrial and industrial arts, the original emphasis. Hence, the title has been changed to TEACHING INDUSTRIAL EDUCATION: PRINCIPLES AND PRACTICES. The text is now more adequate to serve industrial educators in all types of instructional settings, regardless of their individual programmatic emphasis.

Undertaking the revision of such a standard reference necessitates that each change be thoroughly scrutinized and each addition critically evaluated. All chapters of the original text have received some alteration. Some of the shorter chapters were combined if they were concerned with related material. Substantial additions have been included in Chapter 1: Effective Teaching; Chapter 4: Course Construction; Chapter 6: Program Emphases; Chapter 11: Media and Technology; Chapter 13: Evaluation of Student Achievement; and Chapter 15: Professional Development. These changes were necessary to incorporate contemporary theory and practice. Chapter 2: Historical Perspective, and Chapter 3: Curriculum Trends, are new and have been included to increase the scope of the text in the areas of curriculum foundations and innovations.

Robert C. Andrews

Excerpts from Prefaces of Previous Editions

The activities of industrial arts teachers may be divided into two general classifications. The first of these consists of analysis and planning; the second covers presentation of teaching material. The chief concern of this book is to encourage teachers in service, and those who are in preparation for teaching, to recognize and analyze the many problems and opportunities that confront them as teachers, and to offer suggestions that will lead to a more effective and satisfying teaching career.

To this end this book is practical in viewpoint, and deals with teaching situations and personal relationships rather than with backgrounds and psychological principles. Patterns of organization, class management, teaching methods, and lesson planning, while presented in detail, are not considered to be final, but serve as examples of definite planning and organized procedure.

From Emanuel E. Ericson's Preface
to the First Edition of TEACHING THE INDUSTRIAL ARTS

Emanuel E. Ericson's book, TEACHING THE INDUSTRIAL ARTS, . . . deals in basics which are not subject to rapid change. In addition to his fundamental approach, he was decidedly thorough. His book was a continuing challenge to him, proved by his eagerness to solicit reactions on educational concepts from his colleagues and students. His writing . . . demonstrates his ability and comprehensiveness as an educator and author. After providing leadership to the profession for nearly half a century, it is not likely that we who are to follow should or could put aside the work of this great man.

His book has for many years served as a guide for prospective teachers as well as for those who have taught. It is appropriate that the book . . . should continue to provide advice and direction to the profession.

From Kermit Seefeld's Preface
to the Third Edition

Acknowledgments

The sincere appreciation of the revising author is expressed to his parents, Edwin and Valerie, for their support and encouragement; to David Townsend and Roy Hayward, for their inspiration and direction; to his wife Emily, and sons Michael, David, and Peter, for their patience and understanding.

Acknowledgment of assistance is addressed to a colleague, Robert B. Hawes, for new material in Chapter 13 concerning measurement and evaluation; to students Geoffrey Robarge and H. Alan Pasour, for reading the revision and offering their suggestions; and to Maurine Ericson and the Chas. A. Bennett Co., Inc., for the opportunity to revise such a renowned basic text in the field.

It was a privilege to author this latest edition, knowing that the result will keep the memory of Emanuel E. Ericson in the place of respect so rightfully deserved. His excellent reputation, and that of his book, is the result of his many years of outstanding leadership in industrial education and his service to the teaching profession.

The publisher wishes to express appreciation to Drs. Kermit A. Seefeld, Ralph K. Nair, Robert A. McCoy, and Paul L. Scherer for their past assistance in preserving the currency and usefulness of this text. Gratitude is extended also to the many others, both teachers and students, who have offered suggestions that have increased the effectiveness of this text as a viable educational tool and a valuable reference.

Table of Contents

Preface 5

Excerpts from Prefaces of Previous Editions 6

Acknowledgments 7

Chapter 1: Effective Teaching 10
    Teaching as a Profession, 10; Learning to Teach, 11; Qualities of the Successful Teacher, 11; Teacher Preparation and Certification, 13; Teaching Loads and Teaching Efficiency, 15; Counseling Students, 17; Extracurricular Involvement, 18; The Public and the Schools, 18; Publicity and Public Relations, 20; Discussion Questions, 22; Additional Readings, 23.

Chapter 2: Historical Perspective 25
    Beginnings, 25; Philosophical Evolution, 25; Program Growth and Refinement, 26; The Mechanic Arts Movement, 28; Scandinavian Sloyd, 28; Manual Training in the United States, 29; The Manual Arts, 30; Vocational Education, 31; Industrial Arts, 32; Two in One, 33; Discussion Questions, 34; Additional Readings, 36.

Chapter 3: Curriculum Trends 37
    The Search for Relevance, 37; Unitary Teaching, 38; Analyzing Industrial Organization, 39; Classifying Types of Industry, 41; Universal Themes and Problems, 42; Clusters of Occupations, 44; Career Education Concepts, 46; Elementary School Programs, 49; Emphasis on Technology, 50; Evolution from Revolutions, 52; Discussion Questions, 53; Additional Readings, 55.

Chapter 4: Course Construction 57
    The Course of Study, 57; Sources of Subject Matter, 58; Selection of Content, 60; Organizing Course Content, 61; Subject Matter in Elementary Schools, 62; Course Content in Intermediate Grades, 64; Course Work in Secondary Schools, 65; Forms and Formats, 66; Discussion Questions, 68; Additional Readings, 69.

Chapter 5: Goal Orientation 70
    Goals and Objectives, 70; The Learning Process, 70; Analysis of Student Needs, 72; Educational Imperatives, 72; Establishing Goals, 75; Writing Performance Objectives, 78; Emphasis at Educational Levels, 79; Discussion Questions, 80; Additional Readings, 80.

Chapter 6: Program Emphases 81
    Program Development, 81; Operations and Processes, 81; The Project Method, 82; Project Selection, 83; The Unit Method, 87; Industry and Technology, 88; Occupational Information, 89; Outline for the Study of an Occupation, 92; Coeducational Programs, 92; Interdisciplinary Cooperation, 93; A Balanced Program, 95; Discussion Questions, 96; Additional Readings, 97.

Chapter 7: Facility Design and Management 98
    Evolution of Modern School Laboratories, 98; The Single-Unit Laboratory, 98; The General-Unit Laboratory, 98; The Comprehensive Industrial Laboratory, 99; The Mobile Laboratory, 99; Facility Design, 100; Check List for Lab Planning, 100; Floor Space, 101; Class Demonstration Areas, 102; Office Space, 102; Tool Storage, 102; Tool Identification and Control, 104; Equipment Needs Survey, 106; Materials and Supplies, 108; Inventories, 110; Supply Requisitions, 111; Equipment Maintenance, 111; Laboratory Sanitation, 114; The Honor System, 115; Exploitation, 115; Further Suggestions, 117; Financing Industrial Education, 118; Discussion Questions, 118; Additional Readings, 120.

CONTENTS

Chapter 8: Beginning the School Year 121
The Basis for Teaching Success, 121; Each Year a New Challenge, 121; Preliminary Considerations, 121; Getting Acquainted, 123; Class Records and Homeroom Duties, 125; Checking Inventories, 126; Conditioning Equipment, 127; Ordering Equipment and Supplies, 127; Checking One's Readiness, 128; The Instructor Meets the Class, 129; Establishing a Cooperative Attitude, 131; "When Do We Go to Work?", 132; The Special Student, 134; Possible Changes, 136; Discussion Questions, 137; Additional Readings, 138.

Chapter 9: Class Organization and Discipline 140
Management and Discipline, 140; Bases for Effective Management, 140; Student Participation in Management, 142; The Disciplinary Role of the Teacher, 144; Environmental Conditions Affecting Discipline, 145; Maintaining Effective Discipline, 147; Discussion Questions, 149; Additional Readings, 150.

Chapter 10: Teaching and Learning 151
Teaching Methods in Common Use, 151; Presenting a Demonstration, 151; The Class Demonstration, 152; Small-Group Demonstrations, 154; Demonstrating to the Individual, 155; The Lecture, 155; Seminars and Discussions, 157; The Discovery Method, 158; Planning for Instruction, 159; The Lesson Plan, 161; Annoyances and Distractions, 163; Techniques for Maintaining Effectiveness, 164; Evaluation of Instruction, 165; Discussion Questions, 165; Additional Readings, 167.

Chapter 11: Media and Technology 168
Emphasis on Learning, 168; Printed Media, 170; Display Media, 183; Projected Media, 186; Recorded Media, 192; Discussion Questions, 196; Additional Readings, 197.

Chapter 12: Accident Prevention and Safety 199
The Importance of Safety, 199; Accident-Causing Conditions, 199; Accident Prevention, 200; Laboratory Improvement, 200; Instructional Improvement, 201; Student Hazards, 202; Safety Precautions, 202; Industrial Safety Education, 203; Discussion Questions, 205; Additional Readings, 206.

Chapter 13: Evaluation of Student Achievement 207
Measurement and Evaluation, 207; Evaluation Terminology, 209; Skill Development, 211; Knowledge Acquisition, 212; Personal Behavior, 213; Test Construction, 214; Subjective Tests, 217; Objective Tests, 217; Performance Tests, 221; Item Analysis, 222; Determination of Grades, 224; Characteristics of Efficient Grading, 224; Marking Systems, 226; Recording Achievement, 227; Discussion Questions, 228; Additional Readings, 229.

Chapter 14: Closing the School Year 231
Maintaining Organization, 231; Laboratory Maintenance, 232; Equipment Inventory, 233; Supplies Inventory, 233; Requisitions, 233; Reports, 234; Permanent Records, 235; An Orderly Finish, 235; Discussion Questions, 235; Additional Readings, 236.

Chapter 15: Professional Development 237
Occupational Opportunities, 237; Staff Organization, 239; Measuring Instructional Effectiveness, 241; Self-Evaluation, 241; Supervisory Evaluation, 244; Student Evaluation, 245; The Professional Educator, 246; Career Advancement, 251; Discussion Questions, 252; Additional Readings, 253.

Index 254

Chapter 1
Effective Teaching

Teaching as a Profession

The time has passed when teaching as an occupation was open to any person with some college training who was prepared to do nothing else, or who failed to get a position in the work for which he or she was specially trained. Now, specialized preparation is expected and demanded for teaching as distinctly as for any other profession.

With new demands has come also a new and different evaluation of the teacher and his or her work. The public is realizing that the effective teacher is worthy of rewards other than the personal satisfaction of having rendered dedicated service. The teacher is coming to the work with a background of special training, and with the intention of making a career of teaching. With this intention, the teacher proceeds to improve further and to elevate the profession of which he or she is now a member.

While teaching is not a lucrative profession, salaries now are more nearly commensurate with the services rendered and the time used in preparation for the work. They are probably as good, on the average, as those for similar occupations demanding an equivalent expenditure of time and money. Teaching offers a better opportunity at the outset than many of them.

Financial remuneration is not the only determining factor to be considered in job satisfaction of teachers. A true educator finds in the work many other rewards, among which are the following:

• *A chance to use initiative.* Teaching usually offers the freedom to use one's own ideas; to organize the work and the means for carrying it out; to use one's own methods in obtaining results; and to use one's own personality and individuality in accomplishing the job.

• *Job satisfaction.* One who is a natural teacher cannot fail to derive satisfaction from being instrumental in shaping the ideas and ideals of youth. In this opportunity lies much of the teacher's reward.

• *Variety in activities.* Teaching can never become a monotonous, routine job to one whose heart is in the work. An endless variety of approaches and responses will keep the teacher enthusiastic. In the classroom or laboratory, this variety is further multiplied, and the industrial educator's day can never seem too long.

• *Opportunity for outside contacts.* The traditional idea that the teacher is a shut-in, with no chance for contacts outside of school, is not true unless the teacher makes it so. There are many outside associations that may be formed, and the teacher should make time available to foster such contacts.

CHAPTER 1—EFFECTIVE TEACHING

• *Continuous employment.* Very few occupations are so little dependent upon business, economic, political, and other conditions for continuous employment as is that of the teacher. Quality of service is the criterion upon which the teacher's tenure of office usually depends.

Learning to Teach

"forehandedness"

There are four steps by which people learn to teach:

1. *Anticipation.* The person who possesses aptitude for teaching will imagine the actual setting of the contact with the class. And in this imaginative procedure, the person will foresee possible problems and their solutions. The ability to anticipate and "live" through the work of days and hours which are yet in the future is a prerequisite to highly successful teaching in any subject. It is especially so in those subjects in which mental and manipulative work is combined.

2. *Observation.* This is another valuable avenue of success as an instructor. Such observation is not necessarily confined to the type that is controlled and required by teacher education institutions and boards of education. It is probably true that instructional methods of our own teachers have done much to shape the actions and responses that we as teachers now put into effect. Much of this background is, no doubt, used unconsciously or subconsciously. It is, nevertheless, a powerful factor in any instructor's work. The teachers whom we have most admired have, unquestionably, impressed us most; but it might be well to realize that even those might have had their imperfections as instructors.

3. *Internship.* Here reference is made to teaching carried out under direct supervision in a teacher-education institution. If conditions are what they should be, this type of preparation should stand out as a most desirable and basic medium through which the prospective teacher will learn to teach. In this phase of a teacher's preparation, there are more possibilities for practice and refinement than in any other type.

4. *Participation.* It will be agreed that actual performance of work will, under reasonably favorable conditions, lead toward perfection. This is not always true, however, because it is quite possible for one who learns solely through his or her own efforts to persist in wrong practices and inefficient and obsolete methods. Learning to teach on the job, particularly in the first stages of a teaching career, is effective largely in proportion to the amount of criticism and suggestions the teacher receives either from outside supervision or by self-examination and comparison of his or her work with standard practices.

Qualities of the Successful Teacher

From the beginning of organized mechanical activities in schools, the question of the sources of teachers and their background has been an important one. Opinion has been divided as to the relative importance of practical experience, pedagogical training, and liberal-arts education in the training of an efficient industrial education instructor. Even where it has been recognized that such an instructor should have passed through all of these phases of preparation, the question of which is most important has still remained a debated one.

Teachers of industry and technology in public schools have generally come from two main sources: teacher-training institutions, and industries. Generally speaking, each of these types of teacher possesses certain definite characteristics. Each type has made valuable contributions toward the development of the total program of industrial education as we know it today. Each, on the other hand, has lacked certain desirable abilities and characteristics possessed, perhaps, by the other.

The following three qualifications for successful teaching in industrial education are generally agreed upon:

1. *Ability as a craftsman.* Mechanical skill is required on the part of the teacher. Lacking mechanical skill, the instructor cannot hope to accomplish maximum results. It is the duty of the instructor to qualify through sufficient practice and contact with the trade in order that he or she may at all times set the proper example in craftsmanship.

2. *Ability to teach.* A fine craftsman is not necessarily a good teacher. There is a great difference between being a producer and being able to analyze and present instructional material to learners. Successful teaching is dependent upon knowledge of fundamental educational principles and methods. Such knowledge comes from professional work in teacher education institutions and from continued study and research. Requirements are specified by state departments of education, which certify public school teachers. Unfortunately, such requirements are not uniformly stipulated for teaching in institutions of higher learning, not even for colleges preparing the teachers to be so certified. An appreciation of the mental processes by which learning takes place is just as important as knowledge or skill regarding subject matter, and must be so considered by everyone who expects to become a good teacher.

3. *Proper scholastic and cultural background.* Knowledge of a single subject, and knowledge of how to teach that subject, would still not enable a teacher to be of maximum value in the profession. A rather intimate knowledge of other subjects of the curriculum, of social and economic aspects of education, of backgrounds that broaden one's vision and create sympathy for other work and other instructors, is also necessary if the teacher is to be well-educated. In this respect, the special-subjects teacher should be equal with those teaching other subjects.

An examination of each of these requirements should result in a decision regarding the use of the summer vacation, barring, of course, unusual financial or physical difficulties. The teacher who is weak in mechanical skill should go into the trade. The teacher who is too much of a tradesman and too little of a teacher should seek more education in a suitable college. If the teacher lacks background and appreciation, then he or she should study literature, economics, or sociology.

CHAPTER 1—EFFECTIVE TEACHING

Teacher Preparation and Certification

Traditionally, most programs for industrial teacher education have involved the three elements of general studies, technical studies, and educational studies. In the area of educational studies, or methodology, a great deal of emphasis is now being placed on the exacting specification and performance of desirable teacher competencies, to be practiced and perfected for the development of efficiency and effectiveness in organizational duties and instructional activities. The system, known as *Performance-Based Teacher Education* (PBTE) or *Competency-Based Teacher Education* (CBTE), is goal-oriented, and competencies are specified in behavioral terms. Teachers-in-training become cognizant of, and practice, the expected behaviors or skills they must be capable of before being allowed to begin independent teaching. Clusters of behaviors relate to program planning and management; organizing, implementing, and evaluating instruction; counseling and guidance; community involvement; and continuing education for the professional educator.

The first cluster, *program planning and management,* prepares the prospective industrial educator to:

- Identify attitudes, knowledge, and skills that are to be required of students in curriculum offerings.
- Write behavioral objectives for all industrial education courses included in the curriculum.
- Specify long-range equipment and supply needs.
- Prepare a budget.
- Design a laboratory to house a program.

Topics relating to these objectives are included in Chapters 4, 5, 6, and 7.

The next cluster, *organizing instruction,* prepares the future teacher to:

- Assess student needs, interests, and aptitudes.
- Write student-oriented performance objectives.
- Outline subject matter to be included in a unit of study.
- Prescribe student-oriented activities that correspond with objectives and subject matter.
- Specify methods of evaluating student achievement of the prescribed objectives.

Information and activities relating to this cluster of objectives are presented in Chapters 4, 5, 6, 8, and 9.

Implementing instruction is the title of the third group of competencies. These are mainly concerned with offering the opportunity to:

- Specify student objectives to be fulfilled in lessons, demonstrations, discussions, lab activities, or through independent study.
- Plan a lesson and prepare accompanying suitable media.
- Organize and conduct field trips.
- Plan peer teaching activities for the laboratory.
- Plan appropriate projects and laboratory activities.

TEACHING INDUSTRIAL EDUCATION

Teaching strategies and learning opportunities relating to this cluster are described in Chapters 9, 10, 11, and 12.

Procedures for *evaluating instruction* comprise the next cluster, through which the teacher will be more able to:

- Specify expected student performance in relation to attitudes, knowledge, and skills to be acquired following instruction and/or laboratory activities.
- Construct and administer objective and subjective testing instruments.
- Analyze testing instruments, record results, and alter the instruments in accordance with the analysis.
- Design a grading system for recording student achievement.

Evaluation methods and instruments are presented in detail in Chapter 13.

Skills in *counseling and guidance* are also of utmost importance to the industrial educator. Teachers who want to know their students on a more personal basis must be able to:

- Collect data related to student interests, aptitudes, and background.
- Conduct case studies.
- Assist students in career orientation, exploration, and preparation.
- Assist students in analyzing and solving personal problems.
- Refer students to professional specialists when necessary.
- Sponsor a student club or organization.
- Conduct activity periods for students who are unable to schedule regular industrial education courses.

The performance of these skills is described later in this chapter as well as in Chapters 8 and 9.

Recognizing the need for *community involvement* composes the next set of objectives. New teachers should be cognizant of ways to:

- Involve citizens in trade and program advisory committees.
- Exhibit student projects during parent visitations and display articles in local businesses.
- Disseminate news articles concerning programs, projects, and class activities.
- Schedule and conduct adult education programs during evenings.
- Participate in local civic, humanitarian, and fraternal organizations.

Some methods of fulfilling these objectives are mentioned later in this chapter. In addition, Chapter 15 will provide more information and activities in this regard.

Finally, *professional development* and *continuing education* must be considered necessary by the professional educator. Effective teachers must become involved in accepting responsibilities to:

- Participate in local, regional, and national professional and technical organizations.

- Conduct personal behavior in accordance with an accepted code of ethics and morals.
- Express and promote a personal and professional philosophy.
- Study towards advanced degrees.
- Read professional and technical periodicals and journals.
- Attend state, regional, and national conferences and conventions.

Many relevant topics concerned with updating and improving one's professional stature are provided later in this chapter and in Chapters 2, 3, and 15.

Additional competencies can be identified for all of the aforementioned clusters. The competencies presented are a limited sample of the types of behaviors considered essential to effective teachings.

Systems of *Competency-Based Teacher Certification* (CBTC) are also being developed along similar performance-oriented lines, necessitating in-service updating of teaching skills and techniques. Such a system, based on behavioral objectives, requires continuous educational and technical growth on the part of the industrial educator. Every experienced teacher must prove himself or herself worthy of retaining state and/or regional teacher certification, universally regarded as the "license to teach" in most public school systems. The old adage, "one year of experience repeated twelve times," for a teacher who has been in the profession for thirteen years, will become inappropriate in an organized system of in-service continuing education.

Teaching Loads and Teaching Efficiency

Much has been said about the relative instructional load that should be assigned to industrial educators in comparison to teachers of academic subjects. Administrators and teachers of subjects other than industrial education have been inclined to feel that class organization and methods are not necessary in "shopwork." When this feeling is expressed or allowed to influence teaching assignments, it is usually based upon the thought that industrial educators need no preparation for teaching, do not have written papers to evaluate and correct, do not give written examinations, and can let students work with a minimum of attention.

On the other hand, industrial educators are prone to feel that their position in the school is misunderstood, that good teaching in their field requires all that other subjects demand, plus a great many extra details and responsibilities. Usually they confine their reactions to talk among themselves and do very little to clarify their position to those who are not familiar with their instructional procedures. Many teachers in other disciplines would become more sympathetic if they were better informed.

In discussing teaching loads for industrial educators a number of factors must be considered. Among these are the following:

- Number of actual teaching hours—or length of modules—per day.
- Length of periods for this type of teaching.

- Degree of homogeneity of students.
- Size of classes.
- Physical facilities for teaching.
- Types of activity carried on.
- Teaching methods and philosophy involved.
- Cocurricular demands upon teachers.

In many school systems it appears to be the custom to assign the industrial educators to a program of continuous teaching for the full school day, while teachers of other subjects are given some free time. The reactions of the former group to this condition are normal. Modern teaching of technology requires a variety of activities in order to satisfy student interest. While the regular classroom teacher has one topic to prepare for discussion, the industrial educator must have ready a dozen plans and ideas for the day. In addition, materials and tools must be kept in readiness.

There might have been a time when many so-called "shop" teachers, because of lack of training and vision, simply told the students to "go to work." Today, industrial education involves a study of materials and phenomena concerning industry and technology. It includes study about occupational opportunities, safety practices, intelligent consumption of goods and services, and definite training in cooperative living in social and work situations. To make these experiences a part of the industrial education program requires much preparation on the part of the instructor.

The length of class periods obviously relates to the number of hours taught. During recent years a definite practice has been to make the laboratory periods of the same length as those of other subjects. Regardless of the length of the periods, the greatest need is for more planning, more frequent demonstrations and presentations of informative material, and more constant checking on tools and equipment, to say nothing of providing storage space and identification procedures for the work of the added groups. Industry and technology in modern education now receive status equal to that of other subjects in the curriculum. However, no justice can be done to that status unless the industrial educator is given the same consideration as other teachers in regard to teaching assignments.

The load that the teacher can efficiently handle depends upon many factors other than the number of classes or teaching hours assigned. In industrial education, the drain upon the teacher's energies is often increased by unnecessary mixing of pupils of various ages and grades. The possibilities of placing first- and second-year mathematics students or first- and second-year history students in the same class would not enter the minds of administrators and program advisers.

Even though age and ability are generally used to determine the assignment of students to particular classes, such judgments are often ignored when students are assigned to industrial education classes. Thus, students of different ages and talents are often placed in the same class.

CHAPTER 1—EFFECTIVE TEACHING

There is no intention here to claim that in all laboratory classes there must be a single group with reference to age and grade. However, the point needs emphasizing that, as the variety increases, the pressure upon the teacher increases, necessitating more time for planning and organizing the program of activities.

The size of classes that industrial educators should handle has been a subject of much discussion. The teacher might well point out that in this type of work individual contact with students is a prime requirement. Without reasonable opportunities for personal attention to the problems of each member of the class, the most important outcomes sought would be lost.

The administrator, on the other hand, is faced with problems that are not well understood by the teacher. The greater cost per capita in industrial education is an important problem. During recent years a general tendency has been to increase numbers in laboratory classes. Adoption of new teaching techniques by versatile teachers has helped keep major objectives still attainable. However, there is obviously a point beyond which opportunities for any semblance of planned activity cannot be offered.

Two of the chief factors that determine the maximum number for industrial education classes are the size and condition of the laboratory. In general, when class enrollments are increased, reduction in learning opportunities does not come from the increase in numbers as much as from the fact that little or no attention is given to a corresponding remodeling of the laboratory. To place thirty students in a room that was built and equipped for twenty means not only lack of facilities for the added number but also the disorganization of the program for all. Where plans have been made for larger numbers to be accommodated in industrial classes, students are being cared for under an orderly procedure and with good results.

Counseling Students

Counseling students is an important part of a teacher's activities, whether or not the teacher has received a definite appointment for such service. In fact, teaching has always been partly counseling. Youth needs counseling and appreciates it, provided it is constructive.

To deal with classes and groups and yet know and appreciate the individual and be a friend and counselor, requires an ability to communicate something more than craftsmanship. Without having developed an interest in helping each youth form wholesome attitudes toward his or her vocation and associates, an instructor is not fully prepared. Many a student continues to build for himself or herself false ideals and poor social habits because each of his or her teachers are concerned only with teaching subject matter and not with interesting themselves in the students. Every instructor must have the courage to be personal, friendly, and unbiased in assisting individuals.

There is a broad, general, undefined responsibility with reference to the welfare of students that industrial educators must accept equally with other instructors. These duties demand that they show an interest in the students at all times whether in or out of classrooms or hallways, and take an interest in assisting students to follow the rules and regulations of the school. At this point the instructor must consider himself or herself a part of the supervisory force of the entire school, and be willing to stand the unpleasantness that sometimes may come in connection with disciplinary action.

In addition to moral and disciplinary counseling, the industrial educator often plays a key role in helping students discover career alternatives through occupational orientation, exploration, and preparation. The perceptive teacher uses every possible opportunity to notice when students begin to "find themselves" vocationally. Each student's individual needs, desires, interests, and aptitudes are often fulfilled in industrial education activities. Thus, the industrial education teacher is often in a unique position to provide occupational counseling at the most opportune time.

Extracurricular Involvement

To be a member of a professional teaching team in an educational institution involves a greater challenge than to be simply a "shop" teacher. Instructors of industrial education should welcome the opportunity to mingle with students outside of the laboratory, for by dealing with materials and mechanical processes constantly, one stands in danger of becoming narrow, prejudiced, and perhaps unsympathetic.

Special student clubs in which a teacher may take an interest are of two kinds: those organized within regular school hours, forming a part of the student program, and those falling outside of the regular school day. The former are probably more common. In many junior and senior high schools it has become a practice to organize the entire school into a series of groups or clubs for a variety of cocurricular activities according to the choice of the students and the ability of teachers to act as sponsors.

Such activities may range from study of Greek and Latin to camera work and clay modeling. These special student activities offer a challenge to every instructor. To offer the facilities as a club activity for girls or college-preparatory students who cannot otherwise schedule industrial education in their academic programs may enrich their lives with experiences that would not otherwise be theirs. Among activities falling outside of school hours are radio clubs, home workshop programs, stagecraft work, photography, and various types of play programs.

The Public and the Schools

Until the late 1950s, Americans considered their form of education to be the finest in the world. With the onset of the space age, however, the United States seemed to take second place, and a large portion of the blame was directed toward the school systems. An investigation and examination was demanded by the nation's citizens.

The goals of American education had always seemed acceptable. All students were expected to become:

- Participating citizens in a democratic society.

CHAPTER 1—EFFECTIVE TEACHING

- Worthwhile family members.
- Financially independent through occupational preparation.
- Capable of using communication and computation skills effectively.
- Appreciative of the arts and humanities in the culture.
- Knowledgeable consumers of goods and services.

Few educators or citizens had found need to question the practicability of trying to fulfill, or measure the results of, such generalized statements. Yet, when those long-held goals of American education were subjected to close scrutiny, it was deemed almost impossible to state or evaluate the direct benefits or results of such a "general education." Public schools and teachers were challenged to prove that they were accomplishing those things they purported to be doing.

The stage was set for a re-examination of those goals. Primarily, there was a need for more specificity in the statements of educational intent. "Behavioral Objectives" was the name of the new game, and educators began to expend great effort in writing and categorizing thousands of educational prescriptions. During the 1960s, the federal government assisted in the effort by generously funding the planning and implementing of pilot programs and curriculum models designed within the framework of behavioral objectives.

Once in such a program, teachers and students knew exactly what was expected of them. The grandiose goals of earlier years gave way to exacting statements of specific skills, information attainment, and attitudes that could be evaluated after the learning activity. Examples of this specificity for teacher behaviors can be found in this chapter and in Chapter 15. General goals and behavioral objectives for students are described in Chapter 5.

In the early 1970s, the large programs of federal funding came to a gradual close. The plight of teachers was heard throughout the news media. "Militancy" became a common term as teachers sought the benefits of organizing together in professional associations and unions. Through collective bargaining, teachers were able to present their demands for higher salaries and better working conditions. As teachers made their demands on the community, the public also made demands on the performance of teachers. The public sector demanded proof from educators that students were really achieving those things stated in the behavioral objectives. Hence, there was a concern with "accountability."

In such a system, teachers were responsible for teaching, and having the students learn necessary skills, knowledge, and behaviors. Accountability forced teachers to:

(1) State realistic behavioral objectives for each course, unit, lesson or activity.

(2) Provide leadership in presenting relevant instructional activities and learning opportunities directed toward the students' fulfillment of prestated objectives.

(3) Assess and evaluate each student's progress toward, or achievement of, the behavioral prescriptions.

(4) Be held accountable if the students were unable to attain an acceptable standard, or level of performance.

Inherent in the system is the necessity of keeping the public informed of educational processes and progress. Usually, when taxpayers are aware of the benefits derived from their support, there is little resistance to those things that the schools are trying to accomplish.

Publicity and Public Relations

Only recently have educators come to appreciate the necessity for keeping taxpayers and parents informed regarding programs and purposes of public schools. Both teachers and administrators are inclined to become involved in the serious business of carrying out the educational program to the point of forgetting that support and goodwill are essential to the success of the program. If public understanding is needed in regard to the commonly known subjects of the school, it is even more important that such understanding be established for industrial education.

Four reasons may be given why there is lack of publicity in connection with the industrial education program:

- *Teachers consider advertising unprofessional.* There is a feeling that the service is cheapened if news of the work is spread. This attitude is shared by members of other professions—sometimes, no doubt, to the disadvantage of persons who should have certain information.
- *The work should speak for itself.* In feeling this way, teachers fail to realize that however important the work is, students must know about it before they can seek membership in the classes.
- *Some have not thought of it.* Some teachers may not realize the possibility of doing anything other than teaching those who come. Students are sent from the enrollment office, and the instructor considers that he or she can do nothing if the attendance is not satisfactory except to carry ill-feeling against the person who has charge of the student programs.
- *Some need no more students.* In many schools the facilities are overcrowded with students, and the instructors have little incentive to undertake publicity schemes that might tend to make their work even more popular.

If the instructor believes that the program functions as an important part in the education of a large number of students, he or she will be eager for those who may profit from it to know that it exists.

Newspapers

Schools can usually depend upon the support of local news media if that support is intelligently solicited. In spite of such discouraging factors as misprints, exaggerated statements, "flashy" reports, and the like, which have to be dealt with, the newspaper, radio, and television have become important institutions of society, and may be of great assistance in developing any public enterprise. The activities of public schools must be kept before the eyes of those who pay the bills if intelligent support is to be expected. Too little publicity for the program of the school has often led to misunderstanding and lack of confidence.

In connection with newspaper items, as well as other forms of publicity, care must be taken by the individual teacher not to absorb the prerogatives of someone else who may consider it his or her privilege and advantage to handle this phase of the work. Principals may sometimes be jealous of such privileges, and, if so, it is the duty of instructors to cooperate in such practices as may be desired.

Two types of news service may be considered: contributed news items and paid advertising. The second is rarely necessary, but may be used in connection with special adult programs and vocational classes, or in order to advertise publicity schemes such as open nights, special shows, or exhibits.

Items of news may appear at fairly regular intervals telling of new courses, special projects for school and community, special contests, and other activities. A profitable feature has been the writing of a series of short articles telling of the industrial education program, its aims, and services. Such a scheme should first be submitted to the principal for approval. It is well to have the material read by the principal, or by someone else who has in mind the broader viewpoints of the entire school, in order that no statement may be misconstrued or reflect badly upon any other phase of the school program. If the writer's name is to appear with the contributions, the copy should not be altered by the editor without the writer's permission.

School Papers   Too little attention is often given to the school paper as a means for spreading the news of the industrial education program. Laboratory activities furnish interesting themes for youthful reporters, but the difficulty is that those reporters do not normally turn in that direction for material. Consequently, it is the task of the instructor to stimulate the needed interest. The school paper reaches the sources from which future enrollment will come, namely, the students and the homes.

Bulletins   Bulletins issued by the department constitute a valuable type of publicity material. These can be mimeographed or printed, depending upon conditions. They have been used largely in connection with vocational and adult-education programs, but are also useful in spreading news of activities in nonvocational work. Thus, the graphic arts laboratory can handle practical jobs, and at the same time serve the interests of the department and the school.

Exhibits   Exhibits have long been an effective means of stimulating interest in laboratory activities. If the exhibit is an honest one, and so planned as not to disorganize regular activities, it still remains in the front rank as a publicity feature. Permanent exhibits should be used in offices and hallways of schools, while other displays can periodically be set up in prominent windows of banks, stores and other locations in the commercial districts of

TEACHING INDUSTRIAL EDUCATION

the city and suburbs. An annual exhibit at the school may be varied from year to year, or may be omitted entirely, in favor of the types of display just mentioned and other special features.

"Shall I have an exhibit this year?" is the question before industrial educators and supervisors. The answer will vary with different teachers, according to whether they believe the exhibit to be worth while or not, whether they have the interest and initiative necessary, whether the administration calls for one, and whether they have done work of the kind that will stand exhibition.

Open House

In many school systems the "open house" has become an annual affair. On this occasion the entire school is usually run in the evening as in daytime, in order to give the parents and patrons an opportunity to see its varied activities. Needless to say, the industrial education program may be a large part of the attraction because of the very nature of the work. In such programs exhibits may be featured, as may also special construction devices and machines.

The teacher is justified in planning in a limited way a publicity program for the department. Many instructors who are doing splendid work in their laboratories receive no recognition because little is known of their activities. A reasonable program for the purpose of informing the community of the program objectives, procedures, and accomplishments is legitimate. There is little danger that the public will be reminded too often of what the schools are doing in educating youth.

DISCUSSION QUESTIONS

1. From where should the future teachers of industrial education be recruited? What qualifications should they have?

2. In your opinion, who is responsible for recruiting suitable teachers for the profession. By what procedures should they be recruited?

3. List points that might be noted on an observation trip to an industrial education department in a local school.

4. What do you consider the most desirable program of training and experience for the preparation of an industrial educator in junior high schools? In high school vocational subjects?

5. Make a study of the credential requirements in your state for teaching industrial subjects.

6. What can a college-trained industrial educator do to learn about industrial methods and industrial production?

7. How much time do you consider that a teacher can devote to private interests and still be effective and efficient in his or her teaching?

8. How do you feel you have learned teaching methods from your own teachers in high school and college?

9. In what ways does the industrial educator have superior opportunities to teach courtesy, cooperation, and other desirable personal qualities by participating in the programs?

CHAPTER 1—EFFECTIVE TEACHING

10. To what extent do you believe that a teacher should feel responsible for the morals and manners of his or her students?

11. Name clubs you could sponsor in the school, and show the value of such clubs.

12. How has "Competency-Based Teacher Education" changed the program for preparing future industrial educators?

13. What will be the effects of "Competency-Based Teacher Certification" on tenure, continuing education, public subsidy of coursework, and retirement benefits?

14. List possible evening activities through which a teacher might further the growth of his or her industrial education program.

15. Have you known teachers to overdo the matter of advertising? If so, in what respects?

16. Name ways through which the principal, superintendent, and board of education may learn about the work done in industrial education.

17. What publicity value is there for the industrial education program if the teacher becomes connected with youth program activities of a community?

18. A young industrial educator stated that the first thing that he would do when coming into a small community would be to go to a newspaper office and get "written up." What do you think of the idea?

19. List methods of obtaining publicity not mentioned in this chapter.

20. Would Saturday morning "open house" in the laboratory for all students who wish to make things be a good publicity scheme?

21. Make out a complete schedule for the publicity of the industrial education program in a small community where not more than two teachers are engaged in this special work.

22. In what way may industrial films be used to promote the industrial education program?

23. If you were organizing a vocational class in auto mechanics or electrical work, what would you do to build up an enrollment?

24. In what ways may industrial education be publicized through the school paper?

25. List a number of schemes by which the general student body in a high school may be informed about the industrial education program.

26. Do you feel that teachers should be the only ones held "accountable" for student achievement? Explain your answer.

27. What roles do parents, the teacher, the public, the federal government, and the principal play in the education of youth?

ADDITIONAL READINGS

Allen, Dwight W., and Seifman, Eli, eds. *The Teacher's Handbook.* Glenview, Illinois: Scott, Foresman, 1971.

Baird, Ronald J. *Contemporary Industrial Teaching.* South Holland, Illinois: Goodheart-Willcox, 1972.

Burkhart, Robert C., and Meil, Hugh M. *Identity and Teacher Learning.* Scranton, Pennsylvania: International Textbook, 1968.

Cenci, Louis, and Weaver, Gilbert G. *Teaching Occupational Skills.* 2nd ed. New York: Pitman, 1968.

Jordan, Thomas E. *America's Children: An Introduction to Education.* New York: Rand McNally, 1973.

Larson, Milton E. *Teaching Related Subjects in Trade, Industrial and Technical Education.* Columbus, Ohio: Charles E. Merrill, 1972.

Leighbody, Gerald B., and Kidd, Donald M. *Methods of Teaching Shop and Technical Subjects.* Albany, New York: Delmar, 1966.

Littrell, Joseph J. *Guide to Industrial Teaching.* Peoria, Illinois: Chas. A. Bennett, 1970.

Pautler, Albert J. *Teaching Shop and Laboratory Subjects.* Columbus, Ohio: Charles E. Merrill, 1971.

Silvius, G. Harold, and Curry, Estell H. *Teaching Successfully in Industrial Education.* 2nd ed. Bloomington, Illinois: McKnight & McKnight, 1967.

Chapter 2
Historical Perspective

Beginnings

Since the beginning of the human race, some form of basic manual training has been practiced. Mainly concerned with the basic needs of food, clothing, and shelter, early humans survived by making tools and weapons from wood, hides, bone, and stone. From generation to generation, education by imitation was the only viable means of passing on the necessary skills for survival in a hostile environment.

Over the centuries, very little refinement took place in the design of the basic implements until humans began to specialize in the production of a particular article. The development of individual aptitudes, as evidenced by skillfully constructed products, initiated systems of exchange. Thus, each artisan became known for his or her accomplishments and contributions to the common good.

During the fifteenth and sixteenth centuries major accomplishments influenced the destiny of the human race. During those years of crisis and change Europeans journeyed to the New World. With each new discovery in science and nature, new problems were created. New skills were required to solve these problems. Consequently, there began to evolve, in Europe and America, a pedagogically organized system of manual skills training.

Philosophical Evolution

In his writings, *Francis Bacon* (1561–1626) noted that all new learning eventuates through the activities of daily living (work, involvement in nature and the arts)—not from reading others' observations. Bacon's philosophy of realism and his belief in participation and involvement resulted in his coining of the term "manual arts," referring to those disciplines which eventually led to the development of the applied sciences. This is the first recorded use of the term.

John Comenius (1592–1670), a theologian and educator, felt that learning must necessarily evolve from a study of both words and artifacts. The complete learning process would have to be based on a study of the object, as well as on studies of its name and description. Often referred to as the "father of modern pedagogy," Comenius was a prolific writer whose books employed illustrations to assist in the understanding of the commentary. One of the first to divide schooling into segments, his plan incorporated four six-year schools. In the plan, all children were obliged to attend the first two schools (infant and vernacular), while only selected students were privileged to continue through the final divisions (secondary, or gymnasium, and university).

TEACHING INDUSTRIAL EDUCATION

While Isaac Newton and Robert Boyle were establishing the basic foundations of science, *John Locke* (1632–1704) was expounding on the necessity for all education to train boys for practical occupations in trades or professions. "Working schools" were founded in 1697 to provide poor children with training in wool spinning and knitting. Holding such aims as the cultivation of virtue, wisdom, and manners to be as important as learning, Locke advocated a combination of physical, moral, and intellectual education. The physical or manual portion of the curriculum was especially designed to instruct students in the values of exercise, utility, and recreation. Gardening and woodworking were popular activities.

Basing much of his philosophy on Locke's writings, *Jean Jacques Rousseau* (1712–1778) felt that education was becoming too formal. He felt that it should be exciting, natural, and spontaneous. In *Emile,* he professed that all knowledge is acquired through one's own experiences. He advocated that students be provided with materials and activities that would arouse their curiosity. Believing that the search for knowledge is a natural activity and the depth of understanding is increased through the excitement of discovery, Rousseau thought that the teacher should pose questions, and not merely answer them. Rousseau also believed that an hour spent in purposeful handwork was more valuable than a day of instruction. He often used agricultural studies in his programs.

Program Growth and Refinement

Although he had a confused childhood and was a classic example of a student with little direction, *Johann Heinrich Pestalozzi* (1746–1827) eventually became known as "the father of manual training." Even after studying law, his disorientation and disenchantment continued. Finally, he abandoned formal study of academic subjects and turned to the study of agriculture, the most natural of all trades. Soon thereafter, he married a woman of considerable wealth and bought a large farm. Eventually, he failed at farming, too. However, during that time he developed a practical philosophy of education and decided to found a school for poor children, using his wife's property for the educational experiment. Learning experiences in farming, spinning, weaving, and cooking were provided, in addition to the traditional subjects of the liberal arts. Even though the school was an exceptional educational success, financial mismanagement and the resulting heavy debts eventually doomed it to failure.

In spite of his many disappointments, Pestalozzi made several contributions to the development of educational methodology. Since his philosophy was closely allied with Rousseau's belief that education should be based on the study of nature, he believed that one must progress from the study of concrete objects to the study of more abstract subjects. His conviction that one must first build a foundation of experiences, then move to more formal intellectual endeavors, provided that education should serve primarily as a preparation for a practical life.

After working with Pestalozzi in many ventures that failed economically, *Philip von Fellenberg* (1771–1844) developed a similar, but financially successful, system of education. Not believing in social mobility, he felt that people should be educated to perform and serve within their stations in life. He believed that their talents should be nurtured and refined so that they might become capable producers within their own class. Interestingly enough, he also felt that people from the various classes should be integrated in the educational setting. Thus, the upper classes would develop proper sympathy for the lower classes, and the members of the lower classes would develop proper respect for the people in the upper classes.

A poor school for boys was founded by von Fellenberg on principles quite similar to those advocated by Pestalozzi. The program of studies incorporated a great deal of farming and mechanical arts, although formal lessons in more academic areas were held during mealtime. In a similar experiment, von Fellenberg offered girls from the laboring classes a curriculum of domestic occupations, so that they might be better prepared for their stations in life. Boys from the middle classes were placed in an organized program known as the school of applied sciences, which offered agricultural studies through experimentation. Their activities were primarily designed for improving methods of farming and manufacturing machinery, not for training students to be farmers, as was the goal of the poor school program. When the need for teachers became acute, von Fellenberg formed a normal school (école normale or "model"). Its program combined instructional methodology with a thorough study of disciplines. Students working alongside master teachers were instructed in practical subjects.

Building on a philosophy of "self-activity," basically a refinement of Pestalozzi's educational tenets, *Friedrich Froebel* (1782–1852) placed handwork at the center of all school learning. He believed that man was fundamentally born for activity and that learning evolved naturally through participation in activities. His predecessors had used handwork as a means to education in the more traditional disciplines. Working mainly at the kindergarten level, Froebel presented handwork as a separate subject in the curriculum.

Manual education has a rich heritage. However, until the beginning of the seventeenth century there was little development of any formal methods of teaching manual arts. The educators previously mentioned helped to develop viable programs of manual education. They, along with many others, helped to perfect production-type handwork to the point where it helped to foster the industrial revolution.

With the development of the factory system, apprenticeship training soon became an integral part of industry. However, it was seen as a great waste of the skilled laborer's time and the company's materials. To alleviate the problem, school workshops were established throughout Europe and America, providing the opportunity for selected craftsmen to teach their skills to apprentices in an environment separate from that of industry. Relevant manual education served as preparation for entering the factories. Such education largely replaced the more formal instructional activities within industry.

The Mechanic Arts Movement

Founded to train engineers, draftsmen, and chemists, the Imperial Technical School of Moscow was the first to replace the apprenticeship method with a pedagogically organized program of studies employing instruction areas and construction shops. Imitation had previously been the main method of skill and information acquisition. However, *Victor Della Vos* and his instructors began to require students to pass a rigid course of instruction before proceeding with more complex construction activities, such as the building of steam engines and agricultural machinery. The prime result of this new program was the shortening of the time needed to teach the mechanic arts. Grouped into a single class, many students could be taught simultaneously by one master craftsman. Under a system of formal apprenticeship, the same craftsman would have been able to instruct only a few apprentices. The development of a systematic ordering of tasks (from simple to complex) was also possible. Thus, student achievement could be more easily and accurately evaluated by the instructor.

A great deal of influence was exercised on the American system of manual training when, in 1876, Della Vos and his colleagues displayed some student products at the Philadelphia Centennial Exposition. Such items as joints and simple tools were in abundance, illustrating the concentration on basic manipulative operations. Few projects were useful in themselves and by contemporary standards they would be considered drill projects, performed mainly in order to learn tool manipulation.

Scandinavian Sloyd

Scandinavian farming families, needing constructive pursuits during the long winter evenings, found much satisfaction in the useful handwork of woodcarving. Tables, benches, household articles, and handles for farm implements were carved from pieces of native wood. By 1800, the practice of this handwork, known as "sloyd," had become firmly embedded in the lives of the people of Sweden and Finland.

Developing his own particular talent, each farmer-craftsman became known for the implement which he was most skillful in producing. A bartering system, *domestic industries,* soon grew out of *home sloyd* and each farmer offered his finest products in exchange for those he needed.

This system of manufacturing continued until the advent of the industrial revolution in Scandinavia. Mechanized production proved too great a competitive challenge for domestic industries, and an era came to a gradual close. Without sloyd activities, many people turned to other pursuits. One in particular, brandy distillation, became so popular that the government was forced to pass laws limiting such manufacture, fearing that excessive alcoholic consumption would eventually destroy the character and fabric of the citizenry. As an alternative, schools for young boys were established to redevelop interest in sloyd and provide socially constructive activities once again. Products made in these schools were constructed according to local needs, and not necessarily because of the educational values inherent in their manufacture.

In Finland, *Uno Cygnaeus* (1810—1888) developed *folk schools* with studies based on the programs and ideas of Pestalozzi and Froebel. Manual dexterity through handwork was the main aim, not trade competency. Eventually, sloyd became integrated into the elementary schools, which were distinctly separate from the original sloyd schools.

As a refinement of Cygnaeus' work, *Otto Salomon* (1849-1907) of Sweden developed a systematic *educational sloyd,* which was made a part of the general education program in the elementary schools. Educational sloyd was characterized by the usefulness of the constructed articles, an organized analysis of processes similar to the Russian system, and formalized educational methodology, attributed to Cygnaeus. Through this unique combination, Salomon provided Sweden with the most advanced system of educational handwork at that time.

Educational sloyd was directed toward formative and utilitarian objectives not too dissimilar from those of contemporary education. Work experiences were to instill respect and love of manual labor; develop independence; cultivate accuracy, neatness, perseverance, and patience; and promote the refinement of physical and aesthetic powers. Instruction was based on the ability of the student to duplicate a series of models prepared by the teacher. At first these models were made of wood, but later, metal also became quite popular. Because the products of the sloyd movement were useful, and because its program was included in the general education of many youths, the sloyd movement spread throughout the world. It influenced many different types of manual training then in vogue.

Manual Training in the United States

Preceded by the establishment of many private technical and trade institutes, the *Morrill Act* (1862) provided for an endowment whereby land grant colleges could be developed to teach agriculture and mechanic arts. During the ensuing years, while private engineering institutes continued to flourish, many such public "A & M" colleges were established across the country.

At Washington University in St. Louis, *Dr. Calvin Woodward* (1837-1914) sensed a serious deficiency in the educational preparation of engineers. There existed a general lack of practical experience with tools, machines, and materials. This lack necessitated a lengthy post-graduate apprenticeship before a student could be recognized as an independent practicing engineer. Therefore Woodward organized shops in which the college carpenter could supervise those students who wished to perfect their mechanical abilities. The Russian Exhibit of Mechanic Arts at the Philadelphia Exposition of 1876 provided necessary reinforcement for Woodward's ideas.

Facing the same void in engineering education at the Massachusetts Institute of Technology (MIT), President *John D. Runkle* (1822–1902) initiated similar shopwork in woods and metals. The refinement of his and other such programs occurred because of their incorporation of principles associated both with sloyd and the mechanic arts. This resulted in a relatively new system of manual training.

The employment of this new and eclectic philosophy made the spread of manual training inevitable. Secondary schools began to adopt manual training programs. The Manual Training School of St. Louis was established under Woodward's guidance. Amid a great deal of controversy between academicians and educational pragmatists, similar schools were built in many major cities of the United States. The success of practical education continued to illustrate the need for integrating tools, materials, and manipulative activities into the traditional program of academic studies.

The turn of the century ushered in the further expansion of experience-oriented learning to the elementary and secondary schools. As a professor of mathematics before becoming a teacher of manual training, *Ira S. Griffith* (1874–1924) knew the benefits of a textbook that is correlated with classwork. To that date, little had been published in the field of manual training. Therefore he authored a book on basic woodworking that included plans for many small pieces of furniture, each selected for its design as well as for its utilitarian value.

John Dewey (1859–1952) promoted the study of man's occupations as the basis for a method of teaching in the elementary school. These modes of activity (occupations) provided a balance between the intellectual and practical phases of a person's life.

In the same vein, *Charles R. Richards* (1865–1936) of Columbia University structured his elementary education programs to provide learning experiences that would typify situations found outside the school environment. He was perhaps the one who coined the term "industrial arts" as a possible substitute for "manual training." The use of the term "industrial arts" suggests the transition within industrial education programs from purely manipulative operations to industrial occupations and activities.

Before this term was to enjoy wide acceptance, however, two other movements received a great deal of attention. As an outgrowth of the English arts and crafts movement, manual arts emphasized aesthetic creativity in project making. World War I and its associated training needs ushered in the vast expansion and popularity of vocational education and trade preparation.

The Manual Arts

Influenced by the Arts and Crafts Movement of England with its emphasis on creativity and aesthetics, manual training began to evolve into manual

arts. One of the leaders in this transition, *Charles A. Bennett* (1864–1942), instituted a system of the six arts of industry.
- *Graphic arts,* embracing all forms of drawing and illustrations.
- *Mechanic arts,* dealing with product construction in woods and metals.
- *Plastic arts,* including work with ductile materials such as clay and concrete.
- *Textile arts,* with activities in spinning, weaving, basketry, and garment making.
- *Bookmaking arts,* concerned with printing and bindery work experiences.
- *Culinary arts,* dealing with aspects of food preparation.

This structure was so comprehensive that many of the titles are still widely used and accepted in industrial arts and vocational education. With a philosophy similar to that of Dewey, Bennett was mainly concerned with education as preparation for life. He felt that all learning experiences in the schools should be directed toward the fulfillment of that most important goal.

Vocational Education

Although manual training was designed to fulfill the purposes of general education, public interest began to force it in the direction of vocational preparation. In 1881, one of the first schools emphasizing trade instruction opened its doors. Founded by *Richard T. Auchtmuty,* the New York Trade School offered a wide variety of courses in printing, painting, bricklaying, carpentry, plumbing, plastering, blacksmithing, sheet-metal working, and stonecutting.

Auchtmuty used much of his personal fortune to support the school. As the turn of the century approached, many educators began to stress the necessity for all types of manual education to place more emphasis on vocational preparation. The *Douglas Commission Report* (Massachusetts, 1905) expressed the inadvisability of practical education's total commitment to aesthetic and cultural ends. At the University of Missouri, Robert W. Selvidge noted a fundamental deficiency in the instruction of manual arts. He felt there was a general lack of activities that might at least orient students toward industrial occupations.

These attempts to analyze program emphasis came to an abrupt halt with the country's involvement in World War I. Immediately, skilled tradesmen were needed to develop wartime industry. Coincidentally, the passage of the *Smith-Hughes Act* (1917) provided for the development of special schools and training programs for vocational preparation. The establishment of this first federal aid program to vocational education forced the manual education movement to re-examine its goals in light of society's needs for occupational orientation and trade preparation. As time passed, vocational education and industrial arts developed individual identities, through a varied emphasis on common goals and desires.

While educators developed a wider variety of occupational programs, legislators tried to fill the need through the refinement of the original *Smith-Hughes Act* and the passage of new laws. The *George-Reed Act* (1929) provided funds for vocational home economics and vocational agriculture for a five-year period. Soon thereafter, the *George-Ellzey* and *George-Dean Acts* subsidized some distributive education courses in addition to continuing the appropriations of the George-Reed legislation. The *George-Barden Act* (1946) provided for increased flexibility in the use of funds.

The *National Defense Education Act* (NDEA, 1958), which embraced many disciplines and fields of interest, also included some provisions for vocational education. Funds were granted for salaries and travel expenses; purchase, rental, and maintenance of equipment; purchase of instructional supplies and media; needs assessment studies; transportation of students; work experience programs for drop-outs; and related instruction for apprentices.

Designed as a total amendment to all previous legislation in vocational education, the *Vocational Education Act* (VEA, 1963) provided for the extension of all active programs and the cultivation of new ones. It also promoted research and experimentation and established subsidies for work-study curricula.

The *VEA Amendments* of 1968 almost completely revised the original law. The amendments were designed to provide vocational education programs for the training and retraining of all people in need, regardless of their geographical location. Additional priority areas concerned with postsecondary education and with the education of the handicapped and the disadvantaged were also funded within the provisions of the amendments. Mainly because of this legislation, vocational education has continued to expand and flourish. Most recently, with the national emphasis on career orientation, exploration, and preparation, many new types of vocational programs are providing students with knowledge regarding possible careers. Contemporary program offerings are discussed in Chapter 3.

Industrial Arts

During the ten years following Richards' introduction of the term "industrial arts," many others experimented with the development of a curricular division which would better exemplify industry. Considerable confusion existed in terminology. Terms such as manual training, sloyd, manual arts, practical arts, handwork, construction, mechanic arts, and industrial arts were all in vogue, and were commonly used to describe similar programs.

In 1913, *Frederick G. Bonser* (1875-1931) established the framework for establishing the program of industrial arts as a separate subject by changing its previous concentration on *use* as a method of instruction. Working mainly with elementary school students, he promoted the idea that students

CHAPTER 2—HISTORICAL PERSPECTIVE

should become producers before participating in society as adult consumers. Thus, as members of an industrial society they would have a greater awareness and deeper understanding of the methods of industrial production used to fill human needs. His definition of industrial arts as *"those occupations by which changes are made in the forms of materials to increase their values for human usage . . . and of the problems of life related to those changes"* provided a basis for curriculum development.

Thus, the *project* became the principal means of teaching and learning. Teachers encouraged the integration of academic subjects and industrial arts through such projects as the building of birdhouses. Students first learned about the local species of birds before designing and building homes suitable for them.

Throughout the 1920s, 1930s, and 1940s, many educators refined and expanded existing industrial education programs. These same men made lasting contributions to the philosophy and methodology of industrial arts. *John F. Friese* authored many industrial education publications and was instrumental in incorporating guidance activities into vocational programs. *William J. Micheels,* a noted author, analyzed evaluation procedures and served as a curriculum change-agent in Minnesota, Wisconsin, and throughout the country. *Emanuel E. Ericson,* the author of the first edition of this text, evaluated the principles involved in teaching the industrial arts. *G. Harold Silvius* of Michigan, was the coauthor of numerous books and articles. *William E. Warner,* was instrumental in the founding of the American Industrial Arts Association and Epsilon Pi Tau; *Gordon O. Wilber,* was famous for his publications and especially for his definition of industrial arts.

Seven subject areas evolved that were quite similar to Bennett's manual arts. Woodworking and mechanical drawing were the most popular, with metalworking, graphic arts, crafts, mechanics, and the study of electricity incorporated in various degrees. The project method remained the central focus for instruction, with related information and attitudes derived from associated activities.

A re-evaluation of objectives and subject matter occurred during the 1950s and 1960s. An age of experimentation resulted from the technological nature of society. Subject areas expanded to include line production and studies of space travel, industrial plastics, and electronics. In this way, the foundation was laid for the prolific development of innovative programs.

Two in One Much of the confusion in connection with aims, goals, content, and teaching methods comes from a lack of distinction between the fundamental purposes and position of industrial arts as contrasted with vocational-industrial education. While these two activities have common characteristics to the point that they may appear similar when viewed superficially, they are two distinct and independent areas in industrial education.

TEACHING INDUSTRIAL EDUCATION

They must be so recognized if either is to be expected to render its maximum service in the educational program.

Industrial education is a comprehensive title used for all activities that are in some way connected with "education about industry," whether the program be introductory or trade-skill oriented. Therefore, both industrial arts and the industrially related portions of vocational education are embraced within the definition of this term.

The following listing should be helpful in pointing out distinguishing characteristics of each of these two related fields.

CHARACTERISTICS OF INDUSTRIAL ARTS	CHARACTERISTICS OF VOCATIONAL-INDUSTRIAL EDUCATION
• A program based on values attained principally through manipulative activity and study of industrial materials, life, and processes. • Emphasis placed upon exploration and participation, with attention to skill and efficiency. • Open and valuable for all students whether talented or not. • Pupils of all ages eligible. • Aims best served through a variety of experiences with tools and materials representing many industries and crafts. • Equipment need not match industrial conditions. • Classes held for single class periods except in special cases. • Not usually reimbursed through special federal funds, except where some programs emphasize occupational orientation. • Teachers primarily prepared in teacher-education institution. • Course content, length of time, etc., determined by school conditions. • Projects are chosen with reference to student interest and educational needs. • Success measured in terms of pupil progress rather than skill with which work is done.	• A specialized program for the purpose of preparing students for remunerative employment. • Development of trade skills and occupational competence is emphasized. • Students selected with reference to aptitude for the work. • Available to students of high school age and older. • Concentration on one trade or the surveying of a cluster of occupations. • Working conditions and kinds of equipment should basically be parallel to those of industry. • Work usually carried on in lengthy periods each day in trade practice and related subjects. • Reimbursable through state and federal funds. • Teachers selected from trades with professional courses or programs. • Course content and duration of courses arranged through advisory committees. • Work assignments based upon practices in the trade. • Standards of workmanship judged in the light of demands of the trade.

DISCUSSION QUESTIONS

1. How did the early philosophy that learning should be a natural experience that occurs in all aspects of living affect the principal activities of purposeful instruction? How did these activities relate to the character of the prevailing culture?

2. Why is Pestalozzi considered by many to be the "father of manual training?"

3. What type of society was promoted by von Fellenberg's instructional methodology? Give reasons for your answer.

4. What were the major events that led to the apprenticeship system of training.

5. What were the major causes for transferring responsibility for training craftsmen from the factory to the school system?

6. Cite and describe the major contributions of the Russian system of mechanic arts to the overall development of industrial education.

7. Describe the type of project mainly used for the learning and practice of tool manipulation in early manual training programs.

8. What event precluded the acceptance of Della Vos' work in the United States?

9. Define "sloyd" and trace its stages of development.

10. Cite and describe the major contributions of the sloyd system to the overall development of industrial education.

11. Do the objectives of sloyd still have relevance in contemporary society? Defend your answer with a comparison of the two cultural periods.

12. Compare the birth of manual training in the United States with the implementation of the mechanic arts of Russia. Did the two systems have similar causes? Describe.

13. How did Bennett's manual arts areas lead naturally to the development of the traditional areas of industrial arts and home economics?

14. What major events led to the public promotion of vocationally oriented manual training programs?

15. Discuss the main objectives of vocational-industrial education and industrial arts. Are these two curricular divisions totally separate, integrated, or simply mutually beneficial? Explain.

16. Trace chronologically the federal legislation that assisted the development of vocational education programs.

17. How does vocational education fit into the broad spectrum of career education? Does industrial arts also have contributions to make in career orientation? Is it also possible for academic subjects to provide activities in this direction? Explain.

18. How did Bonser provide a philosophical foundation for industrial arts education?

19. In your experience, do contemporary industrial arts programs fall short of, fulfill, or go beyond the original intent of Bonser's definition? Explain.

TEACHING INDUSTRIAL EDUCATION

20. Are typical projects in industrial arts more similar to sloyd, manual training, or manual arts? Provide reasons for your answer.

21. Name and describe the seven traditional areas of industrial arts activities.

22. Define industrial education, industrial arts, and vocational-industrial education. Describe how they are interrelated.

ADDITIONAL READINGS

Barlow, Melvin L. *History of Industrial Education in the United States.* Peoria, Illinois: Chas. A. Bennett, 1967.

Bennett, Charles A. *History of Manual and Industrial Education up to 1870.* Peoria, Illinois: Chas. A. Bennett, 1926.

Bennett, Charles A. *History of Manual and Industrial Education, 1870 to 1917.* Peoria, Illinois: Chas. A. Bennett, 1937.

Evans, Rupert N. *Foundations of Vocational Education.* Columbus, Ohio: Charles E. Merrill, 1971.

Henry, Nelsen B., ed. *Forty-Second Yearbook, Part I: Vocational Education.* Chicago: University of Chicago Press, 1943.

Mays, Arthur B. *Essentials of Industrial Education.* New York: McGraw-Hill, 1952.

Miller, Rex, and Smalley, Lee H. *Selected Readings for Industrial Arts.* Bloomington, Illinois: McKnight & McKnight, 1963.

Olson, Delmar W. *Industrial Arts and Technology.* Englewood Cliffs, New Jersey: Prentice-Hall, 1963.

Roberts, Roy W. *Vocational and Practical Arts Education.* 3rd ed. New York: Harper & Row, 1971.

Thompson, John F. *Foundations of Vocational Education.* Englewood Cliffs, New Jersey: Prentice-Hall, 1973.

Chapter 3
Curriculum Trends

The Search for Relevance

In the late 1940s philosopher-practitioners prescribed many curriculum refinements that were similar in content and method. However, their vision was so futuristic that general acceptance still remains unfulfilled. Program offerings in industrial education are often still very similar to their historical antecedents.

Bonser's definition of industrial arts, mentioned in Chapter 2, was considered by some to reflect pre-war developments in industrial education. In order for industrial arts curricula to become more representative of the industrial-technological society into which the war years had propelled us, Gordon O. Wilber suggested that industrial arts include *"those phases of general education that deal with industry—its organization, materials, occupations, processes, and products—and with the problems resulting from the industrial and technological nature of society."*

Since that time, many have attempted to update traditional program offerings and bring them more in line with the broad scope of that definition. In addition, Wilber suggested many goals, objectives, and activities. Although intended for industrial arts, his writings, because of their comprehensive nature, also found applicability in vocational-industrial education, depending on which goals received primary emphasis.

There were other educators involved in curriculum design at the time Wilber was doing his work. The greatest contributions to the field were provided by William Warner of Ohio State University with "A Curriculum to Reflect Technology." Delmar Olsen proposed an extensive plan for revision and refinement titled "Industrial Arts and Technology."

A Curriculum to Reflect Technology. In 1947, at the annual convention of the American Industrial Arts Association held in Columbus, Ohio, William Warner proposed "A Curriculum to Reflect Technology" as the feature presentation. Resulting from extensive research, six major subject matter divisions were established: *power, transportation, manufacture, construction, communication,* and *management.* Such an organization, although immediately praised as a giant step forward, actually found little general acceptance on a national scale. Regardless, this unique effort is considered the foundation for the curriculum development revolution in industrial education that occurred during the 1960s.

Industrial Arts and Technology. Delmar Olsen was another leader to establish a culture-based program to acquaint students with the technological society around them. In his proposal, "Industrial Arts and Technology," all activities were related to industrial experiences in *power and transportation, electricity-electronics, construction, services, production, organization and management,* and *research and development.* The scope of the program was comprehensive, and curriculum tracks were provided for students of all ages. The use of such comprehensive titles for industrial education activities set the stage for the shift away from historically established names such as "woods," "metals," and "drafting."

Unitary Teaching

In industrial education, units have been used for many years as a method of structuring technical subject matter and the instruction of manipulative skills into convenient sections, chapters, or work periods. During the 1950s, an alteration to this basic method of teaching and learning centered units around personal and industrial themes or problems. At that time, outstanding curriculum projects employing unitary teaching were developed in Massachusetts, Maryland, and Maine.

The Unit Method of Fitchburg State College. An early attempt to organize instructional material according to unitary method was undertaken at Fitchburg State College in Massachusetts under the direction of James J. Hammond. While most traditional industrial teaching had focused on tools, machines, operations, processes, and products, the unit method of Fitchburg State provided more specific themes to unify class and laboratory activities. Topics related to:

- *Two-dimensional puzzles*—providing introductory drafting and design.
- *Toys and games*—including the planning and processing of an article.
- *Christmas decorations*—with life-sized figures.
- *Household accessories*—incorporating the construction of all types of helpful implements for use around the home.
- *Sports equipment*—including the construction or repair of items such as skis and tennis rackets.

The organization of learning activities into such units offered all students the opportunity to pursue individual interests while sharing a common unit theme or topic with others.

The Maryland Plan. In the late 1950s, at the University of Maryland, Donald E. Maley organized an industrial arts program into several themes, or units. Designed primarily to acquaint the individual student with the industrial and technological advancements of society, class activities incorporated the study of mathematics, sciences, social studies, and communications. Intended for use in the junior high school, the seventh-grade program was centered around an *anthropological approach,* so that students studied the historical evolution of *tools and machines, power and energy,* and *communication and transportation.* Emphasizing a contemporary study of industry, the eighth-grade activities involved a *group project,* which dealt with the organization and products of major industries.

It also involved *line production* which, while providing a marketable product, included a complete industrial organization for class involvement and interaction. In ninth-grade, students continued the program through a study of individualized units related to contemporary technological developments.

The Maryland Plan is especially noted for its introduction of *research and experimentation* as an integral part of industrial arts education. This portion of the program was designed for students of high ability, above-average intelligence, and exceptional creativity, but students of all types have found such experiences stimulating, rewarding, and educational.

Industrial Arts Technology. Commonly known as the Maine State Plan, this adaptation by John Mitchell, of the University of Maine at Gorham, combined many aspects of previously mentioned plans. Organized in 1959 and 1960, the program for grades 7–9 included manufacturing industries —with units relating to topics such as *technology and civilization, household accessories, personal accessories, sports equipment, communications devices, tools,* and *furniture.* Construction industries, power and transportation industries, electrical-electronics industries, and service industries were course titles recommended for grades 10–12.

The Maine State Plan incorporated course names established by Warner and Olsen with unit themes allied with Maley and Hammond. The evolutionary process of curriculum development had begun, and the basic industrial topics of manufacturing, construction, communication, service, power, and transportation had become firmly established as the bases for further programmatic refinement.

Analyzing Industrial Organization

In the early 1960s, it became apparent that there was a need in industrial education programs for a series of activities relating to the operation of an ongoing industry. Many programs were developed that attempted to incorporate industrial administrative structures and personnel organizations into traditional subjects. Later developments provided for a conceptual base, promoting insights into the most intricate operations of a contemporary industry. Although there are many programs of this type, only *Functions of Industry, American Industry Project,* and *Orchestrated Systems* are described here to illustrate three possible approaches for developing such a program.

Functions of Industry. Evolving from a review of the industrial teacher education program at Wayne State University in Detroit, the Functions of Industry program offered a conceptual study and activity sequence to assist students in *understanding industrial activities and processes,* and *selecting an occupation oriented toward industry.* The subject matter centered around *goods producing* and *goods servicing,* established as the two basic functions of an industrial enterprise. Aspects of production related mainly to research, development, production planning, and manufacturing. The diagnosis, testing, and correction of industrial problems comprised the servicing portion of the program. Although this program was an early attempt at a fundamental analysis of industry, many similar attempts can be found in later, more developed programs.

American Industry Project. Resulting from U. S. Office of Education and Ford Foundation Grants, the American Industry Project was originated by Wesley Face and Eugene Flug at Stout State University in Wisconsin. The curriculum seeks to assist students in understanding industrial concepts. It also seeks to develop their abilities to understand and solve industrial problems. The program is structured on three levels: *industrial orientation, in-depth study,* and *individualized research and experimentation of industrial problems.* The entire program is intended to bridge the gap between the general education interests of industrial arts and the occupational preparation emphasized by the vocational education of trades and industries.

This complete analysis of industry resulted in the identification of thirteen major themes: *marketing, management, production, materials, processes, energy, communications, transportation, finance, property, research, procurement,* and *relationships.* The conceptual approach to industrial analysis was founded on an analysis of a cultural environment involving government, public interest, competition, private property, and material resources. The comprehensive nature of the American Industry Project, and its use of many available instructional materials has established it as one of the outstanding curriculum developments of the 1960s.

Orchestrated Systems. Concerned with individual development, this program leads the student toward developing habits of self-discipline, investigation, and the discovery of new knowledge. Likewise, self-motivation directs the student toward practice, with the anticipation of the acquisition of new skills and techniques. Developed in 1966 by Lewis Yoho of Indiana State University at Terre Haute, the project is concerned primarily with production and consumption activities relating to industrial goods and services, as man continues to pursue the "good life," which results from the industrial and technological nature of society.

Subject matter is structured through the use of a systems modeling technique titled "Systems Network Analysis Process," or "snap maps." Activities are provided in a comprehensive laboratory designed for the line production of consumer goods. Students become involved in product design, production planning, manufacturing, assembly, packaging, and shipping. Peripheral activity areas include drafting, jig and fixture design, communications, scheduling, specification writing, maintenance, work measurement and methods, quality control, electronic instrumentation and control, automatic systems, plant layout, and materials handling. Upon entering the program for the first time, the students are processed through a personnel department, just as in a real industry. After completing an interview and tests, and after engaging in a variety of basic activities, the student progresses to more responsible positions in the industrial organization as his or her newly acquired skills allow for advancement. In a program of this type, there is maximum student participation. Although there is little time for technical specialization, students do leave the program with a broad conceptual knowledge of industrial production and its place in society.

Classifying Types of Industries

The three plans described in the last section offered a structural analysis of industry as the basis for curriculum planning. Although similar in many respects and utilizing many of the same structural concepts, the *Industrial Arts Curriculum Project* and *Industriology* place primary emphasis on the identification of types of basic industries in order to establish another logical and convenient outline for subject matter organization.

Industrial Arts Curriculum Project. Considered by teachers of industrial arts as the most significant curriculum innovation of the 1960s, the IACP has influenced the redefinition and updating of many standard subject offerings in junior high schools throughout the country. In 1965, after receiving federal funds, Donald Lux, Willis Ray, Jacob Stern, and Edward Towers initiated a joint study effort at Ohio State University and the University of Illinois. The project grew out of a general concern that the traditional industrial arts curriculum was too narrow in scope to acquaint students sufficiently with contemporary industry. Extensive research activity resulted in a rationale, a statement concerning the structure of knowledge, a general study of society and its institutional practices, and a detailed study of industry and industrial technology. It also developed two one-year programs for instructional implementation: *The World of Construction* for grades 7 or 8, and *The World of Manufacturing* for grades 8 or 9.

The first course includes a comprehensive set of activities involving role playing and problem solving. These activities are associated with surveying, soil testing, topography, site and structural design, masonry, electricity, plumbing, plastering, framing and roofing, insulation, interior decoration and landscaping. The second course deals mainly with the planning, organizing, and controlling of manufacturing or production systems. Topics include market analysis, designing, fabrication of prototypes, and setup of production and assembly lines. There are also studies of materials like oil, rubber, and plastic, topics which have previously found little or no inclusion in traditional programs.

Field evaluation centers were set up in junior high schools in Long Beach, California; Austin, Texas; Chicago and Evanston in Illinois; Cincinnati, Ohio; Dade County, Florida; and in the Trenton, New Jersey area. As a result of the feedback collected from this initial period of trial and evaluation, the program was revised many times prior to its final publication and dissemination on a national scale. A complete instructional package of materials is available, including teacher's guides, textbooks, student lab manuals, supplies, and equipment. Through participation in summer workshops, thousands of industrial educators have adopted and adapted the

IACP. This program has found more general acceptance than any other similar curriculum innovation in industrial education.

Industriology. Defined as the "science of industry," the concept of Industriology was originated in 1965 by Jack Kirby and the industrial education faculty of the University of Wisconsin at Platteville. Industriology was intended as a means to update, not replace, the traditional offerings of industrial education. The four-phase program provides a two-track approach to the study of industry in the school setting. The first track, a study of the *types of industries,* categorized all industries into *raw materials, manufacturing, distribution,* or *service* types. The second track, involves the *activities of industry,* with learning experiences dealing with *development and design, purchasing, manufacturing and processing, finance and office services, industrial relations,* and *marketing.* Most of these activities are found in all of the basic industries previously mentioned.

Planned as a continuum for orderly educational growth, *Phase I, Structure of Industry,* offers a general orientation to industry. In *Phase II, Industrial Elements and Processes,* an in-depth study of industrial operations is provided. *Modern Industries, Phase III,* incorporates many activities associated with metalworking, woodworking, power, graphics, ceramics, the textile industries, and electronics. As a culminating experience, *Phase IV, Vocational and Occupational Guidance,* by providing counseling and on-site visitations, is designed to assist students entering the job market. Faculty members and industrial educators have developed instructional materials for much of the program during teacher institutes.

Universal Themes and Problems

Mankind has always been faced with problems. At first, they related mainly to obtaining food, finding shelter from the elements, and obtaining safety from enemies. In contemporary society, however, most of these basic needs have been sufficiently satisfied, so that time is now available for seeking solutions to environmental, societal, psychological, ecological, and geographic problems. Some leaders in industrial education are critical of the shortsightedness of an "industries" approach to curriculum development. They note predictions concerning the relatively small number of men who will be needed in the next century for manufacturing or producing the world's goods. These industrial educators believe that the industrial age will soon give way to a new, super-technological era. To educate youth for today will render them helpless in tomorrow's world.

Many curriculum developers prescribe conceptual approaches for program planning in order to provide students with long-range insights and help them cope with the future. This section, plus others that follow, describes some of the programs that have been designed on that basis. In searching out theoretical and practical constructs, the *Fitchburg-Dracut Thematic Approach* utilized a refined method of unitary teaching, while the *Maryland Plan for Senior High School* attacks contemporary and future problems of society. Both incorporate the unit method of teaching and learning, described earlier in this chapter and also in Chapter 6.

Fitchburg-Dracut Thematic Approach. Few problems encountered in our contemporary society can be solved by the solutions offered by a single discipline. Usually, many areas of study are called upon, to assist in arriving at the best solution. This approach was applied to curriculum design when Fitchburg State College and the school system of Dracut, Massachusetts combined talents and resources to seek a plan for substantial interdisciplinary cooperation between the subject areas of art, science, industrial education, mathematics, social studies, languages, and physical education.

In the thematic approach, *universal themes* such as *communication, measurement, energy, materials, transformation,* and *structures* were selected as teaching topics. Each was chosen because of its generic relationship to all subjects in the school, not just to those of industrial education. Each theme was taught simultaneously to participating classes in a manner that related to the methods and subject matter unique to their particular disciplines. As a result, students were able to integrate educational experiences, find commonalities between subjects, and transfer information and concepts between content areas of the curriculum.

The Maryland Plan for Senior High Schools. Reviewing industrial arts programs across the nation, a researcher would find little attention given to the problems of society resulting from industry and technology. Seeking to fill this void, Donald Maley of the University of Maryland proposed a high school program designed to assist secondary school students in exploring the applications of technology in the solution of major societal problems that face mankind today and in the future. Using four instructional modes similar to the junior high school program of the same name, Maley suggested that the student be involved in the learning process through the *unit method;* the *group process; research, experimentation, and development;* and a *school-community interface.*

Maley called for interdisciplinary cooperation between science, technology, sociology, mathematics, psychology, geography, history, and communications. He stated that education must seek solutions to the pressing problems and issues of *pollution, power generation, housing, transportation, communication, conservation, efficient resource usage, waste disposal,* and *industrial productivity.* While recognizing that there are many other similar problems with which man must deal, Maley established these as most appropriate for study in industrial education.

Generally, such a program provides an exciting experience for both students and teachers. Since the problems will change, the program will change. The program will update itself each time a problem is researched and the method of its solution will reflect new discoveries. As with the junior high school program, major emphasis is placed on the educational development of the individual student.

Clusters of Occupations

Prior to 1960, vocational programs in secondary schools usually prepared a student for employment in a single trade or craft. Although these programs continually updated content and methods to keep pace with important developments in industry, graduates often found themselves occupationally immobile and relatively insecure in the rapidly changing job market. Automated industrial practice often forced a worker into unemployment. While having sufficient skill in a particular trade, a worker found that it was sometimes relatively difficult to change his or her occupation, either by choice or necessity. Some federal assistance programs, like those provided through the Manpower Development Training Act, made retraining possible along with some assurance of employment in another trade.

During the 1960s, a decade of study and renewal, programs were designed to combat vocational obsolescence before it occurred. In secondary schools, educators initiated programs employing a more general approach to training. Associated jobs and skills were clustered, or grouped into comprehensive categories, offering students a series of related experiences for developing their competencies in a broad field of occupational interests. Although many curricula of this type were developed during this period, only five are cited in this section. They serve as examples illustrating progressive refinement of the clustering process. The first three, *Introduction to Vocations, Training for Families of Skills,* and *Occupational, Vocational, and Technical Program,* provide an evolutionary description of occupational clusters. In the late 1960s, as the career education concept became more popular, the *Correlated Curriculum Project* and *Galaxy Plan for Career Preparation* emerged as two plans directed toward the inclusion of all occupational clusters within three or four "career-oriented" clusters.

Introduction to Vocations. This program resulted from a 1963 appropriation by the North Carolina State Legislature. The program was under the direction of Joe R. Clary. Its major objectives dealt with developing in the student a number of attitudes:

- A realistic self-concept through self-appraisal.
- An appreciation of the ever-changing employment market.
- An understanding of the fundamental processes of production and distribution.
- An acquaintance with major occupational clusters and their interrelationships.
- The development of inherent technical specialties.
- The acquisition of desirable attitudes toward the dignity of work.

Specifically, the program was designed to assist students in making tentative, realistic vocational choices as they progressed through school. The six major steps directed toward the fulfillment of these goals were study *of the self-appraisal process, major economic systems, industrial occupations, business occupations, professional occupations,* and *future pos-*

CHAPTER 3—CURRICULUM TRENDS

sibilities. Although an early attempt at the formulation of occupational clusters, this North Carolina State University plan established a solid foundation upon which many future plans were modeled.

Training for Families of Skills. Known as *Project ABLE,* this plan was developed in Quincy, Massachusetts as a result of a 1965 U. S. Office of Education grant. The plan provided the non-college preparatory students, numbering 75 percent of the student population, with more realistic, occupationally-oriented, educational activities. Directed originally by Maurice J. Daly, the project assisted students in gaining vocational competence, becoming responsible citizens, and realizing their own maximum potential in selected fields of employment.

Students entered the program in junior high school. All took a general technology course with study units concerned with *mechanical and electrical principles, spatial concepts, chemical-biological principles, and social relationships.* In high school the student studied the occupational clusters embraced by the fields of *electronics, metals and machines, power mechanics, general woodworking, general piping, food preparation, computer data processing, graphic and commercial arts, health occupations, home economics,* and *business education.* All instructional materials for the program were developed cooperatively in a unique team-teaching effort involving educators in the fields of mathematics, physical science, social science, English, and vocational studies.

Occupational, Vocational, and Technical Program. Initiated in 1964, the OVT was based on the desire of a community to retain a greater percentage of young people in the locale through educational job-entry programs and advanced skill development activities. Jerry C. Olson directed the program in the Pittsburgh Public Schools. Comprehensive, exploratory activities in industrial arts, home economics, and business education were considered the principal components of the OVT program. All junior high students were introduced to the broad occupational areas of *business communications, information processing, merchandising, food and nutrition, clothing and textiles, social and individual services, visual communications, manufacturing, construction,* and *power and transportation.* Following the series of comprehensive learning opportunities in the junior high school, subject matter in grades 9 through 12 offered students many opportunities for increased specialization in the occupational field of their choice.

Correlated Curriculum Project. Although the previously mentioned three programs show a continuous growth in the number and variety of occupational clusters or groupings, these final two are directed toward fewer categories, illustrating another type of comprehensive organization for vocational programs.

In order to provide more meaningful and realistic integration of subject matter, the New York City public schools developed a correlated curriculum under the sponsorship of a Ford Foundation grant. The curriculum was

structured to include educational experiences related to three major career clusters:
- *Business careers*—jobs commonly found in manufacturing, retailing, distribution, and finance.
- *Health careers*—jobs in food services, laboratory services, medical and hospital care, personal nursing, and therapy services.
- *Industrial careers*—job classifications found in electromechanics, building construction, equipment maintenance, and transportation.

Students were rotated through the three career groups during the early high school years. In grades 11 and 12, all were encouraged to concentrate on one or more of the career clusters. Laboratory activities were reinforced with correlated subject matter from the fields of science, mathematics, and English. The emphasis was now directed toward the development of a careers orientation, a cluster style considered to be even more general and comprehensive in structure.

Galaxy Plan for Career Preparation. In 1968, the Detroit Public Schools published a description of the Galaxy Plan for Career Preparation. Directed by Carl H. Turnquist, it was organized around four career clusters:
- *Materials and processes*—metals, wood, ceramics, soil, and plastics.
- *Energy and propulsion*—land, sea, and air vehicles, electronics, power plants, and instrumentation utilizing electricity.
- *Visual communications*—art, drafting, printing, secretarial services, bookkeeping, writing, and information storage and retrieval systems.
- *Personal services*—health, commercial foods, environment, clothing, cosmetology, performing arts, recreation, distribution, and protection services.

Students in grades 7 and 8 participated in introductory half-year courses in each of the four clusters. In secondary school, students were offered the opportunity to specialize in areas of their own choosing. Four paths provided structural uniformity for students in the program. All occupations were classified as *professional, technical, trade preparatory,* or *occupational preparatory.* The Galaxy Plan was another outstanding program seeking fewer, more general categories for the organization of occupational education.

Career Education Concepts

As an answer to the criticisms, problems, questions, and general educational upheaval of the 1960s, the *career education movement* sought to provide students with topics of greater relevancy in their school programs. In 1971, one of the most outstanding promoters of the concept was the U. S. Commissioner of Education, Sidney P. Marland, Jr. Asking all educators to take a long and hard look at their curricula and daily teaching activities, he urged a redefinition and refinement of educational purposes. He proposed that the activities of everyday life be integrated into the school program. It was felt that such a program would provide new realism and excitement in the teaching-learning process and would help to relate the educational environment to the environment outside the classroom.

The entire concept was formulated around eight elements:
- *Career awareness*—an introduction to possible occupations.
- *Self-awareness*—the assessment of personal aptitudes and interests.
- *Appreciations and attitudes*—the development of habits of cooperative and ethical citizenship in a technological society.
- *Decision-making skills*—the ability to evaluate individual potential realistically.
- *Economic awareness*—guidance toward independence in the world of work.
- *Tool and process applications*—experiences with equipment and operations.
- *Employability skills*—acquiring, practicing, and perfecting job performance.
- *Educational awareness*—the realization of continuing education as a fundamental necessity in a productive life.

Based on the assumption that much of what had been termed "general" education was comparatively meaningless to many youths, the U. S. Office of Education proposed *a set of goals* for career education, *a series of fifteen occupational clusters,* and *four models for the implementation of the concept.*

Major goals. In order to provide a unified plan for the development and acceptance of career-oriented education, activities were directed toward several specific goals.
- *Making all subject matter more meaningful and relevant for students.*
- *Providing counseling, guidance, and instruction for self-awareness and direction.*
- *Availing all students of the opportunity to develop entry-level job skills or suitably prepare themselves for further education or employment.*
- *Providing placement services upon leaving school.*
- *Utilizing more community resources in the educational system.*
- *Increasing occupational studies by providing more occupational choices for students to pursue as career goals.*

Occupational clusters. In the previous section of this chapter, different types of clusters were described. In the 1970s, the U. S. Office of Education suggested fifteen occupational clusters formulated to embrace the thousands of vocational possibilities listed in the *Dictionary of Occupational Titles.* Occupations were classified as relating to the following categories:
- *Business and office.*
- *Marketing and distribution.*
- *Communications and media.*
- *Construction.*
- *Manufacturing.*

- *Transportation.*
- *Agri-business and natural resources.*
- *Marine science.*
- *Environmental control.*
- *Public services.*
- *Health.*
- *Hospitality and recreation.*
- *Personal services.*
- *Fine arts and humanities.*
- *Consumer and homemaking careers.*

In selecting the clusters, qualifications were established to assure verifiable comprehensiveness. Each cluster had to encompass existing jobs, and be easily organized into units providing instructional materials and methods. It also had to relate closely to entry-level jobs in the existing labor market, and familiarize a student with a cluster of occupations. Vocational education offers educational programs for a majority of those listed. Industrial education relates mainly to aspects of communications and media, construction, manufacturing and transportation.

Models for implementation. In all, four approaches were proposed to enact career education concepts. These were *a school-based, or comprehensive model, an employer-based model, a home or community-based model,* and *a residential-based model.*

School-based activities included students from kindergarten through junior college years. Career education was intended for all students. An educational treatment system was developed to include certain central strategies necessary for guiding students into rewarding employment.

- *Diagnosis*—assessment of needs.
- *Prescription*—specification of behavioral objectives.
- *Treatment*—development of attitudes, knowledge, and skills.
- *Assessment*—evaluation of results.
- *Decision*—acceptance or rejection of the results and estimation of student's progress.

The *employer-based model* provided an alternative to schooling for teenagers in a work-oriented environment. A closer relationship was developed between the school and the business community by involving public and private employers in the academic program of the local school.

Home and community-based models centered around the development of an educational delivery system in homes through the establishment of career-development programs for adults with community-based counseling services. Other objectives were the preparation of more competent workers through continuous education, and the enhancement of the quality of home life.

In the *residential-based model,* disadvantaged individuals and families were provided with resident programs and services.

Interwoven into all of these models were levels of career education, beginning with *awareness*—becoming informed about all available occupations. Through *orientation* the individual student explores occupational clusters of interest. *Preparation* is the tentative selection of an occupational cluster. Finally, the student's experiences lead to *specialization,* the intensive development of a specific set of skills in one occupational cluster.

Career education includes not only vocational preparation for work, but also the development of those attitudes and skills, and the acquisition of that knowledge necessary for a satisfying and productive life. Career education seeks to achieve this through a total integration of the principles and activities relevant to an individual's occupational, home, and leisuretime environments.

Elementary School Programs

Through the years, many educational philosophers have stated the fundamental importance of active involvement in constructive pursuits. This was of special importance to the very young student in elementary schools. The writings of Francis Bacon, John Comenius, Jean Jacques Rousseau, Johann Pestalozzi, Friedrich Froebel, and John Dewey promote the use of handwork activities to provide a center of interest and to infuse reality into the abstractions of most academic subjects. Brief descriptions of their philosophies of education are provided in Chapter 2.

Historically, activities were related to crafts. Students were mainly involved in the construction of bird feeders and houses, small shelves, novelties, and household ornaments. More recently, with the development of curricular unification, social studies, mathematics, science, and the fine arts have found new realism when integrated with industrial education. Interdisciplinary cooperation benefits industrial education programs by giving practical activities new breadth and meaning. The programs resulting from such integration often deal with industry and technology, for they are inherent in all phases of contemporary life.

The use of clusters is also found in the industrial education programs of elementary schools. Familiar topics dealing with construction, manufacturing of consumer goods, power generation, transportation vehicles, communications devices, and most recently, the career education emphasis, provide an introduction to the world of work.

From many attempts, two established programs are exercising influence on elementary school curriculum development in industrial education. The first, *Industrial Arts for Children,* is college-based, while the other, *Technology for Children,* was developed as an elementary school-based model. Both are aimed at providing very young students with an integrated introduction to academic subjects, industry, the world of work, career awareness, and technology in society.

Industrial Arts for Children. At Kent State University in Ohio, future teachers are trained in methods for teaching academic subjects. The

teachers-in-training become involved in an observation-demonstration-research-experimentation-participation sequence. Activities involve:
- *Planning and material selection.*
- *Materials processing.*
- *Historical development.*
- *Present practice.*
- *Contemporary research in industrial arts for elementary schools.*
- *Unit planning for technical topics.*
- *Laboratory and program management practices.*
- *Development of integrated activities for children's understanding of the interrelatedness of all knowledge.*

The primary objective is the motivation of elementary school children by involving them in a stimulating environment providing interesting, and often exciting, activities.

Technology for Children. Commonly called T4CP, the Technology for Children Project was originated by Elizabeth Hunt in 1967 and continued to flourish under the direction of Fred J. Dreves, Jr. The program was planned under the joint sponsorship and support of the Ford Foundation and the New Jersey Division of Vocational Education. Many of the state's elementary school students participated in the program.

Primarily, the project aimed at assisting children in the basic conceptual understanding of traditional academic subjects by involving them in constructive activities and community affairs. Citizens from all walks of life visited the schools to describe their trades and professions. Students visited businesses, industries, and agencies of local government. Through these visits, they were able to acquaint themselves with different occupations.

In this program, students have constructed voting booths for use in social studies units. When learning about the postal system, they have printed, sold, and mailed Christmas cards. They have constructed maps in connection with geography studies; they have built small houses in the classroom; they have printed a weekly newspaper, and produced a videotaped television show. After the adoption of such activities, teachers reported new vitality and increased understanding on the part of their school students.

Emphasis on Technology

Subject matter in industrial education has passed through a series of stages. For years, trades or crafts were the main emphases. At that time, programs were easily adapted to a technical level or to the vocational orientation of the student. Many production systems were structured to instruct students in individual skills.

Substantial mechanization in production lines required a new training emphasis. Industry became the center of interest, and comprehensive programs were developed around clusters of occupations and careers.

More recently, the use of computers and advanced automated systems has necessitated continuous examination, evaluation, redefinition, and

CHAPTER 3—CURRICULUM TRENDS

refinement of curricula. Toward this end, a third generation of program evolution is described in this section. It deals with the development of clusters concerning technology, the main theme and direction of tomorrow's world.

Enterprise: Man and Technology. In 1968, at Southern Illinois University in Carbondale, Ronald W. Stadt originated the *Enterprise* program. Designed as a pre-vocational, generalized, career-oriented program of education, it utilized simulation models as the main method of enabling students to learn about men and technology in the world of work. A conceptually based program in occupational education, it was organized into a series of clusters. Following an introductory experience in the operation of an enterprise, students participated in learning activities related to *visual communications, materials and processes, electronics and instrumentation,* and *energy conversion and power transmission.* Entry-level occupational training was also provided during the high school years.

James A. Sullivan coordinated the project, wherein students became actively involved in planning, financing, organizing, staffing, controlling, testing, and operating a productive enterprise relating to manufacturing, construction, retailing, banking, or distribution. The program was an attempt to simulate the operations of actual businesses and industries in contemporary society.

Processing Centers. This new type of industrial education at Central Connecticut State College is based on a conceptual framework. Originated by Joseph Duffy, the program is designed to incorporate more technological concepts than have been previously included in traditional curricular offerings of industrial education. Clusters involve the following activities:

- *Information processing*—the translation of man's ideas into the industrial-technological languages of graphics and computers.
- *Materials processing*—the alteration of the forms of raw materials into useful objects.
- *Energy processing*—the generation and utilization of energy and power to assist man in work-related tasks.

Man and Technology. Man is the creator of technology. If man's education is to be liberal, it must deal with the social, cultural, aesthetic, physical, and technological aspects of human life. At Oswego State University in New York, Paul DeVore, after exhaustive research, developed a curriculum foundation for industrial arts based on technology as an academic discipline. The examination of the cumulative knowledge base resulted in the formation of a taxonomy, or structure, of technology. It was organized into elements, areas, divisions, systems, categories, types, classes, and order.

Central themes or areas proposed for study were *communication, production,* and *transportation.* These three technological clusters were chosen as the key points for the total program in industrial arts education because they seemed to include all activities relating to the history, inventions and innovations, contemporary problems and practical solutions involved in the study of man and technology.

Tecnol-o-gee. Technology is being blamed for many of the cultural, social, environmental, and political problems of the day. Although technology has sometimes been man's instrument of destruction and decay, man has also reaped benefits from technological progress. Positive aspects of technology are emphasized in the concept *"tecnol-o-gee,"* written in a manner which expresses the enthusiasm and excitement of young students pursuing its study and applications.

This emphasis is substantially an expansion and refinement of Delmar W. Olson's original thesis. It retains his primary directive for American education—to prepare youth to comprehend, wisely use, efficiently operate, control, and alter technology. Industrial education in particular should accept the responsibility for the major fulfillment of that objective.

Content is organized into three clusters:
- *The technical complex*—the materials and processes of technology.
- *The human complex*—man, who has created and who controls technology.
- *The culture complex*—our continuously evolving society.

Sample topics in the technical complex include materials, manufacturing, industrial organization and management, engineering, and manpower. The human complex studies creation and invention, planning and designing, aesthetics, and recreation. Incorporated into the culture complex are such aspects as the economic, historical, social, religious, and industrial spheres of man's existence. Total integration of subject matter disciplines is necessary for a meaningful, comprehensive treatment.

Evolution from Revolutions

Over the years, substantial updating and refinement have occurred in the curricula and programs of industrial education. This continuous alteration has resulted from teacher dissatisfaction with traditional subject matter, student and teacher boredom with annual project repetition, and low esteem of "practical" education by academicians and the public. Resultant innovations, or "revolutions," have failed to find wide acceptance, however, and their impact on the profession has been relatively small.

Most of the conceptual clusters relate to individuals in an industrial-technological setting, as they identify needs and seek methods of fulfillment. *Ideation* is the initial step in the process. It generates the necessity for many types of transferal systems for *data communication*. Ideas, in order to come to fruition, call for *production processes,* employing many types of materials and occupations. To alter materials into desirable forms, the processing methods require diversified forms of *energy* and *power*. Although each of these three key processes are unique and independent, industry has combined them into a structure of internal cohesiveness and interdependence. Industrial education can derive career clusters from them.

Data communication. The communication process begins with thought conception, or ideation, resulting from an awareness of needs. Next, research and analysis intervene before messages and meanings are encoded for transmission. The act of communication requires a channel or transfer medium to carry the message to a receiver. Intelligence comes into play for decoding and evaluation prior to trial and experimentation. The process is complete when the original message sender acknowledges feedback from the receiver through observation or implementation. Traditional laboratory areas of drafting and graphic arts have been melded with computer languages to provide industrial education with this more comprehensive cluster of subject matter.

Production processes. These include the processes related to material science, industrial extraction of raw materials, manufacturing, materials processing, building-construction, materials handling methods, servicing, salvage, reconstitution, and conservation of natural resources and man-made substances. Wood, metal, and plastics are the principal materials used in this area.

Energy and power. In addition to the popular study of engines and electricity, the study of power generation by fuels is also of prime importance. Transmission through various media is incorporated into distribution networks. Electronic instrumentation, control, consumption, utilization, and conservation of energy occurs in production systems, transportation vehicles, communication devices, and virtually every technological activity.

This chapter includes only a few of the major curriculum "revolutions" of the past thirty years. Those selected were chosen as examples of programmatic trends.

Whether oriented toward industry, technology, occupations, or careers, curriculum designs have been generally limited to include only a small number of comprehensive topics that can be identified as unique and established as genuine trends. Trends, in curriculum design, are recognizable as those elements that are common to many innovative projects being proposed for adaptation or adoption.

For the practicing teacher, many questions may still remain unanswered. Some sponsors profess their programs to be the only answer to curriculum design problems. In the final analysis, the resourceful teacher, employing an eclectic approach, will provide students with many possible directions for involvement in industrial education and career preparation.

DISCUSSION QUESTIONS

1. Explain why the 1960s have been considered the decade of reflection and revision in American education. What events gave rise to the need for change?

2. Has Gordon Wilber's definition of industrial arts enjoyed fulfillment through traditional programs? Describe how some of the curricular refinements attempt to embrace the entire definition.

3. Have innovations universally updated traditional offerings in industrial education? Explain your answer.

4. List the major differences in topical titles between the traditional and innovative types of industrial education programs.

5. Define "unitary teaching." Provide explanations of various methods for organizing units around (a) subject matter, and (b) themes.

6. Cite the single, most unique topic to which newer programs have addressed themselves. How does this contribute to the refinement of industrial education programs?

7. Contrast the unit and thematic approaches of curriculum organization.

8. Graphically illustrate the line and staff organization of a local industry. Explain how such a structure could be incorporated into an industrial education program.

9. Describe the program (or programs) which seems most appropriate for adoption in your desired or present teaching situation. How would you implement such a program?

10. Is interdisciplinary thematic cooperation practical in a contemporary school? Cite advantages and disadvantages of such a plan to support your answer.

11. Define "clustering." Should all industrial education programs reorganize in this way? Why, or why not?

12. Is it possible to integrate academic subjects into programs oriented toward career education? How?

13. What are the major differences between traditional and contemporary curriculum models for industrial education in elementary schools.

14. List advantages for youth as prescribed in the career education movement. How can industrial education contribute to the concepts of career education?

15. Illustrate the evolutionary refinement of innovative programs in industrial education. Cite additions and refinements.

16. List and describe ten major activities that would be found almost universally in an industry. Could all of these be used in an industrial education program? How?

17. Plan a series of units for junior high youth concerned with (a) materials processing, (b) communications, and (c) power and energy. How do these three clusters of technology embrace all industrial activities?

18. For use in a basic level course, describe general activities you would plan for a short unit of study titled "industrial orientation."

19. Do you feel that current course offerings in industrial education adequately provide youths with entry level job skills and social skills necessary for contributory citizenship? Do you feel that these course offerings effectively orient students to the industrial and technological culture? Do course activities offer opportunities for the student to develop avocational

interests? What experiences would you add to the program in order to achieve these aims?

20. To what extent are you convinced of the necessity for updating of industrial education programs? Explain your answer.

ADDITIONAL READINGS

Amrine, Harold T. *Manufacturing, Organization and Management.* Englewood Cliffs, New Jersey: Prentice-Hall, 1966.

Bailey, Larry J., and Stadt, Ronald W. *Career Education: New Approaches to Human Development.* Bloomington, Illinois: McKnight & McKnight, 1973.

Cochran, Leslie H. *Innovative Programs in Industrial Education.* Bloomington, Illinois: McKnight & McKnight, 1970.

DeVore, Paul W. *Structure and Content Foundations for Curriculum Development.* Washington, D. C.: American Industrial Arts Association, 1966.

DeVore, Paul W. *Technology—An Intellectual Discipline.* Washington, D. C.: American Industrial Arts Association.

Drucker, Peter F. *The Age of Discontinuity.* New York: Harper and Row, 1968.

Ellul, Jacques. *The Technological Society.* New York: Alfred A. Knopf, 1967.

Engineering Concepts Curriculum Project. *The Man Made World.* New York: McGraw-Hill, 1971.

Gerbracht, Carl, and Babcock, Robert. *Industrial Arts for Grades K–6.* Milwaukee, Wisconsin: Bruce, 1969.

Gerbracht, Carl, and Robinson, Frank E. *Understanding America's Industries.* Bloomington, Illinois: McKnight & McKnight, 1962.

Gilbert, Harold G. *Children Study American Industry.* Dubuque, Iowa: Wm. C. Brown, 1966.

Goldhammer, Keith, and Taylor, Robert E. *Career Education: Perspective and Promise.* Columbus, Ohio: Charles E. Merrill, 1972.

Kranzberg, Melvin, and Pursell, Carroll W., Jr. *Technology in Western Civilization.* New York: Oxford University Press, 1967.

Lauda, Donald P., and Ryan, Robert D. *Advancing Technology: Its Impact on Society.* Dubuque, Iowa: Wm. C. Brown, 1971.

Lux, Donald G., and Ray, Willis E. *The World of Construction.* Bloomington, Illinois: McKnight and McKnight, 1970.

Lux, Donald G., and Ray, Willis E. *The World of Manufacturing.* Bloomington, Illinois: McKnight and McKnight, 1971.

Miller, W. R., and Boyd, Gardner. *Teaching Elementary Industrial Arts.* S. Holland, Illinois: Goodheart-Willcox, 1970.

National School Public Relations Association. *Vocational Education: Innovations Revolutionize Career Education.* Washington, D. C. National School Public Relations Association, 1971.

Olsen, Delmar W. *Industrial Arts and Technology.* Englewood Cliffs, New Jersey: Prentice-Hall, 1963.

Olsen, Delmar W. *Tecnol-o-gee.* Raleigh, North Carolina. North Carolina State University, School of Education, Office of Publications, 1973.

Pucinski, Roman C., and Hirsch, Sharlene Pearlman, eds. *The Courage to Change: New Directions for Career Education.* Englewood Cliffs, New Jersey: Prentice-Hall, 1971.

Rhodes, James A. *Alternative to a Decadent Society.* New York: Howard W. Sams, 1969.

Roscoe, Edwin Scott. *Organization for Production.* Homewood, Illinois: Richard D. Irwin, 1967.

Scobey, Mary-Margaret. *Teaching Children About Technology.* Bloomington, Illinois: McKnight & McKnight, 1968.

Swierkos, Marion L., and Morse, Catherine G. *Industrial Arts for the Elementary Classroom.* Peoria, Illinois. Chas. A. Bennett Co., Inc., 1973.

Thirring, Hans. *Energy for Man: From Windmills to Nuclear Power.* Bloomington, Indiana: Indiana University Press, 1958.

Venn, Grant. *Man, Education and Work.* Washington, D. C.: American Council on Education, 1964.

Zetler, Robert L., and Grouch, George W. *Successful Communication in Science and Industry.* New York: McGraw-Hill, 1961.

Chapter 4

Course Construction

The Course of Study

A *course of study* is essentially a guide for the purpose of assisting the teacher in his daily routine. In its simplest form, it may consist of a skeleton outline of topics to be covered in some suggested sequence, with perhaps the addition of assignments and student activities. From this point on, it may be expanded to include a variety of directions, suggestions, and information regarding the teaching process and many other matters more indirectly related to the classroom procedures. A course of study is differentiated from a curriculum principally in that the former pertains to organization of material for a single subject for a definite grade or age level. A curriculum, on the other hand, has to do with groups of courses covering larger segments of subject matter areas or fields, or a series of courses arranged sequentially for a single field. A course of study dealing with electricity might be produced for the eighth grade. The industrial education curriculum would deal with not only all courses in electricity, but all the courses offered in industrial education.

Traced through its various stages, the making of a course of study may involve the following processes:

1. *Statement of definite objectives for the activity.* This will involve not only general goals for industrial education, but the addition of specific outcomes sought, based upon such factors as the subject considered, age of students, time allowance for the work, physical setting, available equipment, and previous experience of students. Care should be taken not to list objectives at random and hope to fulfill them. It is better to concentrate on definite behavioral goals and be able to do something worthwhile toward their attainment.

2. *An extensive analysis of teaching content.* The extent of the survey for suitable content would depend upon the specific objectives of the course. The analysis would cover not only content pertaining to operations and related technical material, but subject matter that would serve at least a number of the less recognized aims.

3. *Random selection of feasible items.* At this point, length of time, ability of students, physical facilities, and the specific objectives will again be determining factors. This list will now contain the selected items without reference to ranking or order of use.

4. *Organize items in instructional sequence.* This process may involve grouping items under various headings for final use in the course outline,

as: operations, processes, technical information, related studies, and occupational information, depending upon the format and organization to be used. When this job is completed, the items will be arranged on cards or sheets of paper in the order in which they are expected to be introduced, although they might again be readjusted when finally put into the outline.

5. *Organize selected materials into the final format.* This material will now become the source from which instructional units will be drawn.

Sources of Subject Matter

After a set of goals or objectives has been stated and accepted, a next logical concern will normally be the problem of locating and organizing suitable content and subject matter for the attainment of these goals.

If it is agreed that industrial education is basically an investigation of industry and its impact upon social and economic life, it would seem obvious that the primary source of subject matter for the program is industry itself. But industry has many facets and ramifications and an attempt to discover suitable content or subject matter through this approach will immediately appear either to fall short of satisfying the needs or become extremely involved. One approach here which has been practiced rather extensively has been that of *trade analysis,* which has been prompted mainly by needs in trade and vocational education. The results have also affected teaching content for industrial education, particularly in advanced work.

It will soon become clear that a study of operations which skilled workers are expected to perform will throw light upon only one segment of the teaching content needed for industrial education. How can other phases of industrial life be explored and drawn upon as promising subject matter and content? In answer to this question, it would seem that the technique of analysis might well be applied to a number of areas or phases of industry in addition to tool processes and operations. Some of these are suggested in the following listing, with brief comments for each.

• *Production of goods from raw materials.* An analysis of production and production techniques requires a viewpoint different from that of trade analysis. While skill in the use of tools and machines would be involved, such aspects would be only a small part of the total program.

• *Mass production and automation.* This should prove to be a fruitful area leading to teaching content for understanding industry, and possible organization of group projects in class so that students would get experience indicative of that offered in industry.

• *Managerial practices.* An analysis in this area could lead to subject matter for helping students to become acquainted with the relationship between management and labor, as well as to appreciate future applications of practices provided in the school shop.

• *Organization of industry.* The complexity of modern industrial organization cannot be presented haphazardly with good results in the limited

CHAPTER 4—COURSE CONSTRUCTION

time available. The application of the analysis technique should furnish a number of items which may later be selected and refined for proper use.

- *Human relations problems.* This phase of analysis might involve personnel problems within industry as well as problems of labor relations and a study of arbitration procedures, sales, and many other problems.
- *Designing and planning.* An analysis in this area might include processes of obtaining patents, design of the product, specifications, lofting, cost estimating, and similar elements. Eventual instructional units resulting from this analysis should apply directly to work in the industrial education program.
- *Materials of industry.* A listing here could include both raw and processed materials used in manufacture and construction. Such a list would furnish a reservoir of available content from which teaching units or information for use with demonstrations would ultimately be drawn.
- *Advertising and distribution of goods and services.* Modern advertising is a very real adjunct of our technological age. Systems and means of distribution affect the occupational and social life of a large number of people. An analysis of advertising and merchandising techniques should result in some valuable lesson materials suitable for industrial education.
- *Consumption and use of goods and services.* Intelligent consumption has been included in most lists of industrial education aims for many years. Very little has been done to segregate and organize teaching content for realizing the aim. An analysis of possibilities here might lead to more conscious effort in this direction.
- *Occupational requirements and opportunities.* This area of subject matter has received considerable attention and possibly needs little if any original analysis from raw data. There may be situations where there is need for local investigation. There would, however, be need for analysis of available literature and information before actual teaching units could be selected for the particular class or age level concerned.

No attempt will be made here to detail procedures for making these analyses. Two sources appear to be available: written material covering the various areas indicated, and personal visitation. The degree of detail of the analyses would, of course, depend upon the conditions causing it to be made. Each analysis should be as thorough as possible, listing many more items than will be used in the final course of study.

While extensive analyses of most of the areas indicated in the previous paragraphs have not been carried out in detail for use in industrial education, there are, however, many existing sources of organized content basically useful to the teacher in search of subject matter. If these sources can be tapped, the material obtained will serve the same purpose as that obtained by original investigation, so far as the listing of possible items or teaching units is concerned. Much of this type of material is available in printed form, while in some cases personal visitation may be necessary in

TEACHING INDUSTRIAL EDUCATION

order to get the necessary information. The following are a number of sources:

- *State departments of education.*
- *Office of Education, Washington, D. C.*
- *National teachers' organizations.*
- *State organizations of teachers.*
- *Professional journals.*
- *Curriculum books for the field involved.*
- *Textbooks and manuals.*
- *Material from manufacturers of school equipment and supplies.*
- *Visits to schools and school systems.*
- *Attendance at meetings and conventions.*

Other sources not falling directly under this classification are:

- *Home maintenance and do-it-yourself needs.* These can be analyzed by surveys of home owners, and student reports.
- *Leisuretime needs.* A study of adult education programs, of home workshops and equipment, and of recreational and vacation activities would help to indicate possibilities for meeting these needs.

The aforementioned are not intended to be an exhaustive treatment of possibilities in the search for subject matter for industrial education, nor the only approaches to the problem. It would seem, however, that any subject matter or content considered should be subjected to analysis and selection in the light of chosen and accepted objectives and other limiting conditions and should contribute to the attainment of those objectives and conditions.

The analysis suggested so far would normally result in a random listing of segregated items. These listings would probably contain many more items than would ever be used in the classroom. It seems best not to attempt to arrange the items in order of importance when the original listing is made. This procedure applies to the treatment of written or published material, as well as to items obtained from conversation or conferences. The written material, whether it be books on industrial organization or items from courses of study, would be scanned for pertinent material and every promising suggestion noted. Using cards and listing one item on each card will save time later when proceeding with the additional steps in the selection of items for use in the course of study and for teaching units.

Selection of Content

The listings of items that will result from this first step in analysis are obviously not valuable for immediate use. The second logical step is to make suitable selections, from these listings, of those items that appear useful as instructional content in the course contemplated. Here some bases for selection will be needed. The proper selection of items would involve a statement of the general objectives of the industrial education program and a study of the detailed objectives for the course in question. The age, previous experience, and future plans of the students would also have to be considered. The time available for the course is also important.

With this information, the selection of subject matter can go forward. The best procedure will probably be to go through the cards or the lists available and pull out each item that appears suitable. No attention is paid to arrangement of the items at this time. Items not used for this course may be useful when selecting subject matter for some other course.

Organizing Course Content

The third step in the process of obtaining organized content is the *arrangement of the selected items into a correct sequence for instructional use.* If the card system is used this will be a simple process. Such a set of items, logically arranged, would then be basic material for the instructional content in the course of study.

The approach to the problem may be made from several basic viewpoints. The following will indicate some of these.

Student interest or need. Interest as a factor in the educative process has been emphasized to the point that it has been given first consideration in organizing teaching material into courses of study. It might be nearer the truth to say that it has been emphasized to the exclusion of a tangible course of study. Under the cover of real or pretended zeal in approaching industrial education through the avenue of student interest, poor teaching methods may be used and students may be poorly educated. Student interests and student needs are not necessarily synonomous. "Needs of students" constitutes a legitimate and major basis for an approach to curriculum making. Recognition of such "needs" should lend a healthy atmosphere to course construction in industrial education.

While shifting interests of students may be dangerous as the controlling factor in selecting and organizing subject matter, it nevertheless is true that subject matter should be tested by measuring student interest. If there is no chance that it is or can become interesting, this fact alone should suggest its omission or reorganization.

Projects or articles to be made. If the free choice of projects is practiced, this approach might be a logical one. It was in practice in the early days of sloyd teaching in elementary schools, although the models upon which it was based were usually compulsory and allowed for no choice. In this case the articles to be made were arranged in a series, in ascending order of difficulty, involving what was assumed to be a logical sequence of tool processes.

Sequence of tool processes. Historically, this is the established approach. It was practiced in its most rigid form in connection with the use of graded series of exercises and practice jobs, each exercise or job more difficult than the one before. The entire program was based upon a graded series of tool practice and techniques. While modern concepts of teaching industrial education have discredited the practice exercise for its own sake, the listing of tool processes has persisted, with some justification. When this approach can be coupled with suitable projects, it furnishes a basis for orderly planning.

Acquisition of knowledge. This approach has been generally adopted in elementary schools. Where formerly the industrial work even in the lower grades involved the formal construction of articles by individual students, these activities are now guided toward interpreting and vitalizing work in terms of social studies, expressions of arts and crafts of primitive people being studied, and similar projects.

Future usefulness or adult needs. For the general home-mechanics lab, particularly, surveys have been made in order to determine the frequency of future demands upon tool and operational skills. The frequency of the recurrence of repair jobs and other home services in a large number of homes over a long period may be used as the determining factor in arranging jobs in the course of study. The great expansion of activities under the "do-it-yourself" slogan has magnified possibilities for both teaching content and personal interest. A number of the commonly accepted goals for industrial education can receive special emphasis under this approach, including intelligent selection and consumption of goods and services, and appreciation of good design.

The organization of the teaching content in the course might also be influenced by an investigation of industry and the occupational distribution of the workers in the community, and by the general attitude of the community towards its educational program.

The aforementioned is not meant to indicate that any single factor or approach is likely to be used alone and to the exclusion of all the others. The question will be mainly one of emphasis, as decided by the course maker or teacher and by the physical arrangement of teaching content in the course.

Regardless of the type of course of study used, it will be necessary for the teacher to break down the items listed into small teaching units and plan each of these units separately for presentation to the class. And in these presentations the teacher can use an endless variety of techniques and aids to keep the subject fresh and alive. The course of study may be the same, but the projects, the approach, the point of contact, and the visual and other teaching aids need not be the same. Lesson planning is discussed in detail in Chapter 10.

Subject Matter in Elementary Schools

While no attempt is made in this book to treat comprehensively the work of the grades below the seventh, a brief discussion of subject matter for industrial education in elementary schools may be helpful.

In the organization of activities in the grades below the seventh, formal work with tools and materials is not the prime objective. The woodworking program that once was common has given way to other types of activity with

CHAPTER 4—COURSE CONSTRUCTION

less demand for skill and more direct relationship to the study program of the classroom and to the life of the child. This means also that the supervising teacher of industrial education is consulted in these grades, and that the activity carried on usually comes under the instruction and supervision of the regular classroom teacher. Special teachers are prone to feel that this lowers standards of work, and probably develops poor habits in tool manipulation. In some larger schools, special rooms are used for the laboratory activities, with a special teacher in charge. However, in modern settings these activities are not confined to formalized work. The equipment of such rooms may be quite varied.

Young boys and girls find constructive exercises fulfilling. Their involvement in the learning opportunity is increased, and greater relevance is established through their participation in the class enterprise.

The everyday environment of the child—with much emphasis on the world of work—forms the core of the subject matter. Mental and manipulative activities relating to the following topics provide realistic projects for class participation.

Shelter. As the cultural foundation of youth, the home and family living are very important ingredients in the elementary school curriculum. Likewise, they should form a basis for many industrial education activities at that level. The health and safety of the child are important facets of family life. In addition, occupational orientation to the world of work is provided through a study of the job activities of craftsmen and tradesmen such as farmers, architects, builders, plumbers, electricians, masons, interior decorators, and landscape gardeners. There are also laboratory activities associated with materials that these people use in their work. The contemporary home offers an outstanding opportunity for diversified activities.

Clothing. A study of clothing and textiles of all types forms another base for elementary subject matter. Raw materials, as well as man-made fibers, are used in the laboratory activities, and occupational information is given regarding many people, from the cotton farmer to the laboratory technician working with plastics, glass, and paper.

Foods. To the growing child, this topic is probably the most important. Many exciting units of study can be derived from a study of foods, where they come from, and how they are processed and prepared for consumption. All types of primary agricultural workers, in addition to butchers, bakers, cannery and freezer plant workers, offer world-of-work investigative possibilities. Cereal processors, grocery sales and advertising people, grain traders, breeders, packagers, cooks, chefs, and many others provide relevance in the study of the things we eat.

Power. Also connected with the home, sources and uses of energy comprise another element of subject matter. Without electricity, fuels of all types, muscle power, and basic machines and tools, much of the modern world's work could not be accomplished.

Communication. The studies of all types of devices used for communication are exciting inclusions in the elementary curriculum. From early forms of graphical expression to contemporary microwave transmission, students can find alternative constructive activities in this field. It is very important for elementary children to have a fundamental understanding of language, the telephone, and radio and television, in order to be technologically literate.

Transportation. The study and construction of boats, planes, automobiles, rockets, and other modes of transportation is included in this unit. As with communication, various types of energy form important aspects of transportation. Ecological study, and its interrelatedness with power and transportation, find inclusion in elementary-school subject matter as well.

The integration of curricula in the elementary school is the prime objective of handwork and industrial education activities at that level. They are seldom treated successfully as separate courses. Social studies—including geography, consumer economics, and history—can effectively utilize laboratory activities. The fine arts, sciences, and mathematics often employ industrial education for activity-oriented learning. Language arts and graphic arts also find the integration of their subject matter mutually beneficial.

Children ought to understand the importance of technological development and its impact on cultural change. The provision for concrete, manipulative learning experiences in an otherwise totally academic atmosphere is of utmost importance to the elementary school student.

Course Content in Intermediate Grades

Traditionally, the junior high school or middle school has provided students with their first experiences in industrial education. Typical coursework has centered around instruction dealing with woodworking, drafting, metalworking, electricity, printing, and small gasoline engines. These programs are now being improved through the addition of basic courses in plastics and craftwork. The instructional emphasis has changed substantially, but project construction is still an important activity in these programs.

Many contemporary courses have become aligned with the fundamental organization of industry and its dependence on technology. These courses deal mainly with:
- *Man,* creativity and ideas.
- *Materials,* and the processes and operations needed to change their shape into intended designs.
- *Power,* its utilization in machines for materials transformation, as well as its importance in the transportation of both the ingredients and the final product. Three activity centers, related to communications, materials, and power, usually comprise the general laboratory facility.

In information communication, students are offered course work dealing with basic graphic design, product planning, reproduction (graphic arts), and industrial organization.

CHAPTER 4—COURSE CONSTRUCTION

Courses in materials processing relate not only to woodworking, metalworking, and plastics, but to all industrial materials. These courses are incorporated into units of study associated with the fields of extraction, manufacturing, and construction.

Learning opportunities in power and energy include instruction in principles of transportation and propulsion. However, the traditional service orientation is not excluded. Additional subject units concerned with the control of power—through the use of electronics, hydraulics, and pneumatics—are easily included in an expanded program.

This relevant, contemporary, junior-high or middle-school series of course offerings provides youth with a more diversified investigation into occupational opportunities than has been fostered in the traditional "six shop" approach. Boys and girls in their early teens now have the advantage of flexible courses of study to orient them to literally hundreds of occupational possibilities. In this way, it is hoped that students will be more capable of making realistic choices regarding secondary-school courses. They will also be better prepared to consider the choice of an industrially oriented occupation.

In the junior high school or middle school, occupational orientation should not be placed in a subsidiary position to manipulative activity. For a discussion of aims and objectives appropriate to both the intermediate and secondary school industrial education programs, refer to Chapter 5.

Course Work in Secondary Schools

In the high school, although curricular offerings include more electives, many students may be unable to take advantage of these learning opportunities because of college entrance requirements, parental disposition, or course scheduling difficulties. Yet all students, regardless of career goals, should be cognizant of the advantages of participation in such programs. Conversely, industrial educators are challenged with the task of providing contemporary relevance in the subject matter they present.

For the relatively small high school, course offerings similar to those mentioned for intermediate grades are appropriate, especially for grades nine and ten. Problems sometimes arise, however, when teachers attempt to define the emphasis for more advanced course work. Career preparation must necessarily be one of the foremost goals of courses during the final years of secondary school. Students completing their education should be prepared for employment, while students planning for collegiate study ought to be introduced to fields of occupational interest in which they think they wish further study.

Regardless of the occupational plans of the individual student, flexibility and open-endedness should be the guiding principles of course planning. For those students placing emphasis on career preparation, industrial educators should not try to focus on skills as specific as those desired by machinists, carpenters, plumbers, electricians, welders, press operators, or

TEACHING INDUSTRIAL EDUCATION

auto mechanics. Since most individuals alter or completely change their occupations during their lives, it is imperative for all students to understand educational flexibility. For example, the press operator, although deeply interested in making a particular contribution, is usually a better citizen and a more effective contributor to society and his or her job when he or she has gained a necessary perspective regarding his or her occupation. Motivation and contentment, so important to the effective industrial enterprise, are easily understood by the worker who knows the value of his occupation.

Until recently, many young people planning careers in engineering and technology have not had the opportunity to investigate these fields during their secondary school years. The future electronic, mechanical, civil, architectural, chemical, manufacturing, industrial, or design engineer can benefit from participation in a quality industrial education program.

Needless to say, some college-bound students oriented toward purely academic subjects may find little relevance in traditional programs in industrial education. For such students, courses such as cabinetmaking, welding, sheetmetal fabrication, and plastics-forming seem to hold only a general, or avocational, interest. Of course, the true value of these courses lies in the fact that craft experience is a strong link between theoretical-technical knowledge and a general understanding of industry. Nevertheless, challenging subject matter relating to applied physics, materials science and processing, product design, and communications electronics can be developed to provide relevance and interest to college-bound students.

Forms and Formats Most courses of study are put into the form of booklets or folders with page sizes varying from 6" x 9" to 8½" x 11". For certain types of course material, the card file system may be used to advantage, particularly where the principal interest is in the course material useful for daily teaching. However, for the comprehensive type of course, the book form in the size of 8½" x 11" appears to be favored.

The organizational structure for arranging parts of the course of study is conveniently accomplished as follows:

1. *Title page.* This page gives the exact title of the course, the school or school system where the course will be used, the grades or school level for which the course is planned, and the date of publication.

2. *Acknowledgments.* This will state names of persons and committees who have worked on the production of the document and also list administrative personnel under whose direction the work was done.

3. *Table of contents.* Some types of brief course outlines may not require a table of contents, but it should be kept in mind as a regular feature of comprehensive course construction.

4. *General statement of philosophy.* A definition of the instructional area under study, in addition to the instructor's own point of view or

CHAPTER 4—COURSE CONSTRUCTION

professional beliefs, comprises an appropriate statement of educational philosophy.

5. *Objectives.* These may be expressed in statements of two different types: a general expression of aims and purposes for the educational field or area represented, and a presentation of specific behavioral objectives inherent in the specific course to be offered. The second of these is often used as introductory material to the main body of the course, which contains the various phases of teaching content.

The list of these preliminary or introductory aspects of the course is not exhaustive, but will call attention to the major elements of an introductory nature. From this point on, the emphasis will be on the instructional phases of the teacher's job which will logically constitute the main body of the course of study.

6. *The teaching content.* This will involve arrangement of content in some selected form showing what students are expected to learn and experience and the various means by which the prescribed learning experiences may be acquired.

7. *Suggested projects.* Most courses will furnish lists of suggested projects or activities which would be suitable for the type and level of learning indicated.

8. *Instructional media.* This section will indicate types of instructional materials that may be used and sources for obtaining them.

9. *Methods and instructional techniques.* Here suggestions may be made concerning special teaching procedures, use of demonstrations, and assignments.

10. *Occupational information.* This section may indicate to what extent the industrial educator is expected to assist in general and occupational guidance in keeping with school policy.

11. *Safety instruction.* Here attention is drawn to the need for constant attention to the teaching and practice of safety and to regulations that must be followed in case of accident. Chapter 12 is devoted to a discussion of this subject.

12. *Class organization and management.* This section covers suggestions under the following headings: orderly arrangements of the school laboratory, tools, supplies, attendance check and roll-call procedures, management and student personnel organization, lab inventory records.

13. *Evaluation procedures.* The final portion of the course of study should explain in detail the objective and subjective methods for evaluating the student's performance relative to the behavioral aims stated for the course. These methods would include procedures for the observation of the students attitudinal development and skill acquisition. They would also include measures for testing the student's knowledge of course material.

DISCUSSION QUESTIONS

1. Are there situations in which industry and real life are not reliable sources for furnishing subject matter for the course of study?
2. Should the cost of the installation be taken into consideration when planning to introduce new subjects?
3. Do you consider it logical to use leisuretime interests of people as a source for teaching content in industrial education?
4. Make a list of activities that industrial educators may initiate in order to keep their teaching content up to date.
5. To what extent should occupational-training content be considered for industrial education courses?
6. Name some lab activities that do not represent a sufficiently broad field to justify themselves in the school curriculum.
7. What subject matter would fit into a program stressing self-activity in the elementary school?
8. What values do you see in studying methods of industrial production?
9. Name some subjects for which materials would be too expensive.
10. To what extent should an activity taught in school relate to the industrial life of the community?
11. Are there any inherent dangers in a rapid expansion of subjects in the industry and technology programs in the schools? If so, what?
12. If a survey of home-mechanics activities of parents were made, to what extent would you consider it valuable in furnishing subject matter for a home-mechanics course?
13. How can one justify the practice of going to industry for subject matter for industrial education courses?
14. Make a list of twenty-five instructional units or operations that would be suitable for rural schools.
15. If the teacher has had extensive practical experience, should he depend upon that experience as a source for teaching content as the work progresses, rather than make a definite course of study?
16. To what extent, if any, should students participate in making up the course of study?
17. By what means may a teacher keep his course of study from becoming static?
18. Is there danger in having a course of study worked out in too great detail? If so, what is that danger?
19. In what respect would the teacher's previous training and experience determine the type of course of study that he or she would need?
20. How often do you think a course of study in industrial education should be revised?
21. Can you recall having seen a teacher do excellent work without the use of a course of study?

22. To what extent do you feel that student interest should determine content of courses of study?

23. In what form may course material best be kept for easy revision from time to time?

24. What are some of the values in encouraging groups of teachers to participate in producing courses of study?

ADDITIONAL READINGS

Bakamis, William A. *Improving Instruction in Industrial Arts.* Milwaukee: Bruce Publishing Company, 1966.

Cenci, Louis, and Weaver, Gilbert G. *Teaching Occupational Skills.* New York: Pitman Publishing Company, 1968.

Friese, John F., and Williams, William A. *Course Making in Industrial Education.* Peoria, Illinois: Chas. A. Bennett, 1966.

Giachino, J. W., and Gallington, Ralph O. *Course Construction in Industrial Arts, Vocational and Technical Education.* Chicago: American Technical Society, 1967.

Olson, Delmar W. *Industrial Arts and Technology.* Englewood Cliffs, New Jersey: Prentice-Hall, 1963.

Scobey, Mary-Margaret. *Teaching Children about Technology.* Bloomington, Illinois: McKnight & McKnight, 1968.

Silvius, G. Harold, and Curry, Estell H. *Managing Multiple Activities in Industrial Education.* Bloomington, Illinois: McKnight & McKnight, 1971.

Silvius, G. Harold, and Bonn, Ralph C. *Organizing Course Materials for Industrial Education.* Bloomington, Illinois: McKnight & McKnight, 1961.

Silvius, G. Harold, and Curry, Estell H. *Teaching Successfully in Industrial Education.* Bloomington, Illinois: McKnight & McKnight, 1967.

Wilber, Gordon O., and Pendered, Norman C. *Industrial Arts in General Education.* 4th ed. Scranton, Pennsylvania: International Textbook Company, 1973.

Chapter 5

Goal Orientation

Goals and Objectives

Much has been written concerning the similarities and differences between goals and objectives. The terms are often used interchangably. For this reason, it is important for educators to agree on terminology, definitions, and the methods of working toward the fulfillment of word meanings.

Goals are usually considered to be general statements of educational intent, sometimes quite philosophical in nature, and usually quite difficult to evaluate in terms of the degree of student fulfillment. For instance, a diploma is a goal. High social status is a goal. Such pronouncements as "The student will become a better citizen," or "Each student's potential will be developed to the limit of his or her individual capacity," specify goals often stated in educational circles. In reality, these statements tell very little about the specific behavioral changes that are expected to occur as a result of the student's experiences in the classroom or laboratory of industrial education. Still, goals have an important place in curriculum development. They can be used in course descriptions when general, overall predictive statements are necessary. However, the general goals of a course must be made practical for use through restatement in operational terms.

A *behavioral performance objective* is an exacting pronouncement of an overt act that the student should be able to accomplish after performing a certain learning activity. Performance objectives such as, "The student will be able to list and describe three methods of making steel," or, "The student will be able to safely and correctly operate the radial arm saw" determine each action to be performed. Such activities can readily be observed and evaluated.

To achieve accountability in the classroom, it is necessary for teachers to prescribe short-range objectives in addition to the traditional statements of general educational goals. Because of the inherent practicality in industrial education, teachers find little difficulty in being accountable for observable, measurable, terminal behaviors in their programs of laboratory activities.

The Learning Process

In industrial education, student progress is often measured only through an evaluation of the end products of laboratory activities. Most teachers, however, profess that the student's command of information is of more benefit in the total learning process. Others consider the acquisition of positive attitudes and appreciations to be the most important outcome of an educational endeavor. Realistically, all three aspects of learning contribute significantly to the total learning process.

CHAPTER 5—GOAL ORIENTATION

Attitude. For our purposes, readiness is defined as the state of the student's intellectual aptitude and psychological predisposition. That is, one must have both the mental capability and the personal desire to gain from a learning opportunity. Of course, attitude has much to do with successful motivation. The motivation to learn is basic to efficient and effective learning in that it involves values and appreciations. Contemporary learning theorists are deeply concerned with the student's desire to learn. It often becomes necessary for teachers to initiate interest in the subject.

Through attractive school facilities, inspired and enthusiastic teachers, and relevant curricula, students can find the process of education an enjoyable activity. A positive attitude or "state of mind" is the first condition for effective learning.

Knowledge. The sharp, willing student finds the acquisition of information a relatively easy and enjoyable task. Through self- or teacher-initiated motivation, the cognitive process becomes a natural second step toward a beneficial change in behavior.

In the past, much desirable subject matter in industrial education had often been classified as "related information." Such material included topics pertaining to industrial methods, the reading of drawings, knowledge of kinds and quality of tools and machines, characteristics and sources of many materials, and the degree of knowledge in mathematics and science necessary for successful work experience. Actually, this type of knowledge is essential to, rather than related to, efficient work. The curricular offerings should give major attention to mechanical intelligence and technical knowledge. Information regarding furniture styles, the composition of alloys, and the production of lumber could be profitably given. While such information may not be essential for the performance of the required work, it is, nevertheless, valuable in developing a broader understanding of the craft and a pride in the task performed.

Performance. Putting the acquired knowledge into practice completes three-step educational process. In the performance of a skill, habits of order and safety, and the use of correct and successful procedures are observable indications of achievement. From the time of their inception, industrial education programs have placed emphasis upon tool operations, projects, and manipulative experiences. "Learning by doing" was a slogan used in advocating industrial education subjects as a part of the curriculum of both elementary and secondary schools. While this slogan is still applicable, the concept of putting it into practice has grown greatly in scope and comprehension. One result of this growth is increased emphasis on a broadening of opportunities for learning experiences in the program.

In industrial education, all facets of the learning process are developed through a series of practical experiences relating to the industrial environment. Many activities reflect aspects of personnel management. Most activities demand research and problem solving, and an understanding of the principles of design, production, inspection, analysis, diagnosis, and machine operation.

Analysis of Student Needs

It has been a major goal of industrial education to assist the student to become a happy, useful, and successful citizen. Here, because of the nature of its subject matter, and because of the close personal contact existing between teacher and student, industrial education has a unique opportunity to make a contribution. However, these conditions, of themselves, do not always produce the desired results.

Psychologists and learning theorists have long studied human motives and their relationship to behavioral patterns. As we know, a review of their findings can help educators gain a deeper understanding and appreciation of the adolescent student, and how his or her needs and wants determine types of behavior in the school setting.

The need for physical comfort is fundamental to any constructive activity in the classroom environment. Relatively little can be accomplished when students are hungry, thirsty, or have dietary deficiencies. Environmental considerations of temperature and safety are also important.

Once the basic physical requirements have been satisfied, the teacher and students can work toward the fulfillment of the students' psychological needs. Many students need to develop a personal identity. This identity implies acceptance of self as well as positive acknowledgment by others. Self-esteem is second in importance only to considerations of physical comfort. It should be so considered by the teacher. The industrial educator should take every opportunity to bolster the student's self-image and to help recognize and evaluate physical and mental potential.

The truly contented person is termed "self-actualized." Only when it is possible for a person to do those things in life which are most enjoyable, will he or she experience security in a life-style. Many in society are disenchanted with their homes, jobs, salaries, and surroundings. Some of these problems evolve from the lack of understanding, acceptance, or preparation for the most suitable mode of living. It is imperative that industrial education should acquaint all students in some depth with those phases of our industrial and technological society in which they are to participate. It is also important that industrial education assist them in identifying personal goals that are realistic, achievable, and satisfying.

Educational Imperatives

The consideration of goals from the standpoint of educational needs will aid the instructor in deciding on desirable course content and suitable teaching methods. In considering the area of "needs" as basic to goals, it seems apparent that such needs will fall under at least two classifications: general needs that are common to youth, and individual needs that vary with the individual, the school, the community and the area of study under consideration. A listing and examination of these needs relative to common goals will be made in the following paragraphs. The manner in which these

CHAPTER 5—GOAL ORIENTATION

needs might be served by programs in industrial education will also be examined.

- *Students should develop those attitudes, understandings, and skills necessary for intelligent and productive participation in our contemporary society.* The contribution of industrial education to this need will presumably be not so much in furnishing trade skills in a specific occupation as in offering opportunities for understanding basic requirements in any type of employment. The development of general employability traits, work habits, attitudes of cooperation, resourcefulness, and responsibility have long been stressed in industrial education. It is generally known that the great majority of those who lose their jobs in industry and business do so not because they lack the ability to do the required work, but because they lack the personal attributes necessary to enable them to fit into the organization or the personnel setting in which they find themselves. Much can be done in the majority of industrial activities to develop an atmosphere and a work program in which there will be opportunity for cooperative participation that will give actual practice and application of general employability traits. More advanced tool and operational skills can be offered in advanced courses or in some job situations, if basic work habits have been previously acquired by the employee.

- *Students should be informed regarding the maintenance of good health and physical fitness.* The phenomenal development of new materials and new processes in industry is carrying with it a constant need for study and understanding, which in many cases can best be satisfied in the area of industrial education. Facts about chemical products such as paints, bleaches, solvents, fuels, and exhausts and fumes are normally included as direct or incidental learnings in the industrial setting. If safety education is also implied under this need, another wide area of applications is at hand in the industrial education program, both with reference to those safety practices that must be employed in the school laboratories, and in the broader application of safety practices in the home, on the road, and in employment.

- *Students should learn acceptance of the rights and responsibilities of citizenship in a democracy, including a respect for others.*

It is imperative for youth to appreciate and accept racial similarities and differences. Racial harmony is necessary in society. Each person should be measured by his or her ability to contribute to the betterment of society. The changing role of the American woman must also be considered when designing curricular alternatives for industrial education.

The modern school endeavors to offer more opportunities for youth to participate in democratic procedures and group cooperation. Service to this need is rendered in many ways in industrial education. However, as with most other stated goals, such a contribution is not an automatic outcome of haphazard class organization and procedures. Mass production jobs, group projects, student organization for class management, and evaluation by the students of their own and other students' work can lead to growth and maturity in citizenship. It has long been claimed that industrial education furnishes superior opportunities through group organization, cooperative use of tools and materials, and an informal work atmosphere conducive to social adjustment. Social values are enhanced whenever the teacher takes advantage of the inherent opportunities for giving class members important parts in class management. The assigning of supervisors, tool clerks, tool checkers, materials clerks, and finishing room superintendents leads to the necessity for cooperation and promotes a feeling of community.

● *Students should learn to reason properly and communicate effectively.* Here, the industrial educator has unique opportunities to serve youth. Materially, the end product of industrial teaching is often a product made with tools and materials. Under the best practices, at least the following procedures would be performed by the student:

1. Selecting a project after investigating possibilities.
2. Making a detailed drawing showing all dimensions.
3. Composing a bill of materials showing the size and cost of each part.
4. Listing the steps and operations necessary for the construction of the project.

All these procedures require the ability to make decisions, retrace and review a line of thinking, and make judgments concerning structural problems, tool operations, and sequencing of the work. A valuable aspect of the procedure is that mistakes in judgment will reveal themselves in construction failures.

● *Students should develop a respectfully critical attitude toward science and technology.* Science and the rapid advance of technology obviously go hand in hand. Industrial education draws its basic instructional content from the processes of industry, as well as from those social and economic considerations brought into focus by our industrial and technological age. The approach to all activities in industrial education consists basically of analyzing operations and evaluating their results. Tangible evidence usually remains in the form of a product or project indicating the degree of success attained by the student or the group. An understanding of industry and the organization of industry should develop some understanding of science and technology and the influence of industry on human life.

● *Students should develop the ability to purchase, use, and maintain goods and services, and understand the interrelationship and interdependence of producers and consumers.* The teacher who is impressed with the broader objectives of industrial education will find many occasions to organize the classwork to meet these objectives. Attention to the cost of various materials used in projects and attention to appropriateness of design are but two of these. The proper care and maintenance of the home, its furnishings, and mechanical equipment will suggest much additional content for study and investigation.

Aspects of this need are covered or implied in several of the goals listed previously. Practices pertaining to household maintenance should develop in the student sympathetic understanding of material aspects of home life. Judgment and resourcefulness in selection, purchase, and care of industrial products should contribute to those conditions conducive to successful family life. If the teacher will analyze the implications involved in this need he or she will no doubt be able to discover many learning situations that satisfy it, particularly in classes on the secondary school level.

- *Students should develop an aesthetic appreciation of beauty in art, music, literature, and nature.* Appreciation of the arts is best brought about through some degree of participation. An appreciation of good design and the ability to discriminate in the selection of consumer goods can undoubtedly be stimulated in industrial education, provided that the teacher has had the necessary preparation in this area and is impressed with the values of stressing these elements of instruction. Here, as in connection with other phases of coordinated study and discussion, two approaches are available to the teacher: (1) The application of principles of beauty and good taste in connection with all articles made, and (2) the provision of time for the deliberate study and discussion of such principles, with particular reference to examples that may be analyzed.

Reference material for use in the laboratory would be a necessary addition to the program. Consultation would also be helpful.

- *Students should learn to use their leisure constructively.* Probably no one would want to relieve industrial education of the responsibility of attempting to meet this need. A goal pertaining to preparation for the constructive use of leisure has been emphasized in the literature of industrial education for many years. Whether the phenomenal increase in the use of home workshops for recreation and enjoyment can be attributed to the almost universal exposure of present home owners to industrial education has probably not been determined. However, it would seem likely that the basic knowledge of the use of tools in the school program has greatly influenced the movement.

Establishing Goals

In various preceding statements, stress has been placed on the need for setting goals as bases for instructional activities and programs in industrial education. It has also been emphasized that these should evolve from the concept that industry and technology are integral parts of education. While this general concept is widely accepted in principle, there is much need for further clarification and interpretation of its meaning and practical applications.

Much criticism has been directed against the tendency to declare aims on paper and then to ignore them in the teaching process. Some of this criticism is justified. A teacher who has stated a set of aims is more likely to work for their consummation than is a person who has never stated definite goals. Carefully formulated goals imply procedures for their attainment.

With the thought in mind that it is more fruitful to think of final outcomes than initial declarations, the following statements are presented as desired goals for industrial education.

- *Understanding of industry, technology, and methods of production, and of the influence of industrial products and services upon the pattern of modern social and economic life.* The typical industrial education lab probably falls short of giving maximum service to this goal. However, industrial education has, within its areas of instruction, opportunities greater than those afforded by most other subjects in the school curriculum. Industrial education teachers should be alert to take advantage of these opportunities. Line production jobs in the school, visits to industry, suitable films, and class organization patterned after factory management are but a few of the possibilities leading to realization of this goal.

- *Discovery by the student of his or her own abilities and aptitudes, leading toward maturing life interests.* Self-discovery as interpreted here goes far beyond the mere opportunity for exploring a few mechanical occupations and perhaps selecting one of them for a life career. In the informal setting of a well-conducted industrial education program, students are relieved of much of the strain and stress of the formal classroom or counselor's office. In a program of industrial education, students can more objectively discover their likes and dislikes, their aptitudes, and limitations, both in regard to occupational choices and personality traits.

- *Judgment and resourcefulness in selection, purchase, use, and care of industrial products, and services both in the home and in occupational life.* In our society, every person's well-being is dependent upon the efficient use of the machines, mechanical devices, and appliances produced by our technology. Some firsthand experience with materials, tools, and machines will better enable a person to solve the problems that pertain to the purchase and use of such devices. The teacher must keep in mind, however, that to teach only routine tool processes will not in itself guarantee that students will attain this goal.

- *Developing of mature work habits, feelings of responsibility, and the abilities to plan and execute work both independently and in cooperation with others.* A criticism commonly directed against young people taking their first jobs is that they have not established work habits acceptable in business or industry. The industrial education laboratory is probably the best place in the school for the development of such work habits. However, it is essential that the teacher understand that good work habits do not automatically result from his or her teaching. By making the student's position in the laboratory analogous to that of a workman on the job, mature work habits, responsibility, and good judgment can be developed, even by young adolescents.

CHAPTER 5—GOAL ORIENTATION

- *Basic experience in the use of tools, machines, and materials of value in carrying on future educational and professional work.* Advocates of industrial education have long maintained that this program is of value to all children. It has been made compulsory in most junior high schools. However, in secondary schools, there has been insufficient recognition of the value of shopwork for the student who expects to go into advanced work in science or technology.

The value of basic mechanical resourcefulness has been increasingly apparent during the recent rapid expansion of technology and science. Technical competency has become as important as the ability to think clearly. Often, discovery, research, and planning can be carried out only piece by piece to the degree that mechanical and manipulative work accompany theoretical developments. When this is more fully recognized, colleges and universities will be more willing to recognize mechanical ability as one of the legitimate qualifications for entrance.

- *Development of safety habits.* Strenuous efforts must be made to diminish the appalling accident rate. The very atmosphere of the school lab lends itself to the acquisition of good safety habits. Safety instruction can be stressed not only in regard to the use of tools, machines, and materials in the school, but can also be extended to the proper use of cars, home appliances and electrical equipment.
- *Development of communication skills through reading and making sketches and drawings.* This goal needs no justification. However, it needs proper interpretation. Too many teachers confine the opportunities in this area to a few exercises in lettering and to meaningless practice in the use of tools and instruments. If communication skills are to be developed by every student, the learning experiences ought to be expanded and made relevant for everyone, not just for the few who will go into professional work in fields such as architecture and engineering.
- *Satisfying experience in self-expression through creative efforts leading to material accomplishments.* The industrial education laboratory is rich in promise for such opportunities. It can be equally rich in results if the teacher will guide student enthusiasm in productive channels and see to it that formality and lack of vision do not prohibit the attainment of this goal.
- *Appreciation of principles of good design and good workmanship and the application of these principles to the evaluation of manufactured products and the techniques involved in their construction.* It has been argued that it is not possible in the limited time available in industrial education classes to make any significant contribution toward this goal. This might be true if attitudes of proper judgment and good taste were to be fully developed in students. However, the most basic principles and attitudes can be established with young students in a limited amount of time, leading them to pursue their own investigations and studies in this increasingly important area.

Writing Performance Objectives

Just as goal orientation is important to the curriculum planner, the statement of specific performance objectives is necessary to the planning and implementation of everyday teaching and learning activities in the classroom and laboratory. Industrial educators generally have a pretty good idea of where they are going with their students. Many feel that the objectives of such practical work are self-evident, and that specification of behaviors is a waste of time and effort. In reality, however, the lack of prescriptions for intended terminal behaviors often leaves teachers and students in a disoriented pattern of activities. The fulfillment of long-range curriculum goals becomes more assured with the detailed specification of short-range performance objectives.

Goals, as noted previously, are conveniently expressed through the use of general statements. Behavioral or performance objectives, on the other hand, necessitate the exacting prescription of three separate parts including the educational *setting* in which the learning is to take place; the *behavior modification* to be developed by the students; and the *conditions for acceptability,* the minimum desired level of achievement.

1. *Setting.* Although the events of daily life provide randomly organized instructive experiences, formal education is a series of carefully designed learning experiences. Therefore the first step in planning a learning activity is to describe the situation in which the desired alteration in the student's attitude, knowledge, or skill will take place. Introductory remarks such as "Given fourteen different types of metal fasteners . . ." or "Prefaced by a short demonstration in the correct operation of the spray gun . . ." provide the teacher and students with a starting point on which the complete learning experience may be based.

2. *Behavior modification.* With the stage set, the next step in composing a complete behavioral objective is the exacting statement of the overt act which should be accomplished by the learner. "The student will operate the spray gun," or "The student will identify the fasteners by name and common use" are exacting enough, since they require specific behaviors or performances.

Such general terms as "know, learn, realize, appreciate, and do" fall short of specificity. Because of the practicality inherent in industrial education, the list of possible action verbs is vast, including such words as "list, describe, correctly hold, safely operate, analyze, compute, construct, fasten, sketch."

3. *Conditions for acceptability.* Industrially oriented production, endeavors, in order to be successful, must practice effective quality control. A similar practice is found in effective and efficient teaching. Once the setting has been established and the behavior change specified, a certain level of performance or quality is usually required of the students. With a traditional marking system, for instance, a student must answer correctly 65 percent or 70 percent of the test questions in order to obtain the lowest

passing grade. This lowest passing grade is the minimum level of acceptability. Answering the question, "How much?" the third portion of a behavioral objective states: "Twelve of the fourteen metal fasteners must be correctly identified," or, relative to the use of the spray gun, "an even coating of paint, without runs, is to be applied to the product's surfaces." A specification of a course aim will relate setting, behavior modification, and conditions for acceptability in a statement similar to the following examples.
- "Given fourteen different types of metal fasteners, the student will be able to identify at least twelve of them by name and common use."
- "Following a demonstration in the correct operation of the spray gun, the student should be able to operate the gun so as to spray an even coating of finish, without runs, on the product's surfaces."

For purposes of brevity, industrial educators often rely mainly on a shortened version of a behavioral objective. By combining the behavior and performance criteria, it is possible to be concise in specifying terminal behaviors. The use of simple examples such as, "The student should be able to operate a spray gun," may not represent a complete behavioral objective, but it does establish an end toward which the teacher and student can direct their actions. Such short statements find their best practical application in daily lesson plans as discussed in Chapter 10.

Emphasis at Educational Levels

Not all of the goals and objectives listed in this chapter are of equal importance for all ages of students. In elementary schools, many new, exciting programs relate to industry and occupational orientation. Here the manipulative work is done in close coordination and integration with the total academic program of the school. Self-expression and self-discovery are important outcomes. Sheer joy experienced in doing things at this age is in itself valuable but can be made moreso if the experience is related to a "unit of work" or a theme with social and educational value. High interest developed in manipulative work also tends to carry over into other fields. Investigation in geography, history, arithmetic, reading, science, and social studies, is often stimulated through the desire to construct things in material form.

All of the goals are attainable at the junior high school level. Here industrial education is taught in its most comprehensive form, without the restrictions imposed by a highly technical emphasis. However, attention is again called to the fact that to state a desirable goal is one thing and to attain it is another. These goals are student goals and whether they will be reached will depend upon the degree of effort contributed by the student, and the extent of promotion by the teacher.

In the senior high school most of the goals discussed take on an extended meaning. At this level, the acquisition of skill will necessarily receive more attention. Developments of maturing work habits, and independent and cooperative effort may be expected to reach more advanced stages at this age. Since there is more likelihood that the student has made at least a tentative choice of an area of occupational work, he or she can now choose subjects in industrial education that will strengthen his or her background for further education or occupational training.

DISCUSSION QUESTIONS

1. Do you consider leisuretime crafts and hobbies to be more or less important than they were a generation ago? Why?

2. By what procedures can safety habits in the home be developed in industrial education?

3. List ten industrial education activities that would develop in the student that degree of judgment necessary to purchase and use the industrial products produced by our technology.

4. Do you think that the goals presented in this chapter are equally suited to all communities? Explain your answer.

5. To what extent do you think that industrial education has special values for personality adjustment that other subjects do not have?

6. What is the basic difference between a "goal" and an "objective"?

7. Why is it so important to specify goals and objectives in a contemporary educational system? Can education become directionless without such specificity? Explain.

8. Write five examples of complete behavioral objectives. Discuss and evaluate these examples in class.

ADDITIONAL READINGS

Ackerman, J. Mark. *Operant Conditioning Techniques for the Classroom Teacher.* Glenview, Illinois: Scott, Foresman, 1972.

American Vocational Association. *A Guide to Improving Instruction in Industrial Arts.* Washington, D. C.: American Vocational Association, 1969.

Bloom, Benjamin. *Taxonomy of Educational Objectives: Handbook I—The Cognitive Domain.* New York: David McKay, 1956.

Bloom, Benjamin. *Taxonomy of Educational Objectives: Handbook II—The Affective Domain.* New York: David McKay, 1956.

Clark, D. Cecil. *Using Instructional Objectives in Teaching.* Glenview, Illinois: Scott, Foresman, 1972.

Kibler, Robert J., et. al. *Behavioral Objectives and Instruction.* Boston: Allyn and Bacon, 1970.

Mager, Robert F. and Beach, Kenneth M. Jr. *Developing Vocational Instruction.* Belmont, California: Fearon, 1967.

Mager, Robert F. *Goal Analysis.* Belmont, California: Fearon, 1972.

Mager, Robert F. *Preparing Instructional Objectives.* Belmont, California: Fearon, 1962.

Tyler, Ralph W. *Basic Principles of Curriculum and Instruction.* Chicago: University of Chicago Press, 1949.

Chapter 6
Program Emphases

Program Development

In industrial education, "program" refers to the mode of operation when concerned with a practical approach to implementing curriculum. To provide direction in the development of program alternatives, basic objectives concerned with attitudes, information, and performance must be kept in mind.

Based on the foundation of these objectives (refer to Chapter 5), the design of the program in industrial education can be developed and enriched. Some aspects of this development are elaborated on in succeeding paragraphs. The introductory topics are concerned with elements of structure (operations and processes, projects, units, and themes), while the final sections deal directly with contemporary emphases used by industrial educators. These aspects are segregated only for the purpose of discussion. This treatment is not meant to imply that all the elements discussed should be separate topics of instruction.

Operations and Processes

Since the early days of the mechanic arts movement, craftsmanship through the skillful use of tools has always been an important objective of industrial education. Constructive exercises in tool manipulation have provided students with opportunities to shape and join materials into objects that will serve as evidence of acquired information.

Many modern industrial education laboratories have elaborate equipment inventories. Hundreds of physical operations can be performed through the use of intricate tools, jigs, fixtures, instruments, and machines, yet the best-equipped materials-processing facility is really capable of only a relatively small number of fundamental processes. For example, the process of cutting, or material removal, can be accomplished in many ways. The shearing, chiseling, burning, or chemical action of the process occurs through the operation of numerous hand and machine tools. The operation, therefore, is only the physical means of using tools and procedures in implementing the overall process. Measurement is also a basic process essential to most fields of study. Although a basic process, measurement may involve the use of literally hundreds of instruments, from the basic ruler to fixed and variable calipers and highly complex electronic devices.

Teachers of basic courses can select projects to provide students with introductory experiences in operating many tools and machines. The project outcome may be very useful, but the main criteria for its selection are the inherent operations, not the consumer values.

If the project has little practical interest, or if the operations are as simple as those of threading a shaft or joining two pieces of wood with a splined miter joint, the project is usually known as a "drill" project. Although the drill project has fallen into disfavor with many industrial educators, its use can still be justified in trade-oriented programs, such as courses for training machine operators. Also, many persons find satisfaction in manipulative accomplishments. Students planning on employment in industry after graduation from secondary school will find such programs very beneficial in helping them to attain their occupational objectives. A curriculum designed for continuous progress (ungraded), with evaluation based on student fulfillment of performance criteria, can advantageously utilize the operations approach through drill projects and exercises. This allows students in trade preparatory programs to progress independently toward job entry competency. Likewise, the employer will be aware of those skills which have been satisfactorily mastered by each applicant.

The Project Method

Throughout the historical evolution of industrial education, the project has been the main program device for providing realistic, educational-industrial experiences for students. Because of the time and attention given to the project, its use should follow an established structure directed toward the fulfillment of meaningful goals. The student may be allowed to choose from a number of projects assigned by the teacher, or the student may be allowed to make his or her own independent choice of a project. Projects assigned by the teacher may involve, of necessity, a limited number of manipulative experiences. Those chosen by the student alone may often involve manipulative experiences which are either too basic or too involved. Both of these methods of choosing a project leave much to be desired.

Many leading industrial educators view the project as being an outdated learning experience and campaign vigorously for its elimination. Others believe the project is essential to practical education. Regardless, some reappraisal is necessary regarding its importance and the rationale governing its use. Rather than eliminate the project, its advocates would revise the outdated usages and arguments that seem to weaken its defense in the educational courtroom. An imaginative reconsideration of the project's content and scope might establish realistic guidelines for improving its use.

In industrial education programs, the planning and construction of projects normally consume the largest part of the student's time. It is through them that interest is maintained and the students educational and social growth is nurtured. Often, however, too little attention is given to the important task of careful and analytical project selection. Thus, projects have been kept in school programs long after their usefulness has vanished. Some teachers have continued to assign projects they themselves made in college ten or twenty years before. Projects should be updated and made relevant.

CHAPTER 6—PROGRAM EMPHASES

It should be said, however, in all fairness, that many good ideas for projects have been proposed in recent years. Industrial education teachers are now more familiar with the principles of good design. And, while most industrial educators may not be able to produce good original designs, many of them are able to distinguish between good and bad designs. More importantly, they are able to point out these distinctions to their students. Students should be instructed toward an appreciation of good design. Some students may be able to contribute new or altered designs for projects. All projects considered should be analyzed in relation to the principles of good design.

In a project-oriented program, valid student performance outcomes may be assured. These deal with originality or relevance of design, cooperative attitudes through working with peers, abilities to follow plans and directions, leadership in setting a standard for other students, and persistence in the completion of a teacher-established or self-determined task. Such are the true ends of all program emphases. The product that the student manufactures experimentally as a laboratory project is but the means to these ends. It is also a medium by which the student may express himself or herself.

The following paragraphs discuss many alternatives for structuring individual and group experiences with drill, production, and problem types of projects.

Project Selection

Of the many types of projects employed in experiential education, the following three categories have been used extensively in industrial education programs: drill projects, production projects, and problem projects.

Drill Projects

As previously noted under "Operations and Processes," the exercise, or drill project, still finds valuable use in introductory laboratory experiences as well as in advanced trade training. Allowance must be provided for the need to "do things right," rather than banning such an objective. *Craftsmanship is important.* The fundamental purpose is to offer students an opportunity to develop manipulative skills in the use of tools and machines. Also, the student ought to develop respect for and recognition of values inherent in the performance of basic mechanical processes. Projects within this category are selected principally for the operations required, rather than for design characteristics, consumer acceptability, or student interest. Examples may range from lettering exercises and the making of wood joints to the fabrication of weldments, and the manufacture of turnings and threaded shafts. Excellence in operational efficiency is the desired result of such activities.

Production Projects

Since the sloyd movement with its emphasis on the construction of more meaningful articles, the production-type of project has been the hallmark of most industrial education programs. The production (extraction, manufacture, construction, or reconstitution) of a *useful* material object is paramount.

Individual projects within this category have been both teacher-assigned and student-selected. Those assigned by the teacher closely resemble "drill" projects, except that the item produced will always be a useful object. Projects of this type usually reflect those facets of tool and machine operation in which the teacher feels all students should participate. The greatest disadvantage of such projects lies in the possibility that they may become standardized within the framework of a curriculum.

Student selection of projects can be accomplished in two basic ways: by offering a series of similar projects with calculated learning content, or by allowing broad freedom dictated by student interest. For the beginning teacher or student, such freedom can result in haphazard learning, due to the lack of target knowledge. As teachers and students gain experience with the materials and equipment in the laboratory, motivation can be heightened through student-oriented activities. Initially, the teacher should provide direction toward the completion of the selected object. Demonstrations of necessary operations can be presented in film, "live" by outside experts, by the teacher, or by experienced students. Personal development can be evaluated by degree of fulfillment of the original purposes or aims of the student and teacher.

Group production projects usually take the form of either *team* activities or *line* activities. Because *team-type projects* are usually of complicated design, carefully planned assignments and the cooperative participation and efforts of many students are required. Products such as boats, model homes (or model simulations of the roof or other sections), and sets of furniture are but a few of the more common possibilities. At another level of difficulty, telescopes, other scientific apparatus and instrumentation, wind tunnels, electronic game boards and animated or automated robots have proved quite challenging for scientifically minded students. When weather and climate permit, complete houses can be constructed by industrial education teams. These houses can later be sold by a student sales staff. Team activities usually follow a sequence similar to the following: (1) selection of a problem or project; (2) research to establish design and cost parameters; (3) specification of fabrication techniques; and (4) final assembly, with inspection wherever appropriate.

Line-type projects are joint endeavors for manufacturing a large number of a single article through an efficient organization of people combined with a sequential arrangement of production machines. Inherent within the structure is an intricate social order that is the most important single element in the production activity. A primary goal of industrial education is the interpretation of industry. To be familiar with this aspect of industry, one must be conversant with the typical industrial organization of people, the human element in line or mass production. This structure usually includes a director of production, an engineering coordinator, a production planner, a chief inspector, and a public relations director. These positions exist in

CHAPTER 6—PROGRAM EMPHASES

industry, and they could be adopted in the industrial education class. Positions concerned with safety, labor relations, education, and other aspects of industrial organization can also be established according to need and the size of the class. In addition to being responsible for a staff position, each student also fills one of the production-line personnel stations. In this way, self-discipline, leadership, and followership may be cultivated.

Besides providing a realistic imitation of the line production aspects of modern industry, a project approach of this type also fulfills many of the prime objectives of all types of industrial education programs. Activities involving problem solving, consumer efficiency, and manipulative skills can provide valuable learning experiences, as well as promoting extremely important interpersonal-relationships. The school is primarily concerned with the educational benefits of those enterprises, which are based on experiences in industrial production. Such activities offer the individual opportunities to experience a variety of roles in an educational environment. These activities also offer an entire class of students the unique opportunity to participate in an active model of a manufacturing industry.

As a summation and comment:

- *It is the method of industry.* One of the objectives of industrial education in schools is always to provide the student with an opportunity to explore and study various occupations. Individual work, where one person completes an entire product, is not common in modern industry.
- *It puts incentive into the work.* Students who have difficulty in realizing time values when working on individual articles for themselves are now matched against other students in such a way that work habits can be easily compared. If this is not enough, the student will probably be told in plain words by his or her classmates to "speed up."
- *It raises standards of workmanship.* The student may make a bad joint on his own piece of furniture and expect to remedy it. But if the student cuts all tenons too thin for twenty tables he or she will face a different situation. When the student is made a working member of an organization, many things which the teacher has been helpless to impress on him are impressed by force of circumstance.
- *It develops cooperation.* The spirit of give and take is very necessary in life and in employment. Individual work for individual profit is not likely to develop it; production work may.
- *It discovers and develops managerial ability.* Leadership qualities are found through this type of organization, where the class is divided into groups, with students acting as team leaders and managers.
- *It gives an opportunity to less-talented students.* There are many conscientious, willing students who cannot, with all their effort, produce a completely finished article of which anyone can be proud. In a production job they can be placed according to their level of ability and be happy and successful. They will contribute in their way to the finished product and be

TEACHING INDUSTRIAL EDUCATION

proud of the job. They may also be counseled toward an occupational choice in semiskilled work in industry.

The use of team leaders, bills of materials, instruction sheets, and audio-visuals, will seldomly replace direct instruction by the teacher. If the members of the class are fully accustomed to the use of machinery, a brief review of important points in regard to the machine involved may be sufficient; if not, a complete series of demonstrations is essential. Much of the basic instruction that every member of the class must have can profitably be presented to the entire group. While there is truth in the argument that such instruction should be given at the time when students are ready to apply it, it is also true that it is much easier, and takes less time, to refresh the memory of individual students or groups through a later review than it is to teach such subject matter to one or two individuals at a time when specific problems are at hand.

Furthermore, in a production job of this kind, it is probable that all the students will not have a chance to perform all of the operations. However, it is still profitable for students to see as many fundamental processes of hand and machine work as possible. To have seen a demonstration of the setting-up and operating of a machine is valuable education for all students whether they are likely to apply it to an actual problem today, next week, or not at all.

Problem Projects

This type of project has attracted general interest from industrial educators. By engaging in activities involving troubleshooting, servicing, research, and experimentation, exceptional students can find challenging opportunities to develop mathematical and scientific concepts pertinent to experimental problem-solving. The activities involved may test principles of operation, but they need not produce a three-dimensional product. *The problem is the project.* The discovery method, discussed in Chapter 10, offers unique possibilities for the utilization of problem-type projects.

The project must be an educational experience. The student should be encouraged to define a problem and seek its solution, rather than follow a set of prepared plans and operation sheets as in conventional laboratory work. The student must organize and revise his or her thinking throughout the process. The teacher may suggest alternative methods for solution, but should avoid the role of "answerer." Emphasis is placed on habits of inquiry and freedom of physical movement, not teacher control. Thus, in a learning experience of this sort, individualized project activities replace a traditional teacher-directed program.

Pure science and mathematics provide the foundations for industry and technology. Since one of the main curricular objectives of industrial education is the study of the processes and activities of modern industry, it follows that industrial education must look to the fields of science and mathematics for much of its programmatic substance. It should be a reciprocal process.

CHAPTER 6—PROGRAM EMPHASES

The program in industrial education should enrich the scientific disciplines, just as science and mathematics should aid in the meaningful presentation and explanation of practical phenomena. The laboratory environment provides a unique opportunity for the application of scientific and mathematical principles. Industry today, more than at any other time in history, is becoming oriented toward research, problem solving, experimentation, troubleshooting, and servicing, while a correspondingly smaller percentage of the labor force is being utilized on the production line. With this in mind, student projects can include such activities as testing, analysis, invention, investigation, and design, all of which have become processes fundamental to industry.

Problem projects offer a wide variety of learning experiences, all of which may be gauged to the level of difficulty appropriate to the individual student's aptitudes. The original designing of a consumer product from its basic components might provide a challenging experience for some, while a study such as that of the airfoil principles utilized in airplane design might interest other students. The study of woods, metals, plastics, and glass offers many opportunities for chemical and structural analysis and testing. The principles of basic machines such as levers and pulleys can be incorporated into the design and development of work-saving devices. Contemporary problems of housing, communication, urbanization, energy conservation, and pollution, should suggest realistic problem projects. Student involvement in projects such as these would be socially relevant, since today's youth will have to solve these problems in the future.

The Unit Method

A unit of study is defined as a group of varied individual learning activities organized around one central theme or class problem, and directed toward the attainment of realistic, life-oriented goals. Generally, a traditional program can be strengthened when a group of students select a common center of interest prior to extensive planning by and with the instructor. Thus, the unit provides the opportunity for students to take part in the initial stages of program implementation, with their interests and needs influencing the ultimate selection of the class theme.

The goals of the teacher, as well as those of the students, are established at the outset to give that direction necessary for the provision of learning opportunities. Fundamental concepts, skills, appreciations, attitudes, and ideals help to define a set of desirable terminal behaviors and other outcomes. The effectiveness and degree of organization of a unit depend upon the value and arrangement of its activities. These activities ought to be structured and ordered so that they motivate, invite participation, enrich, and lead to an accurate assessment of goal fulfillment.

1. *Motivation.* The first activities of a typical unit have the primary purpose of motivating class interest in a theme. Films, field trips, talks by class visitors, and inventories of student interest can often be effectively

employed for this purpose. At this point, it is important for all students to become aware of the central purposes of the unit of study, and to begin the process of selecting a project, problem, or experiment that is related to some common interest of the class.

2. *Participation.* The second set of learning activities is formulated to provide all students with the opportunity to engage in group and individual laboratory activities. Each student carries out the laboratory phase of the chosen activity, based on individual manipulative capabilities.

3. *Enrichment.* At this point, students are encouraged to share their experiences through seminars, discussions, and presentations. Each displays a project or problem and establishes its relevance within the parameters of the theme. Seminars, discussions, and presentations provide all members of the class with an awareness of the breadth of educational and manipulative experiences possible within the unit.

4. *Goal fulfillment.* The final activity, evaluation of goal fulfillment, requires participation by all students as a group, because it deals with both a personal and a class estimation of growth.

By providing learning experiences associated with the planning, designing, construction, and testing of industrial products, and by using industrial materials in the construction of those products, the unit method can develop student skill. A learning program utilizing the unit method may also increase the student's participation in society. It may inform the student of worthwhile leisuretime activities and develop consumer proficiency in purchasing. The development of latent interests and abilities may specify to the student occupational opportunities of which he or she may have been previously unaware.

The unit method is appropriate for popular industrial education units dealing with themes involving sporting goods, home furnishings, personal accessories, communications devices, propulsion systems, and hand tools. The unit method is also useful in interdisciplinary involvement, providing exciting experiential opportunities for both students and teachers.

Industry and Technology

An understanding of industry, technology, and the society basic to American life has come to be an accepted goal of industrial education. While this goal is undoubtedly shared with many other areas of instruction in our schools, industrial education should offer unique opportunities for contribution to its attainment. The teacher who is impressed with the value of this goal will find many opportunities to do more than give lip service to it. Organization in industry can be illustrated and simulated through student participation in laboratory management. Production jobs will call for cooperative effort and managerial organization. It should be kept in mind, however, that it is necessary to make definite comparisons to industry and to enlarge the vision of the students by additional means, such as field trips,

CHAPTER 6—PROGRAM EMPHASES

motion pictures, and relevant reading material in order to get the greatest value from the learning experiences provided in school. It should not be assumed that young students will automatically relate their experiences to remote situations without having points of similarity emphasized.

Another aspect of this discussion is the impact made by our technology upon modern social and economic life. Rapid advances in mechanization, technology, and automation are making it essential that serious attempts be made in school to assist students in adjusting to adult life in a rapidly changing society. The impact of technological change on society is widely publicized, and the implementation of a program for learning to live and work in this new social order can be considered a challenge to our schools and our society. This challenge confronts the industrial educator and his or her program, and should suggest a new emphasis in certain areas of teacher education.

Realistic experiences concerned with industry, its organization, environment, occupations, processes, products, and problems can be presented only by a teacher who has had previous education in these areas. The education may have been acquired through formal coursework, industrial employment or both. Industrial education is, by definition, education about industry. The relative importance of industry and technology in industrial education program development can be better appreciated through a review of those curriculum foundations explained in Chapter 2.

Occupational Information

Assisting youth to learn about occupational opportunities has become an accepted responsibility of the school. And here, again, the industrial education program is accepting its share of the challenge and is in a favored position to meet it. Two approaches to the problem are suitable and available: occupational exploration through the regular program, and occupational information and study through varied auxiliary means.

The first approach is relatively obvious. Students who participate in a varied program in industrial education have the opportunity to see some of the basic tools, materials, and operations pertaining to the occupations represented. But the instructor's opportunity does not end with the practical work at the bench or at the machine. There is much valuable information about the occupation represented, and about related occupations, that will not naturally be presented through the limited amount of manipulative work that is possible in the school. It is the duty of the instructor to analyze such informational material, and to select from it such phases for presentation as will help the student not only to make a more intelligent occupational choice, but also to learn more about the many aspects of the technological society in which he or she lives.

Information, whether for the purpose of enriching the general course content or for giving an insight into occupations, may be given to students

TEACHING INDUSTRIAL EDUCATION

in a number of ways. The methods of procedure and sources of information are identical in a large number of cases. The following means have been used successfully:

- Presentations by the instructor.
- Research assignments and student reports.
- Talks by men and women from industry and business.
- Visits to industry.
- Videotapes, slides, sound recordings, and films.

Oral presentations by the instructor. The most obvious method, but in many ways the least effective, is for the instructor to give the class the information which he or she thinks they need about the work or about the occupation. there are, no doubt, topics for which this is the most desirable method. However, in general, other methods are more desirable and produce a more permanent effect.

Assigned research and student reports. If the library is at all complete, it should have in it some good books on occupations. Students may be directed to such books for valuable information from which they may draw material for brief oral and written reports. Study of occupational information in this way has a distinct advantage in that it enables students to cover more ground than can be covered by class presentations alone. Government bulletins and pamphlets published by private agencies are available for this study program.

Presentations by outside speakers. A series of talks by outstanding people in the field of occupations under consideration has been used in many schools. This type of approach creates interest among students, unless it becomes commonplace. Extreme care must be exercised in selecting the persons who assist in such a program, or it may result both in waste of time and in unfortunate reactions on the part of the students. Even with the best speakers possible, it is necessary to impress them beforehand with both the purpose for the arrangement and the most effective procedure for presenting their information. A definite outline for studying and presenting an occupation is of value in stimulating discussion.

Visits to industries. Well-organized visits to industrial plants, buildings under construction, drafting rooms, and other industrial environments are valuable in broadening the students' views of occupations and their possibilities. Such visits also help to develop an understanding of the impact of industry and technology upon social and economic life. Next to actual participation in the occupation, this method is probably the most effective in presenting a true picture of an occupation and the conditions under which the work is done.

To be most effective, such visits must be planned in advance. The instructor should first visit the plant to note those phases of the work that will

CHAPTER 6—PROGRAM EMPHASES

be most valuable. He or she might next make out a form for the students to fill in with the information gathered on their visit. Unless the class knows beforehand what they should look for, there is danger that the trip will not be instructive.

Videotapes, transparencies, and films. Some prefer films and slides to any other means available for studying occupations. Even if the numerous difficulties in the way of industrial visits were eliminated, it is argued that pictures are preferable, and for this the following reasons have been given:

- The program can proceed without interfering with the schedule of students with reference to their other studies. This cannot be done when visiting industries, because the period usually devoted to the class is not of sufficient length.
- The attention of students can be concentrated more easily upon the subject. On a visit there are always competing attractions that draw attention away from the important points.
- On a visit, it is rarely possible for all students to obtain a true picture of existing conditions. This is because it is difficult for all of the students to get near enough to those important phases of the work which may be in progress.
- Explanations given in connection with films, slides, and transparencies can easily be heard. Because of noise levels, it is often difficult to hear the explanations given in industrial plants.
- Films can often be slowed down, or stopped where necessary, for further study of details.

While these advantages are worthy of consideration, it can hardly be agreed that pictures are in every respect more desirable than actual visitation. In most localities there would be no pictures available of most of the local industries which students of the schools might expect to visit. Even in the largest cities, only a few of the most important industrial plants can furnish films showing the scope of activity engaged in. Even when such films are produced, advertising qualities rather than true occupational conditions may have been given first consideration.

Educational films, as well as many other types of audiovisual material, do have a definite place in the program of modern industrial teaching. While films are generally thought of as pertaining to occupational and related information, there are valuable films available for giving instruction in manipulative processes as well.

In the study of an occupation, the instructor must have a plan for discovering and organizing that information most valuable to the students. The outline which follows is used to indicate one type of analysis. An outline of this type is equally valuable for use where the study is made auxiliary to the total industrial education program, or where the study of occupations has been organized independently on a broader basis.

Outline for the Study of an Occupation

A. *General statement concerning the occupation.*
   1. Value of the occupation as a social service.
   2. Duties of one engaged in it.
   3. Number engaged in it in local community.
   4. Relative number engaged in it, in general, with its probable future development.
   5. Relative capital invested in it.
B. *Personal qualities demanded.*
   1. Qualities of manner, temperament, character.
   2. Mental characteristics.
   3. Physical demands.
C. *Preparation required.*
   1. General education.
   2. Special or vocational education.
   3. Apprenticeship conditions.
   4. Experience required.
D. *Wages earned by workers.*
   1. Range of wages (table showing distribution of cases).
   2. Average weekly wage.
   3. Relation of wage to length of experience and preparation.
E. *Length of working season, working week, working day.*
F. *Health of the workers.*
   1. Healthful or unhealthful conditions.
   2. Dangers, accidents, or risks.
G. *Opportunities for employment.*
   1. In local community.
   2. In general.
H. *Organization of the industry,* including the relations of the worker to his or her fellow workers, employers, and the community.
I. *Status of workers.*
   1. Opportunities for advancement.
   2. Time for recreation and enjoyment.
   3. Adequate income for recreation and the comforts of life.
   4. Any other items of peculiar interest in this connection.
J. *Biographies of leaders in the vocation.*

Coeducational Programs

More emphasis needs to be placed on the necessity for giving all students the necessary preparation for living in an age of machines and appliances, as well as for enjoyable leisuretime activities. In general, areas of activity involve household mechanics, industrial drafts, architectural design, furniture construction, upholstering, and seminar courses in related topics concerned with the society-technology interface. Definite organization on the part of the teacher will establish proper cooperative attitudes.

CHAPTER 6—PROGRAM EMPHASES

The most opportune way for initiating a coeducational program seems to lie in class exchanges. Students in art or home economics classes are the most easily transferred. In this way, industrial education classes offer the opportunity to gain skills and techniques not normally open to all students within the confines of the curriculum schedule.

Often, activity periods and clubs offer all students the means to enter into the industrial education program and participate in manipulative activities associated with creative problem solving. As mentioned elsewhere in this chapter, interdisciplinary studies provide another excellent means for the industrial education program to serve more youth with relevant learning opportunities in the academic educational environment.

Interdisciplinary Cooperation

Many common problems of everyday life—and of the classroom and laboratory—often defy solution when investigated by the methods of a single discipline. The solution of such problems may often require the use of many different methods from several disciplines.

Many valuable and interesting educational activities can be arranged for students through the cooperation of instructors and classes within and between departments of the school. Correlated activities, team teaching, and integrated curricula offer three possible approaches to providing more relevant learning experiences for students. Fundamental to each of these approaches is the premise that teachers must be willing to share their talents as well as their classrooms. They must be willing to accept the responsibility for any problems, just as they must be willing to share the reward of any success. Through such cooperation, the "pigeonhole" effect of the traditional separate-subject curriculum can be lessened and many interesting educational activities can result.

Correlated Activities

Only a part of the scope of natural student interest and desire for expression lies within the work of any single lab. Unless the teachers of separate single-unit labs correlate their work, they will deprive youth of some of the fine opportunities for expression now offered in the comprehensive laboratories of industries.

There is no reason why some parts of a project cannot be made in one lab area, and other parts in another, even though the product will be individually owned. Nor should there be objection to having certain parts constructed in one lab one semester and the complete job finished in some other lab at a later time. For example, the hull of a model boat can be constructed in the woodshop, while the boat's motor might be manufactured in the power-systems center. In project construction, several single-unit labs can be utilized as efficiently as the general lab, provided that the teachers involved are aware of the need for correlation of the program.

Correlated and coordinated projects can and should be arranged between various departments of the school. The line of least resistance is to plan one's own work for the class. However, always to do so might limit the experiences of the group. Consider, for instance, the project of making scenery for a school play. This is a problem with which most teachers are familiar. Instead of considering such a piece of work a necessary evil, why not welcome it as an opportunity for a splendid, correlated project? If such an undertaking is properly appreciated, it can easily provide experience and knowledge far beyond what the woodworking lab alone can give.

"Yes," you say, "*but*—I am teaching woodwork!" However, ten years from now the skill in making a mortise-and-tenon joint will not be of great value to nine out of every ten of your students. Besides, if that skill can be related to activities of the art department and the drama class, it will present a learning opportunity more meaningful than a series of formal, manipulative assignments. The teacher who wishes to popularize and vitalize his teaching, then, might well investigate opportunities to correlate his work and integrate it into a larger sphere of educational activity.

Team Teaching

Many programs lend themselves well to the utilization of the multiple-staff organization known as team teaching. In this structure, teachers are selected to represent their particular areas of knowledge to the class. These presentations are scheduled as information is needed for problem solution.

In a building construction study unit, for instance, the woodworking instructor can best plan the production activities. Computations necessary in architectural estimating might be offered by a mathematics teacher. Blueprint reading is a specialty of the drafting teacher, while design aesthetics might best be handled by an industrial design, art, or perhaps a home economics teacher. The woodworking teacher, in addition to conducting demonstrations and supervising laboratory activities, would act as team coordinator and organize and schedule presentations by other members of the team. All team members, however, would be responsible for planning, implementing, and evaluating the entire unit of work.

Another established practice in similar situations occurs when the instructor invites members of the community to present their occupational interests to the class. In this way, the most current information on industrial personnel, processes, and products can be provided for the students. This involvement of community guest lecturers can also provide other advantages. All educational programs are substantially supported by local taxation. The involvement of local residents will enable them better to appreciate the value of the curricular contributions to youth. When called upon, much vocal and financial support can be spontaneous.

Most recently, *differentiated staffing patterns* have come into use in industrial education. As a refinement of the team teaching concept, differentiated staffing offers many levels of instructional roles. The master teacher (a professional educator with post-graduate preparation) establishes curriculum directions. His or her staff teachers are responsible for the instructional

CHAPTER 6—PROGRAM EMPHASES

phases of the curriculum. These instructors also usually have degrees, but prefer the classroom activities to those associated with curricular coordination. Laboratory technicians, employed because of their experiences with materials, tools, and machines, usually participate in the activity and manipulative performance phases of the program. Intern and student teachers find it easy to gain entry into such a school personnel organization. These beginners find it comfortable to fill the role of a laboratory teacher or small group discussion leader, whereas the more seasoned professional educator usually fits more easily into the roles of lecturer and coordinator. The "new role" of the teacher as facilitator of learning is especially evident in the differentiated staff.

Integrated Curricula   This type of program structure offers the unique opportunity for an entire school, or school system, to select a unit of study, or theme, around which all educational activities will be centered for a predetermined number of days or weeks. Most student activity relates to their home life, their employment, and their use of leisure. A study of these three spheres of activity will provide a means for cross-disciplined inquiry into life-oriented problems.

The theme of the unit of study would suggest those learning activities that might take place in different courses. For example, the selection of "Introduction to Industry" as an integrated unit of study would suggest specific activities. The mathematics classes might study selected topics and problems associated with measurement, wages, and employment. They might engage in time and motion studies. They might also examine economic factors relative to waste, taxes, income, overhead, and transportation. In social studies, the organizational structure of industry and the social interdependence necessary for success in the free-enterprise system would provide topics for realistic discussions. Topics related to the industrial revolution, inventions, and patents would be part of the history offerings. In English classes, students could write technical reports on products, occupations, and industrial visits, while stressing the types of communication basic to all industry. Home economics classes, to encourage consumer competency, might examine standards of quality and methods of price comparison. Product design could be a part of market research conducted in the community by students in the business education department. Plans and production schedules would be completed in the drafting room, while the actual manufacture of the item would be the responsibility of the materials-processing laboratory students. Sales and other associated activities could be a challenging assignment for the students in distributive education. All activities in the separate classes would operate simultaneously and relate to the student's broad understanding of the theme.

A Balanced Program   Even though there is great value and importance in giving general, industrial, technological, and occupational information to the industrial education class, it still should not be made into a discussion subject of an academic type. Conversely, restricting the classwork to the practice of basic, manipulative processes would limit its educational value. The effectiveness of industrial education is measurable in the operational phases of the program. Under systematic supervision of the professional educator, the work periods become a laboratory setting for the practice and application of the facts, principles, and information learned in the programmatic aspects of the curriculum.

Increasingly, we recognize that personal development—leading toward rewarding work habits, social maturity and awareness, self-discipline, and the willingness to accept responsibility—constitutes the major goal of the industrial educator. With this overall standard in mind, the teacher should correlate the entire instructional program toward the goal's attainment. The various student learning activities should also contribute to the same end.

DISCUSSION QUESTIONS

1. Discuss the relationship of "program" and "curriculum."
2. Is it possible for the project to become the only "end" in industrial education activities? Explain.
3. Describe how the enterprising teacher can allow student choice in project selection while remaining assured that all students will perform similar tool and machine operations.
4. Select five projects of varying difficulty which incorporate the same basic operations. List and describe the operational similarities.
5. Select fifteen experiential themes, five each from the work world, home life, and leisure activities. These themes are to relate to studies that might be pursued in a comprehensive laboratory of power and propulsion technology.
6. Explain why "processes" are emphasized in industrial arts, while "operations" are stressed in vocational preparation.
7. Describe an educationally sound "drill" project for a basic class in woodworking.
8. Cite advantages and disadvantages of team teaching in the industrial education department.
9. Is it possible to combine operations, processes, and project construction within a unit theme? Suggest implementation.
10. What type of project activities are possible when teachers cooperate through "correlated" activities?
11. How could class projects stressing opportunities for "understanding industry" be selected?
12. In what ways might usual teaching procedures be reorganized to place emphasis upon personal interests of the student?
13. At what age do you believe that students should be urged to make a tentative selection of their life's work?
14. How permanent do you consider occupational choices that are made by students fifteen years of age or younger?

CHAPTER 6—PROGRAM EMPHASES

15. List the procedure that a teacher might follow in arranging a unit study for his class.

16. In what respects, if any, are industrial visits superior to films for imparting occupational information?

17. Make up a sheet of information and suggestions that one might give to the class before going on an industrial visit.

18. Make an outline for the students to follow in their reports of industrial visits.

19. How would you go about preparing a person for giving a talk on his or her occupation?

20. Is there, in your opinion, danger in being too explicit in suggestions to one who is to speak to a group of students? If so, what is the danger?

21. What are some advantages in having students, and not the teacher, find and present occupational information?

ADDITIONAL READINGS

Billett, Roy O.; Maley, Donald; and Hammond, James J. *The Unit Method.* Washington, D. C.: American Industrial Arts Association, 1960.

Cenci, Louis, and Weaver, Gilbert G. *Teaching Occupational Skills.* 2nd ed. New York: Pitman, 1968.

Giachino, J. W., and Gallington, Ralph O. *Course Construction in Industrial Arts, Vocational, and Technical Education.* Chicago: American Technical Society, 1967.

Kilgore, Alvah M. "Research in Technology: An Experiment in Independent Study." *Industrial Arts & Vocational Education.* May 1969, pp. 73–76.

Leighbody, Gerald B., and Kidd, Donald M. *Methods of Teaching Shop and Technical Subjects.* Albany, New York: Delmar, 1966.

Marovich, Milton J. "Experiment in Curriculum Coordination." *Industrial Arts & Vocational Education.* February 1968, pp. 74–77.

Olson, Delmar W. *Industrial Arts and Technology.* Englewood Cliffs, New Jersey: Prentice-Hall, 1963.

Scobey, Mary-Margaret. *Teaching Children About Technology.* Bloomington, Illinois: McKnight & McKnight, 1968.

Seal, Michael R. "Go Gunning for Mass-Production Enrichment." *School Shop,* February 1969, pp. 51–53.

Silvius, G. Harold, and Bohn, Ralph C. *Organizing Course Materials For Industrial Education.* Bloomington, Illinois: McKnight & McKnight, 1961.

Silvius, G. Harold, and Curry, Estell H. *Teaching Successfully in Industrial Education.* Bloomington, Illinois: McKnight & McKnight, 1967.

Sredl, Henry J., and Travis, Evan. "Mass Production—Unit of Study or Method of Teaching?" *Industrial Arts & Vocational Education,* May 1968, pp. 43–44.

Wilber, Gordon O., and Pendered, Norman C. *Industrial Arts in General Education.* 4th ed. Scranton, Pennsylvania: International Textbook, 1973.

Chapter 7
Facility Design and Management

Evolution of Modern School Laboratories

The evolution of modern laboratories has been prompted by new interpretations of industrial education. The period from the time when a dark room in the basement was considered good enough for the shop class, to the present, when often the most accessible area of the building is devoted to industrial education, has been a period of progress that has provided evidence of courageous leadership. Every industrial educator needs to become acquainted with modern trends and practices in school plant planning in order to be ready to respond to opportunities in connection with planning new facilities or remodeling old ones. Following is a brief discussion of various types of laboratories in use.

The Single-Unit Laboratory

The oldest type of industrial education laboratory is based on a single unit of industrial activity. As the name implies, this laboratory is designed for only one type of work, such as patternmaking, the study of automatic transmissions, machine drafting, welding, sheet metal working, plumbing, carpentry, or letterpress printing. In modern practice, the unit plan is usually found in those secondary and post-secondary school facilities that are large enough to necessitate several classes under the supervision of several teachers. Programs are usually directed toward vocational objectives, and the educational orientation provides trade training.

The General-Unit Laboratory

To provide for the attainment of contemporary aims and objectives, it became necessary to develop and expand opportunities for experience and exploration within industrial education programs. This need prompted the gradual development of the general-unit laboratory, which now exists under a variety of classifications. This type of facility can be readily recognized by its inclusion of many related activities of one particular industry. In general metals, for example, related activities involved might be metal casting, sheet metal working, welding, working with art metal, spinning, machining, and the study of metallurgy. Graphic arts would embrace not only the more traditional activities such as type composition, platemaking, and letterpress work, but would also include bindery work, silk screening, lithography, and photography. General woods would have space for the inclusion of carpentry, furnituremaking, cabinetmaking, boat construction, and the study of material science. As another example, graphic science or drafting, would deal with the techniques necessary for the freehand and instrumental

CHAPTER 7—FACILITY DESIGN AND MANAGEMENT

drawing of products associated with architecture, manufacture, power, and electronics.

The general-unit laboratory is especially appropriate to secondary school industrial education programs which have either an industrial arts or vocational preparation orientation. In junior high schools, the generalization can be broadened further to provide only three laboratories for housing the entire curriculum. Such a facility is based on the technologies of graphics (including all drawing and graphic arts), materials (testing and processing of metals, woods, plastics, fluids, and ceramics), and power (engines, power transmission, control factors, and electronics).

The Comprehensive Industrial Laboratory

A comprehensive laboratory is usually thought of as one in which several unrelated types of work are taught simultaneously by one teacher. In its most expanded form, this type of facility provides for a large number of work areas, which may not necessarily all be in operation at the same time.

The evolution of the comprehensive laboratory has brought about greater opportunities for broadening and enriching the program in industrial education. At the same time, however, comprehensive labs will usually multiply and complicate problems of organization, management, and teaching procedures, all of which will require special consideration and planning if the educational objectives are to be fulfilled.

The comprehensive lab has found favor mainly in smaller schools where several unit labs are not economically feasible. Comprehensive laboratories are used effectively to offer short exploratory courses in high schools. There, activities involving basic exploration and investigation can aid in assisting the student in occupational selection.

As suggested previously, it is likely that the very nature of the facility will create problems in class management and teaching procedures beyond those present in a unit laboratory. The teacher might well proceed with caution in the selection of the kinds and the number of separate activities to be included. It is better to succeed in the handling of three or four activities than to fail in attempting a much greater number. Just how many and what kinds of activities should be attempted will depend upon several factors, some of which would be: the variety of craft skills possessed by the teacher, his or her experience and ability in organization and management, and his or her ingenuity and resourcefulness as a teacher.

Under efficient management the comprehensive industrial laboratory can become an effective instrument for expanding the concept of industrial education. The resourceful teacher who is willing to invest the necessary time and energy in organizing the students for participation in the management of the facility will render further service to this concept.

The Mobile Laboratory

The mobile facility has become popular for service to small rural schools. A bus or moving van is equipped with the tools and machines necessary for the manipulative work planned. When the van arrives at the school, some equipment may be unloaded for use in the building. The rear door of the van may be lowered as a ramp so that students may enter the "lab on wheels" and work with equipment which is not readily movable. This arrangement, as well as providing various schools with additional tools and equipment, also furnishes more work space.

Facility Design

While it is true that good laboratories and good equipment do not guarantee efficient teaching, it is also true that good physical facilities greatly improve the possibilities for teaching success. Every industrial educator is likely, sooner or later, to have the opportunity to participate in the planning and equipping of new laboratories or in the remodeling of old ones. When that time comes, his or her effectiveness will depend largely upon the knowledge he or she has regarding the various aspects of the challenge that confronts them. Such knowledge should include factual information covering efficient lab planning. The teacher should also know how to proceed to impress his or her views upon those who are in official charge of planning and approving buildings and equipment.

Since the laboratory serves as the industrial educator's classroom, the teacher must not be too timid in offering suggestions regarding its plan. However, he or she should offer such suggestions tactfully and methodically. School administrators who propose policies, school boards that approve them, and architects who plan the buildings will all be glad to have proposals from the teacher, provided that those proposals are sensible, clear-cut, and based upon a knowledge of modern educational practices. The earlier the teacher presents his or her views, the better chance he or she will have of getting a hearing. In presenting needs and requirements for a program and facility, it is well to make out not only a floor plan, but a complete model showing the layout and placement of all equipment.

The accompanying check sheet includes many of the important points that must be considered when planning laboratories. If this or a similar list is used seriously by a person planning individual labs or entire facilities, there is greater possibility that most of the essential features will be incorporated.

Check List for Lab Planning

A listing of items to keep in mind when planning new labs or remodeling old ones includes:
- Funds available, immediately and in the future.
- General and specific objectives of the work to be taught.
- Types of subjects to be taught, unit or comprehensive.
- Age or grade levels of students.
- Location of facility with reference to other rooms or buildings.
- Possibility of future additions, or of internal rearrangement.
- Ceiling height 12'–14'.
- Platforms for materials and finished projects.
- Adequate seating arrangements. Place for demonstration bench.

CHAPTER 7—FACILITY DESIGN AND MANAGEMENT

- Locations and sizes of doors. Enough outside entrances. Double doors for labs.
- Special driveways leading to doors providing access for deliveries.
- Provisions of state and local building codes. Special school codes.
- Architectural style prescribed, factory or ornamental.
- Interior color scheme.
- Safety precautions legally required.
- Types of flooring materials: wood, concrete, asphalt tile, linoleum.
- Hoses and fire extinguishers conveniently located.
- Office or desk space for teacher. Separate office preferred.
- System of locks and master keys.
- Sizes and locations of windows.
- Blinds or shades for windows. Venetian blinds preferred.
- Adequate artificial lighting, 30 to 50 footcandles.
- Floor space available per pupil in activity areas and auxiliary areas.
- Stockrooms, accessible and easily supervised.
- Finishing rooms, provided with special exhaust fans and heat dryers.
- Space for planning and drawing. Library table in planning area.
- Provision for storage of tools. Tool cabinets with door preferred.
- Adequate locker space. One locker for each student.
- Space for exhibits in cases which open into the hallway.
- Separate supplies and storage areas for evening classes.
- Chalkboard in the seating area.
- Accessible bulletin boards.
- Provisions for projection of film material in lab facility, if a central room is unavailable.
- Washroom facilities located near main activity areas.
- Hot and cold running water in all rooms.
- Drinking fountains in activity areas.
- Foundations adequate for the size of the equipment.
- Sufficient service connections and electrical outlets.
- Conveniently located master switches for machines.
- Sufficient outlets for compressed air connections.
- Sufficient gas outlets.
- Good exhaust and ventilating systems. Shavings exhaust for woodworking machines.

Floor Space The most common error the teacher is likely to make at the outset is to underestimate the required amount of floor space. After the square footage has been agreed upon, it becomes very difficult to add to it. It is much easier to eliminate space if there should be some to spare.

A good way to arrive at an accurate estimation of the amount of floor space needed is to divide the facility into two sections: the activity, or "open," area and auxiliary areas. The activity area refers to that main part of the shop which is used for the operational phases of the program. Since project assembly takes place here, it is here that workbenches, machinery, tool cases, and lockers will be located. Auxiliary areas include stockrooms, planning rooms, finishing rooms, washrooms, and storage space. In recent years, considerable study has been devoted to the amount of floor space needed for school labs. This study has resulted in the recommendation that space for labs ought to be increased, due to the increasingly important function of industrial education programs. Usually the most acceptable minimum standard for spatial requirements per student is 100 square feet for activity areas and 50 square feet for design rooms and other auxiliary areas.

The proportion of the length of the lab to its width has considerable bearing on effectiveness in teaching and learning. In general, it is a mistake to plan a square-shaped laboratory.

The best proportion is probably from three to five to two to four. A smaller lab can well be twice as long as it is wide, but when an area is 3,600 square feet or more, a little more width should be used to prevent the room from becoming too long. The location of stockrooms, offices, and lavatories at one end of the room, reduces the floor area as far as length is concerned and should be compensated for in determining proportions.

Class Demonstration Areas

Space for demonstrations and areas for seating the class should be provided. In some cases, it is possible to have a classroom which is shared by one or more laboratories. In woodwork, electrical studies, and most other beginning lab work in junior high schools, it is desirable to have a place in the lab or a separate room for the students to sit in. Loose chairs may be used so that they can be removed if the area is needed for a large assembly or other purposes.

Office Space

Whether the teacher wishes to use a separate office or have a desk in the lab might be a matter of individual preference. The size of an office, particularly when it is to store some supplies and special tools, should not be less than eight feet square.

Tool Storage

Whether a separate toolroom is needed will be determined by the type of facility and by established policies. For laboratories where heavy tools are used, such as auto and transportation, the toolroom may be justified. In most settings the floor space provided for the toolroom can be used to better advantage for other purposes, and tool cabinets can be employed with equal or better effectiveness.

Many systems and schemes for taking care of small tools have been used by different teachers with varying degrees of success. The type of scheme used is probably not so important as is the practice of that scheme which has been adopted. The mental attitude of the teacher has much to do with whether one type of organization or another will be the most successful.

CHAPTER 7—FACILITY DESIGN AND MANAGEMENT

Generally, it is expected that the instructor conform to whatever scheme happens to be used in a system or a school. If no other teachers are affected, it is legitimate that the instructor should be allowed to use his or her favorite plan. The following procedures for keeping tools are in use:

The Central Toolroom Wherever several labs can be served by one toolroom, the central toolroom has been used extensively. Under such an arrangement, one toolroom may serve laboratories for automotive work, machine-tool practice, and woodwork. However, objections to this scheme have been raised because the amount of equipment prohibits it from being efficient. Also, there is a tendency to favor the tools of certain types of facilities. When such toolrooms are in operation, an employed attendant is usually in charge, and has full responsibility. This chief tool clerk may be assisted by students. Salaried tool clerks add to the per-capita cost, and, for small schools particularly, some other plan becomes necessary.

The Individual Toolroom Separate toolrooms for each lab provide a convenient arrangement. The individual toolroom is preferred by many teachers for a number of reasons. Responsibility for its condition is fixed upon each instructor. It is also easier to place responsibility for lost tools, because fewer students are using the equipment. Pride in proper condition of tools and the toolroom is more easily maintained—woodworking students caring little for metalworking tools, and vice versa. Less opportunity is offered for using tools for wrong purposes, such as checking out machinist's calipers for the wood-turning lathe.

The Tool Cabinet The cabinet with doors is like the toolroom, with the difference that, when it is opened, all the tools are exposed to view and easily checked. While it is possible to have a tool clerk for this facility, and it is sometimes done, it is customary to apply the honor system and to allow each student to remove and replace the tools as needed. It is quite feasible to let students have a set of checks for the purpose of checking out their own tools. In this way it can be determined at all times who is using the tools that have been removed, provided, of course, that everyone is conscientious in following the scheme.

If such a cabinet is constructed with solid wooden doors, tools can be fastened on the inside of these, and in this way the capacity is substantially increased. Experience indicates that tools are as safe in a cabinet of this kind as in a toolroom. When the saving of floor space is considered, the justification for a separate toolroom may well be questioned.

The Tool Panel An open panel, with tools accessible at all times to persons in the laboratory, has been advocated and used by some teachers. The necessary tools would be placed on this panel, with an outline of each tool painted on the board to emphasize its absence when removed. Students would then be

TEACHING INDUSTRIAL EDUCATION

placed upon their honor and allowed to use the tools freely. Under the influence of some instructors this scheme has proved very effective. No one will deny that it promotes efficiency. If persons other than the instructor do not possess keys to the facility, or if it is not open in the absence of the instructor, it may be a desirable scheme. However, most teachers like the idea of being able to lock the door to a toolroom or a tool cabinet, and thus assure themselves that the tools are safe.

The *tool rack* that stands in an open place on the floor is merely a variation of the open tool panel. Such a rack or stand should be constructed so that every tool has a definite and conspicuous place. It is possible to put such a rack on rollers so that, if desirable, it can be moved into a separate room for safekeeping, at least during vacation time.

The Tool Kit

To avoid difficulties resulting from the random use of hand tools, the issuing of individual tool kits will be found most effective. To furnish each student with a few of the most necessary tools for his or her own use and keeping is an excellent practice. Such sets of tools may be kept in individual drawers in workbenches, or may be fitted in pigeonholes in a case on the wall or in the toolroom. Such sets are most effective in woodwork, automotive work, and in other laboratory activities where success depends greatly upon the availability and condition of a few smaller tools. Cost must be considered wherever a number of classes come to the facility each day, and particularly where various shifts are scheduled during the week.

In woodworking it has often been a practice to arrange tools in a rack upon the bench. This kind of tool rack has lost its popularity because of the obstruction it offers to the handling of the work. It was found extremely difficult also to keep tools in their places in these racks, since they were too easily accessible to students working at other benches. A drawer in the desk serving all students who work at that particular location is superior to the tool rack, although it does not give the satisfaction of the individual tool drawer or kit.

Tool Identification and Control

The more clearly the tools of the laboratory are marked for identification, the more likely they are to stay in their places. Because of this, it is unacceptable to depend upon marking with small steel numbers or letters. Using paint for marking is much more effective. Such marking will also eliminate unintentional mixing of school tools with those belonging to students. Where there are several laboratories in a building, different colors can be used to correspond to the different labs. This is especially advantageous in large systems.

In the individual toolroom the tools are usually handled by a student tool clerk, a member of the class who serves in the toolroom for a brief period, after which he is relieved by another member. If, for instance, there are twenty weeks in a semester, and twenty students are enrolled, each student

CHAPTER 7—FACILITY DESIGN AND MANAGEMENT

will be assigned one week in the toolroom, and curriculum will be planned for nineteen weeks.

The tool clerk spends the entire time in the toolroom, and checks in and out all tools required by the class. Since this does not usually occupy the full time of the student, the problem of how to supplement these activities always presents itself. The student should take the opportunity to become familiar with the tools.

Responsibility for checking broken tools and ordering repair parts will give valuable training that may be useful in later life. Forms for keeping a perpetual inventory of tools and their condition should be furnished. If such information is kept up to date, the teacher should have a much lighter task at the time for taking inventories. At the same time, the student learns responsibility. Sharpening edged tools and other similar duties would be justifiable activities for the tool clerk's spare time.

If the instructor will plan for the types of work mentioned, there will be little danger of lack of interest or activity for the week the student will spend in the toolroom. To have the tool clerk attempt to carry on lab work in the toolroom, as some teachers do, is likely to result in irregularity in the service and lack of attention to it. The week's work in the toolroom may be more valuable than any other week in the laboratory when interpreted in terms of possible future application.

Various means for keeping a complete check on tools may be used. Some teachers prefer to have students write on a paper the name of the tool they wish to obtain. This may help them learn the correct name of the tool and how to spell that name, but it wastes time, and tends to diminish interest because the student is interested in doing his or her job.

A better way, in some respects at least, is the practice of using checks made of metal, or metal-bound paper tags. A certain number of these, stamped or numbered with identifying numbers to correspond, perhaps, with the student's workbench and locker are assigned to each student. The checks may be given to the student for a certain deposit covering their cost, or they may be kept on a rack in the toolroom. If the student carries the checks, he or she presents one of them at the tool window as he calls for the desired tool. Somewhere in the vicinity of the location of the tool there is a hook upon which the check is placed when the tool is removed. When the tool is returned, it is up to the student to see to it that his or her check is removed and returned.

If the checks are kept in the toolroom—which in some ways is less confusing since it eliminates loss of checks—the tool clerk simply moves the check from the rack to the tool as the student gives his or her check number and calls for the tool. The tool clerk returns the check to its location when the tool is returned. This method is subject to the objection that it is too easy for the tool clerk to forget to return the checks, and thus a student may eventually be held responsible for tools that he or she once returned and that have been called for by someone else. In spite of this objection it is probably the easiest and most satisfactory method to handle, particularly with younger students.

Equipment Needs Survey

In the approach to the problem of selection of equipment, an evaluation of basic factors and considerations must be made. Among such considerations might well be the following:

Types of machines. In most laboratories with average equipment budgets, single-operation machines are purchased for use by the students. However, machines designed for a variety of operations are also available for school use.

There is opposition to their use for a number of reasons. It is usually dangerous for more than one operator to be at the machine. Also, there is delay whenever the machine must be converted from one function to another. Machines designed for several operations are usually not as sturdy as single-operation machines. In most industrial education classes, there are usually enough students to justify separate machines.

One of the primary arguments for the use of multi-operation machines is that it is not always economically feasible to buy those separate machines tooled for performing all the operations that could be provided for through the combination setup. It must also be considered that a small delay in the use of machines is not always a serious problem, since other work can be assigned while the students are waiting. Even though they may have to wait, their work is still done more quickly than if they had carried it out by hand. It should always be remembered that only one student should be permitted to operate the machine at one time.

The question of using small, portable machines for schoolwork is not easily settled. Varied conditions deserve individual study and consideration. In many cases portable machines and light, stationary equipment do adequately all the work that larger devices would be called upon to do. The difference in speed is probably not an important item for ordinary schoolwork.

The number of class hours will also have a bearing on the types of equipment to be used and should enter into the final decision regarding their purchase. Costly equipment standing idle increases overhead expense, yet light-duty machines will break down under heavy use. There are, however, conditions under which the purchase of highly specialized tools and machines may be justified. However, the amount of time the equipment will be used should not be overlooked.

Equipment cost. The money available, both immediately and through future budget allocations, must be considered when planning the purchase of equipment. Should all money immediately available be spent on a few quality machines, or should an attempt be made to purchase several machines, with less emphasis on their quality? Any purchasing plan prob-

CHAPTER 7—FACILITY DESIGN AND MANAGEMENT

ably depends partly upon the possibility of purchasing more equipment at a later time. This is why the size of future budget allocations should be considered.

Location of machines. This is a problem that should be considered before the purchase of any large piece of equipment. The determination of exact locations can be done on scaled layouts. Pieces of cardboard should be cut to scale or models should be made representing each piece of equipment. These silhouettes or models can be placed in various positions for a complete picture of the best possible layout. A *full-scale layout* on the floor is a still better way.

There are a few considerations to be kept in mind when locating pieces of stationary equipment in a lab. The service of equipment is materially reduced by the poor placement of equipment. In a definite plan for placing equipment:

- *Consider safety.* The quality and effectiveness of a machine's guards, pulleys, and power connections ought to be carefully evaluated before the machine is purchased.
- *Consider the operating space.* There should be enough space around machines to permit the operator to work safely and efficiently. Room for handling the material without strain or crowding is essential. This working space should be so arranged that interference from other students or workers is not invited.
- *Consider lighting conditions.* The present location of windows will be the main consideration here, unless additional windows or skylights can be installed. Artificial lighting must also be considered.
- *Consider the routing of work.* The location of some machines is highly dependent upon this consideration. Where machines must be coordinated in a series of operations upon the material, a logical sequence must be considered.
- *Consider room for later additions.* Many laboratories have lost efficiency because all available space has been utilized by a few machines. Thus, when a need develops for additions, a costly scheme for reorganization is necessary.

Schedule for purchase. While teachers would not agree upon the order of necessity in the purchase of tools and machines for any lab, there is evidence that in some cases no serious thought has been given to the problem at all, and that the mechanical equipment has been randomly selected.

Serious consideration should be given to a plan for buying equipment for immediate needs and adding future pieces so that the floor space may be efficiently planned.

Methods of specification. Every teacher should be familiar with standard procedures for making out specifications for equipment. Such specifications are often necessary in order to comply with legal requirements in asking for bids from various firms and vendors. Even more important is the use of specifications for the purpose of obtaining equipment of the type or quality desired. In order that inferior substitutions may not be made, it is essential to write out all important requirements of a machine or other piece of equipment. Among points that must be covered are size, weight, horsepower ratings, table sizes, belts, pulleys, types of bearings, and the complete list of all accessories expected to be furnished. The purchasing agent for the school will be helpful in indicating the type of specifications expected by his or her office.

Materials and Supplies

In junior high school laboratories, the responsibility for care and handling of supplies usually falls directly upon the instructor. Exceptions to this occur in the furnishing of such small items as screws, nails, bolts, rivets, and the like. These are often kept in the toolroom. Where a tool clerk is used he or she might also provide the members of the class with these articles.

What has been said previously regarding watchfulness by the instructor in connection with care of tools applies to an even greater degree here. Tools are borrowed, and are to be returned. Supplies are not expected to be returned. Because of this, it often happens that no account of them is taken after they are issued. There is unnecessary waste of materials in many school programs. Instructors who allow such habits of waste to continue are subject to criticism because the per-capita cost, which is already high in industrial education, is unduly increased to the point that serious questions may be raised about the justification of the subject. Also, undesirable habits are developed by the students, leading to their lack of appreciation of the value of materials and a lack of respect for the articles produced.

Is it better to charge students for materials, or to have the school furnish them? Probably no considerable group of teachers would agree on an answer to this question. Both plans have advantages and disadvantages. That plan that favors charging students for materials states that the student feels more responsibility for that work whose materials he or she has paid for. Also, the student may waste less material, and develop better habits of thrift and conservation. Thus, the per-capita cost to the school will be lessened, resulting in fewer objections by taxpayers to the high cost of schooling. Since they will be charged for their materials, students will be less likely to select large projects for construction. And, naturally, students will not insist on working with unnecessary and expensive materials.

In arguing for the free provision of materials, it might be stated that the most skilled students, who might be capable of producing large and attractive articles, would be denied the opportunity to do so unless the necessary materials were freely provided. Also, since public schools should offer educational opportunities to rich and poor alike, a policy of charging for materials would limit learning opportunities and discourage those unable to

CHAPTER 7—FACILITY DESIGN AND MANAGEMENT

pay. A policy of this type would also keep down the enrollment of industrial education classes.

A reasonable practice is to provide a certain amount of free material for the preliminary and required individual work, but to expect students to pay for their own material in advanced work on the individual basis. It should be neither compulsory nor necessary for students to spend money for materials, since there are always opportunities for turning out a product for the school. Also, there may be individuals in the community who will gladly pay the cost of project materials, as well as pay some profit to the student.

It appears unjust and unreasonable to expect, as some principals and school boards do, that full reimbursement shall be made by students for the value of all materials. When such demands are made, it places the instructor in the position of a factory manager, and forces the teacher to weaken *instruction* for the sake of *construction*. Waste in the school laboratory, or elsewhere, is inexcusable. However, to expect to spend nothing on materials, particularly in classes of beginners and young students, is an unrealistic attitude.

If students are expected to make payments for materials, the teacher is burdened with another detail. Experience has shown that such business transactions give the teacher the least worry, and take the least amount of time, if the teacher allows the money to be collected by some other agency in the school. The financial office of the school or some person in the principal's office can collect the accounts. One procedure would be to issue the materials needed as requested by the requisitions previously discussed. When all the materials have been received and the work finished, the instructor checks the total statement, and the student pays the amount at the office, bringing the receipt back to the instructor as a permit to remove his or her product.

A more satisfactory method is to require payment for materials before the student begins work on the project. The procedure here is similar, except that a receipt for the money is required by the instructor before the work begins.

In such matters as replacing broken tools, and sending for special materials, it may seem desirable for the instructor to collect money for cooperative purchasing. A good rule, however, is not to handle cash in the laboratory, because it takes too much time in bookkeeping. Also, there is the possibility that the money will not be collected or that the teacher will be suspected of mismanaging the money. Neither is it a good rule to appoint students to responsibilities involving the care of funds unless one is in position to supervise the transactions closely. If possible, let the purchasing agent collect from the students.

In larger systems where a paid tool clerk is used, the duties of such a person are often extended to include the handling of supplies. In woodworking labs, particularly, these duties also may involve the cutting of stock in the rough to fill requisitions made out by students. This scheme relieves the instructor of direct responsibility in this regard, and also leaves the materials in the hands of one person. In the use of lumber, this should result in a distinct saving of material, since more economical use of all pieces could be expected.

Another approach to the solution of this problem is to assign students to the duty of supply clerk in much the same way as tool clerks are assigned. The value of such an assignment has been pointed out, especially for high school classes, where one of the objectives is that of training future managers and foremen. In this connection, a rather complete system of bookkeeping can be evolved, including also a perpetual inventory, through which a complete check is kept at all times upon the materials remaining in stock. Where classes are large, this type of work can obviously furnish excellent practical experience in maintaining stockrooms.

Another source of assistance in keeping accounts of supplies is the commercial department of the school. Often this department will welcome the opportunity for practical work and the school laboratories may be made to furnish a setting similar in many respects to that of a commercial plant.

Inventories

In purchasing and using supplies, the instructor should be careful to provide himself or herself with all records necessary for future reference. In the first place, the teacher will profit greatly when ordering supplies for the coming year or for coming classes if he or she has provided a means of knowing how much has been used in the past, and how the materials were distributed in various classes. The teacher can also tell where economy may be practiced through certain changes in courses of study, use of equipment, or through changes in class management and teaching procedure.

It also happens occasionally that teachers are charged for supplies that were delivered elsewhere. For this reason a thorough check should be made of all items received. Without detailed records, the instructor starts each year as a beginner and wastes a great deal of time and effort in getting the work under way. Records should be kept for equipment as well as for supplies.

For convenient handling of records of equipment and supplies, the card file is probably the most satisfactory device. It makes possible easy tabulation and reference, and sheets or cards can be added or changed without difficulty. If forms of the type shown in Fig. 7-1 and Fig. 7-2 are used for recording information, the instructor can obtain at a glance the data likely to be required.

By maintaining complete card files covering previous purchases of materials and tools, the instructor can save a great amount of time both in taking inventories and in making additional purchases. Once the system is perfected it requires very little time to keep its information current.

CHAPTER 7—FACILITY DESIGN AND MANAGEMENT

Supply Requisitions Students should be required to make out and present a bill of materials or requisition for supplies that they wish to use. This should be done whether or not such materials are furnished free. Regularity in this respect is an essential factor in the proper use of materials. Written orders, containing estimated costs, also impress students with the value of materials and make them less likely to ask for additional quantities without good reasons. A simple form for this purpose may be made up as shown in Fig. 7-3. More detailed forms may be used for certain types of work, and special blanks are valuable for some types of laboratories, as for instance, those of the graphic arts. The arrangement of the form is not essential.

Requisition forms should, of course, be filled out in duplicate or triplicate, depending upon the routine involved in their use.

Equipment Maintenance While the larger pieces of equipment cause less worry with reference to loss, a definite system is necessary for their upkeep and care. The class can be organized for definite responsibilities in this regard. These responsibilities can be shifted from time to time. Among the jobs that may be assigned in this way are: oiling machines; checking the condition of machines, with particular reference to their belts, motors, and guards; reconditioning and maintaining equipment; and cleaning tools and machines.

The closest possible supervision must be given to the oiling of machinery, even after reliable students have been appointed to the task. Oil holes should be checked to see that they are not clogged. If the instructor fails to give close observation, the first warning sign of poor oiling procedures may be a burned bearing.

Article_____ Lab_____

Inv. Date	Quantity Good	Pur. Date	Cost	Quantity Bad	Scrap-ped	Bought During Year		
						Date	Quantity	Cost

7-1. Form for permanent record or inventory of equipment.

TEACHING INDUSTRIAL EDUCATION

One student may well assist the instructor in the duties listed under checking the condition of machines. This student works in the capacity of assistant manager, and spends several minutes at the close of each period checking the condition of equipment with regard to usefulness and safety. He or she may often see things that the instructor has overlooked, and may also be more familiar with weaknesses in certain students. If a checking

RECORD OF PURCHASE OF SUPPLIES

Types of Articles _____

Date Received	Quantity	Description	Cost	Where Purchased	Address

7-2. Form for record of purchase of supplies.

CHAPTER 7—FACILITY DESIGN AND MANAGEMENT

system is not used for tools, a student will need to be assigned to check the condition of small tools at the end of each period.

Whether it is legitimate to expect students to assist in keeping equipment in order has been, and still is, a debated question. Since the students have come for machine tool work, woodwork, or whatever the activities of the

REQUISITION FOR MATERIALS

Name of School _____

Sold to _____

Instructor _____ Date _____

Quantity	Size	Material	Unit Cost	Total Cost

Total _____

Approved by _____

Received Payment _____

7-3. Bill of material for student use.

program may be, many teachers believe that it is unfair to devote a part of class time to the reconditioning of machines. Student interest is also diminished if their activities are interrupted for this reason. Also, students are not able to do a first-class job of repair work on the equipment. Since it takes them too long to repair equipment, classwork is unduly delayed.

All of these arguments contain elements of truth. However, there are teachers who point out that the maintenance and repair of equipment gives training that cannot be obtained in regular lab work, training that is likely to prove valuable later. This is because equipment maintenance activities help develop cooperation and a willingness to assist in emergencies. There may be some students who are not particularly interested in the regular class routine and would rather work on special problems. To these students, as well as to others, repair activities may suggest new fields of vocational opportunity.

Some objections to the integration of repair activities within the class can be easily answered. If the responsibility for emergency work on the equipment is organized in such a way that students know that they are likely to be called upon during the assigned period, the objection usually raised, that time is taken up for illegitimate purposes, is obviated.

There can be no question that work on the equipment, whether repairs or new construction, has its value. When overdone, however, and used for saving money, it becomes exploitation, and cannot be tolerated under the name of education.

Laboratory Sanitation

How much cleaning of the laboratory, if any, should be done by students? There are various answers to this question. Most teachers insist that students should sweep floors in the labs, so that they will not have to do it themselves. There seems to be good reason for demanding that floors in laboratories be swept by students.

There is, however, some question as to where the students' responsibility leaves off and that of the janitor begins. To make the janitor responsible for cleaning the tools and machines would be unwise even if it were possible. Students in materials processing labs, after collecting the loose scraps of metal, plastic, wood, or concrete waste materials, should clean the lab, even if only as a safety precaution. Extensive clean-up following a day, week, term, or school year is not the responsibility of the class, except, perhaps, in small schools. A custodial staff is provided by the school system for such tasks. Many student jobs are described in Chapter 9.

Student personnel systems of sanitation are usually organized in one of two ways. Either the teacher assigns each individual to a particular piece of equipment or task, or a group of students is required to maintain a portion of the laboratory. The first method provides an easy system for checking student responsibility for various individual items, whereas the second system promotes teamwork and gives the team foremen valuable super-

CHAPTER 7—FACILITY DESIGN AND MANAGEMENT

visory experience. In both systems, the teacher acts as general superintendent.

The Honor System

The so-called honor system applied to the care of the laboratory is favored by many teachers. Under the full utilization of this system, the students are made individually responsible for the tools, equipment, and materials they use. This scheme, to be successful, must be launched only after proper preliminary preparation. To attempt it without first preparing the students fully, and obtaining a popular acceptance of it, would be unwise. However, if the individual members of the class are put into the frame of mind that makes them zealous in carrying it out, there is little danger of failure.

Full use of the honor system might suggest that all tools and materials be made readily accessible to students. The system may also be used in a more restricted form. In the latter case the most common tools and materials are kept within reach of everyone. Special equipment, or that needed less often, is kept in a separate place and handed out by the instructor or some appointed student. In making the change from a strictly supervised checking system to the honor system, it might be well to adopt and practice limited supervision for a season, until a measure of success has been obtained.

The key to the success of any system lies in the hands of the instructor. It is the instructor who makes a success or failure of it. No system is self-sustaining for any length of time. The student tool clerk might or might not be conscientious. Even if the tool clerk is conscientious, he or she might lack ability and experience. The honor system which advocates open access to tools and supplies has many advantages and implements many modern ideas of education.

However, the success of any of these methods depends upon the instructor. His or her vigilance is essential to success. The less obvious such vigilance, the more effective it will be. Attention to small details is the most important thing. To leave responsibilities to students whenever possible, and yet to give proper and sympathetic supervision to all activities, is the task that lies before the instructor.

Exploitation

A majority of teachers feel a strong resentment against taking care of odd repair jobs in their classes. Seldom do a number of such instructors get together without the conversation directed toward this important topic.

The common complaint against the superintendent or principal who wishes to have some cafeteria chairs repaired in the woodworking lab, or who comes to the electronics lab when a switch fails to operate is that such requests interfere with the course of study and with organized instruction.

Objections are valid insofar as they are true, and the sad part is that they are often true. Through personal experience and that of colleagues, it is evident that industrial educators have learned to fear "infringement" upon their plans. There are probably administrators and boards of education who are willing to let utilitarian objectives predominate, and to look upon the industrial education program as an opportunity to get some returns. The exploitive use of industrial education classes by school superintendents and administrators can frustrate the attempts of teachers to present their courses in an organized manner.

That leads us to the question, "What is exploitation, and what causes it?" Does the teacher's poor class organization often invite exploitation of the class? In other words, if the teacher has been careful to lay out his course on the proposition that no such work is legitimate, and has packed his course so full of what he would please to call "instructional" material that no student can afford to spend an hour or two on some special job without failing to complete the assigned work, then it might be easy to prove that any simple outside job is exploitation. And, of course, in such a case, if special jobs of any kind have to receive attention, if often falls upon the conscientious teacher to do the work in preference to using the time of students.

This again leads to a question. Who has decided that it is instructional to build a library table and noninstructional to repair a table for the school cafeteria? Are we not in practical life often forced to quit what we are doing in order to undertake some more urgent task? Have not industry and business sometimes stated that a practical outlook has not been developed?

Of course, no one would insist that definitely planned work should give way to emergency jobs. Such a practice would lead to disorganization. The point made here is that there is educational value of a high order in such emergency jobs. Instructors should look for these values instead of turning the other way for fear that their pet programs might be disturbed. Up to certain limits, such jobs furnish unequaled opportunities for students to do independent thinking and planning and to diagnose situations. Such jobs give students experience in adjusting to those situations in which they are called upon to perform work of a technical nature for people who are unable to perform the work themselves. Jobs of this type may also develop organizational abilities in students, in that they may be asked to commence and continue several different jobs within a short period of time.

The following is a suggested organization for making a number of odd jobs instructional and educational in any technical program:

- In the absence of meaningful projects, such work can furnish realistic jobs that come into the laboratory.
- When the course of study is made up, leave a definite, unscheduled amount of time in each student's program for taking care of special jobs.
- Prepare the students for such work by pointing out the added values that come from it. The students' enthusiasm will follow closely that of the teacher in this respect.

CHAPTER 7—FACILITY DESIGN AND MANAGEMENT

- Arrange the work schedule so that one or two students, depending upon recognized needs, are scheduled each day for special emergency work. These students may also do special jobs on tools or equipment and new work for the schools. Keep them busy on this type of work for the assigned time and make no exceptions, but see to it that the work has educational value which is recognized by the student.
- Rotate such work fairly among all students. Any impression that favors are shown will injure the program.
- Have students study special problems in connection with such assignments, write notes on the work done, and in some cases make reports to the entire class in seminar sessions.
- Check such work closely, take an interest in it, and give definite and separate grades, after first having applied the practical test, "Does it work?"
- Finally, accept no repair work or production work for the school unless such work has recognizable educational value for the group or individual student carrying it out as part of the program.

Further Suggestions

Teachers with limited experience, and sometimes others, report difficulties in receiving proper attention to their needs from administrators. Lack of interest on the part of the administration may sometimes be genuine and beyond alteration. However, in many cases where teachers are complaining, the root of the difficulty lies with themselves. They have failed to analyze their own problem and organize it into a definite form for presentation. Hence, the following suggestions:

Keep the administration acquainted with progress. If the administrative office hears of the teacher's activities at no other time than when money is to be spent, there may be a poor chance for getting what is wanted.

Have definite reasons for expansion of new organizations already in mind and be ready to state them. Administrators will demand information. If the teacher appears uncertain and wavering in his or her replies, the chances for favorable action are diminished.

Show how the plan in question will increase facilities for better teaching. Seeking personal favors, or stressing inconveniences to the teacher, are poor approaches to the problem. Administrators hear too much of self-pity. Industrial educators should relate their interest in better education to their desire for better facilities.

Know what you want. Talking in generalities, without a definite plan, leads nowhere. Administrators should be approached with definite, well-formulated propositions. Have a list of the desired equipment and its proposed uses worked out before asking for the equipment. Incidentally, keep in mind earlier suggestions regarding the use of scale models when presenting plans to administrators.

Know the exact cost. One of the first questions asked by the administrator is, "What will it cost?" A definite answer to that question goes far toward securing results. If there is not a ready answer, the issue may be postponed and no definite action taken. Exact quotations from reliable firms are most convincing, but estimates from catalogs and price lists may be sufficient. Such estimates should, however, be reasonably correct.

Financing Industrial Education

The increasing cost of education is a serious problem that cannot be ignored. In industrial education, the per-capita cost is particularly high. It can easily be shown that technical teaching, because of the very nature of the instruction, must necessarily cost more than the instruction in most other subjects. However, it is also worthwhile to consider any possible means for keeping the expense down to the lowest possible figure consistent with efficiency in teaching. Aside from the possibility of increasing the number of students in laboratory classes—and this number is now great enough in many places—the following possibilities are offered for consideration in connection with solving the problem of costs and possible reductions:

- *Consider the purchase of good used machinery and equipment.* Much of the standard machinery changes very little in principle in a few years.
- *Solicit free material and equipment from manufacturers and industrial firms.* Such material and equipment can often be obtained for teaching industrial education if the manner in which it is to be used is fully understood by the manufacturer or supplier.
- *Salvage material.* Obtain automobile parts at the wrecking yard. Make use of packing boxes, and obtain odd pieces of lumber at the mill.
- *Stop all waste in the classes.* Teach students the value of materials. Have a definite location for all kinds of odd material, and require students to go to these sources before using the new stock.
- *Have students make less pretentious articles in programs where the school pays for the material.* A smaller article using less material may, and often will, serve the same purpose educationally.
- *Manufacture articles for the school, where it can be done without exploiting students.*
- *Apply for financial aid through various federal, state, and local programs and through appeals to local industry.*

DISCUSSION QUESTIONS

1. Plan a laboratory for a high school with a total enrollment of 400. This is to be the only laboratory in the school.

2. What reasons may be given for preferring the general materials lab to a series of unit labs in a large junior high school?

3. Have changes in industrial and social conditions brought about new forms of industrial education activities in the past ten years? If so, what?

4. What separate-unit labs and what general-unit labs would you recommend for a junior high school of 1,600 pupils?

CHAPTER 7—FACILITY DESIGN AND MANAGEMENT

5. What do you think of the idea of having a separate industry and technology room for elementary schools?

6. Explain why the planning of a new facility should be the result of, rather than the cause of, new courses in the school.

7. What are the means by which one may learn what equipment exists in other schools?

8. Make out a sheet showing points for inquiry in connection with a visit to study school equipment for the purpose of getting basic information for your own situation.

9. If a complete course of study were already made, just how would you use it when making up the list of equipment?

10. What are some ways of making the administrator acquainted with the work of the industrial education program?

11. Name some machines which you think should be in school laboratories even though they are seldom used.

12. Make a list of firms manufacturing: (1) metals-processing machine tools, (2) woodworking machines, (3) printing equipment.

13. Work up a complete list of tools and equipment for a ten-week course in one of the common junior high school technical subjects, and show the cost.

14. To what extent, if any, is a knowledge of the industries of the community valuable in buying equipment, after the course of study has been made?

15. What would you consider to be a reasonable expense for new tools and equipment for a junior high school comprehensive laboratory of industries? A senior high school woodworking laboratory?

16. Make up complete specifications for two woodworking machines or for two machines for metals processing.

17. Write a requisition for twenty-five small tools for any industrial laboratory. Be sure to include all necessary data.

18. What reasons would you give a principal for not wishing to have the students sweep floors in the laboratory?

19. Should high school students be called upon to assist in taking inventories? Why, or why not?

20. Make a form for recording a perpetual inventory of supplies.

21. At what age would you expect industrial education students to sharpen edged tools for the laboratory?

22. Do you believe that school repair work has a tendency to take away from or add to interest in the program? Give several reasons for your answer.

23. Make a list of suitable troubleshooting jobs that might be cared for in high school industrial education classes.

24. List in detail all of the duties that may be performed by the tool clerk.

25. To what extent should tools and equipment for industrial education duplicate those of industry?

26. How would you deal with a student tool clerk who was found to be dishonest?

27. What advantages may be listed for the honor system in the use of tools?

28. Would you, as a teacher, spend your own money to satisfy needs of the class? If so, under what circumstances?

29. In what ways can it be said that the teacher may be the cause for the loss of tools, equipment, or supplies.

30. What should be the practice in regard to lending tools to students for doing work at home?

31. List the different age levels at which you would allow various power machines to be used in the lab.

32. Of what educational value is the use of requisition forms for students?

33. List the various duties in the upkeep of the facility and equipment which may be shouldered, in part at least, by students.

ADDITIONAL READINGS

Brant, Herbert M. "Check Out Your Shop Planning." *Industrial Arts & Vocational Education,* March 1967, pp. 36–38.

Campbell, Edward A. "Coordinated Laboratory Storage," *Industrial Arts & Vocational Education,* October 1968, pp. 86–87.

Finsterbach, Fred C. "The Multiple Dimensions of School-Shop Planning." *School Shop,* May 1969, pp. 38–41.

Finsterbach, Fred C., and McNeice, William C. *Creative Facilities Planning for Occupational Education.* Berkeley Heights, New Jersey: Educare Associates, 1969.

Friedlander, David. "Put a Pupil Personnel Plan Into Action," *School Shop,* September 1968, pp. 54–60.

George, William F. "Rotational Team Teaching Using Mobile Laboratories," *Man/Society/Technology,* March 1973, pp. 247–251.

Gerrish, Howard H. "The General Shop—Enigma of Plethora." *School Shop,* March 1968, p. 37.

Hutchings, Gilbert R. "Units of Study for Woodworking Machinery Maintenance." *Industrial Arts & Vocational Education,* May 1968, p. 30.

Modern School Shop Planning. 6th ed. Ann Arbor, Michigan: Prakken Publications, 1972.

Rockwell Manufacturing Company. *School Shop Development.* Pittsburg: Rockwell Manufacturing Company, 1966.

Chapter 8
Beginning the School Year

The Basis for Teaching Success

In industrial education, the successful professional teacher is a person who, besides possessing a native intellectual aptitude and manipulative ability, has received preparation in the art and science of teaching methodology. He or she ought to have formulated a philosophy of life, of education generally, and of industrial education in particular, so as to be able to determine a system of values and attitudes relevant to his or her occupation. A philosophy or system of values dictates goals or objectives. Such goals necessitate methods for achieving them.

In addition, the professional industrial educator must be convinced of the necessity for detailed preparation. At no time is the need for careful preparation more pressing than in the annual process of planning for a new school year. The content of this chapter is organized upon the concept that preparedness is the keynote to successful teaching.

Each Year a New Challenge

Each school year is a unit in itself. Whether a person begins as a new teacher or continues at a position as a teacher with permanent tenure, it is true that with September comes a new school year, new students, and, in some cases, new subjects to teach. Because of these circumstances, beginning the new school year represents a challenge for renewed effort and better planning.

Since the teacher of industrial education is responsible for a laboratory and equipment as well as for the instruction of up to one hundred or more students per day, the importance of planning becomes even more evident. The need for assisting both prospective and experienced industrial education teachers in meeting and solving problems that differ from those of non-laboratory courses lends greater relevance to the theme of this chapter.

Preliminary Considerations

When a contract is signed, or when an appointment is made, a date for the official arrival of the teacher is usually specified. In some cases, this date may be that upon which school convenes. However, the date is sometimes set earlier so that teachers may attend meetings and in-service institutes preliminary to the opening of the school year. It is now becoming more customary to call for the arrival of all teachers, and particularly those working in laboratory subjects, a number of days before school convenes.

With the conscientious teacher, the question should not be, "When am I compelled to arrive according to my contract?" but, "When should I arrive in order to complete all necessary preliminary work?" The answer to the second question cannot be uniform for all teachers and conditions. The nature of the assignment, the status of the course of study, and the condition of the equipment will, among other considerations, determine for the individual teacher the amount of time needed for preliminary preparations.

Arriving on the job ahead of the prescribed time is of little value, however, unless the teacher develops a definite plan for his activities after arriving. Many teachers have responded to the urge to "be on the job" early, but, having arrived, have found little or nothing to do. The reason for this has not been that there were no problems to be solved, but rather that the teacher had no organized method for locating and solving problems that exist in every school lab.

There is a clear necessity for job analysis on the part of the teacher. If the teacher will concentrate upon the details of his or her activities for the first week or two after instruction begins, he or she will become cognizant of jobs to be performed and problems to be solved.

As a further aid in this regard, it is recommended that the instructor make out a written schedule or analysis of the possible duties that may be performed before the actual teaching process is commenced.

Teaching certificates or licenses, granted by the state board of education in the state where the teacher's professional preparation has been completed, are official evidence of the new teacher's academic qualifications. Sometimes, the teacher will fail to realize, however, that mere possession of this official document is not enough. It must be presented to proper authorities before the appointment becomes official and a salary can be drawn. The school administrator who has hired the teacher will give information regarding proper procedure in filing the credential. Teachers moving from one state to another should not assume that their credential is automatically acceptable in another state.

In addition to the details pertaining to the teaching of classes, the new teacher will be called upon to participate in many of the more general activities incidental to the opening of the school year. Some of these are the following:

Faculty meetings. A new teacher is not always given the expected special instruction and notification regarding such meetings. Information methods sufficient to inform returning faculty members of such meetings often fail to inform the newcomer. Whatever the reason for the new teacher's absence from such meetings, the fact remains that he or she failed to appear. While later explanations may partly clarify the situation, the new instructor is at a disadvantage at the outset. It is well then to search for information regarding meetings and conferences and to dismiss, once and for all, the attitude that attendance at faculty meetings is not one of the teacher's responsibilities.

In-Service institutes. Institutes constitute another form of meeting that teachers are asked to attend. Some teachers of industrial education have

CHAPTER 8—BEGINNING THE SCHOOL YEAR

the feeling that these institute programs offer nothing of value for their work. This might be true if those learning activities structured by the teacher were carried out only within the laboratory, and if those activities were unrelated to any other academic subjects. Also, it should be realized that teachers of history, English, mathematics, and other subjects, may have similar feelings regarding institutes. If the lab instructor has a right to stay away, the same right should be accorded other instructors.

In order that the teacher may be of the greatest possible value as a member of the organization, and in order that the school program may be efficiently implemented, it is necessary that each teacher be presented with that general information relevant to administration problems. It is also necessary that he or she be informed regarding the subjects and teaching methods used in other departments. For these reasons, much of the feeling on the part of teachers that institute programs present nothing of value is without justification.

Assisting the administration. Assistance in enrolling, interviewing, and scheduling students are other duties that are likely to be assigned many instructors. In performing these duties, some persons prove themselves more valuable than others. Some shun these duties if there is a possibility of doing so, but in this way they prove themselves less useful to the school organization. Also, it is unlikely that they will be thought of in connection with more responsible positions. A teacher who is interested in building up a department will welcome the opportunity to make personal contacts with students outside of class hours and with prospective students at all times.

Getting Acquainted

The first responsibility of a new teacher can well be that of becoming acquainted with those people with whom he will work and live. He should also familiarize himself with those general conditions that will affect his duties and responsibilities. While problems of laboratory organization may be pressing, it would be short-sighted for the beginning teacher to spend all of his or her time working on solutions to facility and curriculum problems, and thus fail to lay foundations for his or her acceptance into the system as a general faculty member, and in the community as a new citizen and neighbor.

Many teachers overlook the importance of leaving a good first impression on those who are to be their friends and co-workers. In many cases, these first impressions will determine the teacher's chances for finding happiness and attaining success in his or her occupation. Thoughtless words and actions in early dealings with colleagues, students, parents, staff, and custodians, may cause embarrassment later. The same suggestion applies regarding contacts with people outside of the school. It is well to remember that merchants in the stores, real-estate brokers from whom one rents or buys a home, or clerks in the municipal office, might be persons whom one will meet again socially. They may also be individuals who are involved in school affairs. These suggestions are made to emphasize the desirability of maintaining a friendly attitude. They also stress the need to establish friendships within the community and the work environment.

It is obvious that the new teacher should report to the school administrator upon arriving on the job. It is unwise to attempt to learn about conditions in a casual way before reporting officially to the proper administrator. This is true even though the new instructor arrives much earlier than requested. If it later becomes known that the teacher has approached school board members, merchants, teachers, custodians, or staff members for information that should be of an official nature, a suspicion might develop regarding the judgment and ethics of the teacher.

When deciding who is the appropriate administrator to approach, the teacher will need to use the best judgment. Previous visits, correspondence, and official instructions will help to clear this point. In general, the advice would be not to "go over the head" of the person who is the immediate supervisor. If a department head or supervisor has been instrumental in working out the original appointment to the position, that person should be recognized, and be counted upon to make the contacts with other administrative personnel. In smaller communities, the principal of the school or the superintendent might be approached directly.

The length and seriousness of the initial meeting will be determined largely by the administrator. The teacher should obtain a definite assignment regarding the grade level and scope of the subjects he or she is to teach. The teacher will need to be familiar with the layout of the school and with the means for gaining access to the building and lab facility. He or she should be aware of the type and amount of equipment available. The teacher will want to investigate the availability of outlines, invoices, and inventories, as well as the availability of those recorded materials which might relate to his or her course of study. The teacher should be knowledgeable regarding any plans for expanding his or her program or furnishing additional equipment. Finally, the teacher should be familiar with those procedures which might apply to his or her professional routine.

The inexperienced teacher is justifiably concerned with how to respond in these early meetings. Many experienced teachers have apparently learned few desirable techniques. Hence, the following suggestions:

● *Do not prolong the discussion beyond the time indicated by the administrator.* There are few more certain ways of losing the esteem of a superintendent or principal than to display a lack of desire to leave as soon as the business is transacted, or as soon as the time which seems to have been set aside for the meeting has expired. The teacher's standing with the administrator, as well as the ease with which future appointments may be obtained, will both depend on the judgment the teacher exercises in the first meeting.

- *Do not try to be too familiar.* Although some administrators may carry on a very informal type of conference, others will be offended by an attitude of excessive familiarity.
- *Seek a definite statement of budgets.* Chances are strong that if a survey indicates an obvious need, the question of the availability of funds will remain open. This is particularly true if the teacher is dealing directly with the superintendent. However, it also applies to a large extent in a person's contact with a supervisor. A general indication of the size of the budget allocation from the administrator is often sufficient but a definite statement of maximum funds is usually better.
- *Make no definite promises that may later cause embarrassment.* This applies not only to such matters as producing projects and obtaining equipment for the school, but also pertains to cocurricular and social activities. Making tentative promises at this time regarding church attendance and membership in clubs and lodges often leads to later regrets and misunderstandings.
- *Be a good listener.* Talk more after the needed information is at hand. This does not mean, of course, that the opportunity may not come for definite comments by the teacher, but such comments should be offered only upon rather clear invitation.

With the first meeting concluded, the strain of the adjustment process is somewhat relieved, and the teacher is now ready to continue his or her preparation for starting the year's work.

Class Records and Homeroom Duties

Records will probably be available at all schools indicating enrollments and other valuable data regarding students. Such records should be used by the incoming teacher as a means of learning about the number of students in previous classes, the ages of those students, and other details. Such records will furnish information valuable in ordering supplies, planning work, and preparing material for classes.

If previous teachers have fulfilled their duties in regard to the keeping of records, there will not only be available the information already mentioned, but also a record of the articles made by each individual or class. This information may be found in the teacher's record books or in progress charts that also cover the grading of project work.

The assignment of a new teacher as homeroom supervisor demands planning on his or her part. This assignment is likely to be relatively foreign to some teachers of industrial education. For this reason, much preparation may be required for it. While it may be true that not all teachers are required to take on such a responsibility at the outset, the possibility of such an assignment should not be dismissed. Valuable books and references are available on this subject, and some can usually be obtained from the school library. Teachers with experience may be consulted. The teacher who knows that he or she may be supervising a homeroom on the first day of school, can find material and information from which to plan definite procedures and programs for this activity.

Checking Inventories

The new teacher will safeguard his or her own interests as well as those of the school by obtaining copies of inventories and lists of supplies. In examining these inventories, the teacher should make certain that all items listed are accounted for. Since the inventory was made, vacation time has intervened, with the possibility that some of the equipment may have been used by custodians or other workmen, not to mention the fact that, during the rush of the closing days of school, many an inventory may have been hastily compiled and its items carelessly handled by students.

Possessing the inventories of the previous year, the new instructor can proceed to locate the equipment that will be under his or her care. He or she can also determine which items need reconditioning. Too much emphasis cannot be placed upon the necessity for a detailed investigation in this respect. Tools and machinery that will not function during the early days of the semester are obstacles to successful work, and direct evidence of the teacher's lack of foresight.

A method of casually examining the shop premises and equipment and repairing any of those items that require repair will not prove to be efficient. Too many teachers employ this method and, by not properly organizing their efforts, they waste time.

Using the inventory as a guide, one can proceed systematically to check each item listed. A special chart should be made up for noting the condition of each tool or machine, with a column in which might be noted those components whose purchase is essential in order to restore the item to the proper condition. Failure at this time to record numbers and specifications of the parts to be purchased, or of the manufacturers of the article, with all other necessary data, will inevitably cause loss of time later.

The task indicated here may not be a small one, but to perform it conscientiously will result in the teacher's having a new and accurate inventory at the beginning of the school year. The teacher will also be able to order easily all needed repair parts for tools and machines. He or she will also be able to determine that preliminary work which needs to be done on the equipment. Such an examination will help to avoid future misunderstanding regarding equipment condition and quantity. Finally, the teacher's use of a systematic program of inspection will impress the supervisor or administrator with the teacher's businesslike method. This impression can only serve to foster trust and confidence.

It should be said here that unless the teacher returning to a previous school or lab facility has done this work before leaving at the close of the year, his or her job is not essentially different from that of the new instructor.

CHAPTER 8—BEGINNING THE SCHOOL YEAR

Conditioning Equipment

In too many instances students are annoyed and their interest is diverted in the early part of the school year by the fact that equipment is not in working order. Dull tools, machines that are both inoperative and dangerous, paint brushes left drying from last semester, and disorganized toolrooms in which even the teacher cannot find anything are but a few of the conditions to which beginning students are often unfortunately introduced.

The teacher who has experienced the rich rewards that come from time spent in putting the lab equipment in order is sure to invest all the effort needed to give the students a proper start. With the possible exception of some advanced classes, the teacher should not leave tool sharpening and similar work for the student to do as an initial activity. Not only are beginning students unable to do work of this type properly, but such assignments would be misunderstood and perhaps resented by these students.

Attention should be called here to the fact that some larger school systems hire maintenance men to overhaul and recondition all major equipment. This does not relieve the teacher, however, of his or her responsibilities; nor does it excuse the teacher from a great deal of personal work in connection with remaining chores.

Ordering Equipment and Supplies

When the survey of equipment has been completed, the next step should be to obtain the items that have been listed as missing. Also, other new equipment for which there appears to be immediate need may be requested.

While most schools or school systems have some person acting as purchasing agent, it often happens that the instructor is authorized to make certain purchases directly from commercial firms. In either case, the instructor should be aware of the necessity of specifying completely and technically every article to be purchased. Time is wasted by the instructor, and patience is lost by the purchasing agents and merchants when incomplete orders are placed. Such orders also give an unfavorable impression of the instructor. Failure to insert a necessary figure or specification in the original order can delay equipment delivery for months. While students are kept waiting, serious disciplinary and other problems may develop.

The teacher should know how to specify tools and materials. The teacher who does not know should find out before the orders go in. It is not wise or ethical to leave it to the purchasing agent, or even to the supervisor, to check and complete items listed on requisitions. This work is the responsibility of the teacher, and he or she should remember that these requisitions constitute evidence of efficiency, or lack of it. As a help, it is advisable to obtain standard order blanks from firms selling the various types of items and to consult catalogs for all tools. Failure to know, for instance, what "length" means as applied to files, chisels, screwdrivers, and other tools has created many awkward situations.

TEACHING INDUSTRIAL EDUCATION

The problem of estimating quantities of supplies involves additional detail. Records of types of work, past class enrollments, and other details of previous years, as well as those records indicating enrollments and new plans for the coming year, furnish the most satisfactory information upon which to act. Some school systems are demanding that supplies be specified for the entire year or at least for a semester, while others offer the opportunity of ordering quantities as needed. If the former system prevails, the teacher can do nothing but estimate, upon the best available data, the maximum needs, and order accordingly.

However, with this system careful analysis should be used, rather than a blind estimate of requirements. If the instructor will obtain estimates through the detailed process of figuring the needs of one individual student in each prospective class and multiplying this figure by the number of students in the class, he will come close to actual needs.

What has been said with reference to specifications under the heading of ordering equipment applies also to ordering supplies. Too much care cannot be exercised in making requests specific and in conformity with common practices. It is rather late, after useless material has been delivered, to realize that faulty specifications were given; and an attempt to place the blame on the purchasing agent will not help matters.

Checking One's Readiness

The final important touch in the program of preparation is anticipation of the first class meeting. Here the test will come of practically all those qualities desirable in a teacher, as well as of all the acquired skill and adaptability he or she may possess.

One of the first questions that will be asked of the new teacher on the first day of school is "What are we going to make?" or "When do we go to work?" The wise teacher will anticipate these questions, and, before meeting the classes, have in his or her possession some basic courses of study. Even in systems where supervision is provided, teachers cannot expect to be handed detailed instructions and plans for all projects and activities. Hence, it usually falls upon the teacher to furnish instructional material. The teacher who has a collection of blueprints, courses, outlines, and plans for sample projects can draw on them for those ideas and details that may be used as basic material for the opening classes. Later, after the interests and needs of the students have been properly assessed, this material can be reorganized.

As a check upon one's readiness to meet the class for the first time, the following guidelines may be of value:
- Visualize the class as fully as possible as to age, training, temperament, aptitudes, and the like. Previous records will assist here.
- Be certain that equipment and tools are in perfect condition.
- Have a definite plan for the work for the semester.
- Have materials on hand and ready for the first work to be accomplished.

- Have a written lesson plan or procedure for the first class meeting.
- Have the needed tools and other devices on hand for the first lesson.
- Be ready to assign students to working places and lockers.
- Plan a definite method for getting acquainted with the class.
- Prepare to be pleasant as the students arrive. If a teacher is not glad to see the year begin, he should quit and let someone else take his place, for the students will soon acquire a similar attitude.
- Have a definite plan for standards of order and discipline, and be prepared to put this plan in operation from the start.

The Instructor Meets the Class

If the teacher has engaged in a program of preparation of the type discussed on previous pages, he or she will have every reason to anticipate an effective start. If the teacher's foresight has been comprehensive and analytical, and if his or her heart is in the work—in short, if the teacher is a professional—he or she should now be ready to meet the classes.

The importance of the first meeting with the students cannot be overemphasized. At this initial contact, those impressions received by the students and those attitudes established will be instrumental in determining the success of the program. During the first meeting, the students will decide whether or not the instructor is interested, enthusiastic, and deserving of their cooperation. It may be possible for the teacher to change first impressions at a later date. Nevertheless, it is important to structure the first contact with the students so that the results are beneficial and lead to cooperation between teacher and students.

While the personality traits of the instructor count for much in gaining cooperation from students, it is also true that effective teaching methods and organized learning procedures are equally important. Personality is not an adequate substitute for an organized program. However, a teacher with a good personality, and presenting a program of attractive, suitable, and well-considered proposals, can become an effective educator.

The following suggestions are made for procedures in meeting for the first class period a group of from fifteen to twenty students of junior high school or early high school age.

Start something before the students do. When the students arrive they are ready for action; the teacher should be ready also. If the teacher is not in the classroom at the time the class is scheduled to meet, a bad example is set. The class will not obtain that immediate direction necessary for a successful class year. It is easy for the teacher to gain student attention at this time. He or she can attract the interest of the class by handing out information cards to be filled in later. The teacher can talk to early arrivals about some phase of the classwork. To focus the attention of the students on a central point until the class can be called to order is no small task, but it is a very important one. A teacher who begins the first class on time indicates to the students that class time is to be used efficiently.

Get acquainted. This important point is often overlooked. It applies equally to student and instructor. Many timid students will not feel at home in the lab because they do not know the instructor and their classmates. Simply to take the roll call is not sufficient in this connection.

It is just as important for the students to know the instructor's name as it is for the roll of students' names to be in the hands of the teacher. If the latter's name is not clearly presented, this again promotes reticence among some students in approaching the instructor. Let the teacher introduce himself or herself as he or she wishes to be addressed by the students. The teacher should pronounce his or her name so that all can hear, and then write it on the chalkboard as an additional help. The teacher's name imprinted on his or her apron or lab coat will aid in the process. Most students are keenly interested in their teacher, and if the teacher shows an interest in the students, their interest may develop into a deep and profound respect.

Recognize students. In order to develop this acquaintance, the teacher could go so far as to allow the students to introduce themselves to the rest of the group and perhaps tell something of their experiences, particularly in industrial shopwork, both at home and in school. They could also tell about their hobbies and other interests. Such a procedure might well create a new and refreshing schoolroom atmosphere, something surprising in the experience of students. The use of a circular seating arrangement might easily be the means of initiating a spirit of cooperation among the students and between the students and the teacher. Such an arrangement stimulates discussion and encourages student participation.

- *Discuss values and purposes.* Too many students take courses without knowing just why they are assigned to the class or subject. It seems reasonable to assume that much time can profitably be spent during the initial period of any new course in discussing the purposes of the work and the outcomes that may be expected. Such a discussion should obviously be presented to attract student interest.

Students of junior and senior high school age may be expected to take greater interest in the work if they know the reasons why their teachers have decided that a particular subject will make a valuable contribution to their education. Many of the commonly listed aims or outcomes for industrial education are not too difficult for students to understand and appreciate. Incidentally, the teacher can clarify for himself or herself those outcomes desired by listing them in phraseology understandable by the students.

Review course content. As early in the course as possible, preferably at the first meeting with the class, it is well to acquaint the group with the nature of the material to be covered. Some teachers hesitate to do this because they feel that the plans presented will not seem attractive, and the students will tend to drop out. In response to such feelings, it might be said that if the teacher has prepared a course of study that is properly gauged for

CHAPTER 8—BEGINNING THE SCHOOL YEAR

the students to whom it is presented, there should be no danger or lack of interest.

It should also be kept in mind that the attitude the teacher displays in presenting the plan will probably have more to do with its acceptance or rejection than will the content of the plan. A tone of voice or a general attitude that indicates that the teacher is disinterested or uncaring will not assist in the acceptance of the course of study, or of the projects to be made.

Establishing a Cooperative Attitude

To preach constantly about rules of conduct in the school or laboratory is poor practice. To make no attempt to arrive at a cooperative attitude regarding conduct is still worse. Some of the first rules that must be explained to the class are those covering suitable personal conduct and the use of the lab facility. Here, success in obtaining student cooperation comes from explaining the rules and regulations with reference to the conditions which exist in the school and in the lab. A few suggestions that have proved helpful in classes are presented in the following paragraphs.

Show confidence in the students. There is a greater possibility for success within the program if the students feel that they will be treated as responsible individuals. Dealt with in this way, not many students will consciously violate established regulations. The offenses that take place because of lack of maturity and judgment are often not intended, and thus do not offend as greatly as deliberate offenses. Also, the value of putting students on their honor has not been fully realized in schools. That there are exceptional situations under which the applications of these suggestions may be less effective is not to be denied, but with most students their value should not be overlooked. Although this examination of problems of conduct and discipline is brief, it is an important starting point. This topic will be covered in greater detail in Chapter 9.

They come to work. It is wrong to approach a class with the assumption that their chief interest is in playing and provoking mischief. That may be the case if interesting activities are not organized, but the average boy or girl comes to the classroom and laboratory for an opportunity to work and learn. If the teacher will realize this from the outset and provide abundant learning activities, he or she will have little reason to be concerned with anything else. How to get the students away from the work when the class period is over will soon become a greater problem than how to keep them working, if the instructor has the right viewpoint and the right approach. Students should be encouraged to develop mature working habits.

The equipment belongs to the students. A wholesome attitude toward tools and equipment can usually be established through a presentation of the idea that the tools are placed there for the students. They are available for their use. They ought to be cared for as if they were tools in their own or their parent's workshop.

These tools will be only as good as the care that they receive. No student should expect anyone else to treat the tool which he or she will use next any better than he or she is treating the one someone else is to use. Consequently, if tools are properly cared for, there is little or no difference between having a tool kit for each individual and having a much larger tool kit for a group. It simply makes it possible to have many tools which otherwise could not be had, and because of this, opportunities are presented for doing varied and better work.

Such a philosophy presented even to very young students has seldom failed to establish the proper outlook upon the work, and instead of the attitude that they have no responsibility in the care of tools, the students have a new viewpoint concerning public ownership.

Their safety is important. It is not a difficult task to impress students in lab classes with the fact that some rules of conduct are made purely for the safety of the student. Whether students fully understand the reason why they must secure permission each time they wish to use certain tools or machines is not as important as their understanding that their future health and happiness depends on their obeying the rules. This does not mean that explanations of all rules should not be offered, but rather that tools and machines are dangerous if carelessly used, and that for the future good of the individual who is not now mature enough to appreciate the danger, these rules must be respected. Safety practices and procedures are further discussed in Chapter 12.

Instructions must be specific. To talk about matters in general and reach no definite and particular conclusions is probably an important cause of students' failure to respond to suggestions for behavior in the lab situation. Teachers fail at this point, because, in generalizing, they forget that students may not be absolutely sure of precise meanings. Even if students understand the general theme of the statement, they may not be sufficiently impressed to act on what is suggested. Pointed presentations, then, are a basic requirement for success in all teaching. They are even more keenly needed in connection with preliminary suggestions for rules of conduct and response at the beginning of the school year or term. Not too many rules for conduct, but a few rules so presented that they are understood as fully as possible and accepted by the class, should be the objective of the teacher.

"When Do We Go to Work?"

It is of utmost importance to the early success of teaching in the laboratory to permit students to become physically involved in work activities at the earliest possible moment. Let us remember that to the student, the industrial laboratory represents an opportunity to make something. While that conception must be broadened later by tactful planning on the teacher's part, it will still be evident that industrial education makes its unique contribution by providing project activities. To attempt to substitute

CHAPTER 8—BEGINNING THE SCHOOL YEAR

explanations for activities, particularly as an introduction to the semester's work, is to fail to take advantage of that learning opportunity which is the most fundamental and valuable of all those offered by industrial education.

It is highly important that uniform bases for behavior be presented and accepted at the earliest possible moment, before individuals have to be dealt with as offenders or before bad habits have been established. But the custom of some teachers of engaging in theoretical discussions, and teaching names of tools or parts in large numbers as necessary preliminary knowledge, disappoints students and stifles their interest.

Some teachers purposely defer demonstrations and actual work because they expect additional enrollment for following meetings and consider it a waste of time to go on with the work. Such teachers might ask themselves whether they can afford to cool the enthusiasm of 80 to 90 percent of the class while waiting for the remaining few. Of course, it is extra work to repeat instructions to latecomers. But why should those arriving on time be punished for being punctual?

If the first class period consists of ninety minutes or more, then it is quite possible, and entirely feasible, to give a demonstration covering at least one unit of activity, and in many cases, allow the class to begin to carry it out. While lab demonstrations are discussed at length in Chapter 10, it may be stressed here that the first demonstration is probably the most important one that the teacher will ever present to the class.

The demonstration should be fully organized, and based on a complete analysis of the job involved and the responses expected of the students. It should be suitable in all respects to the level upon which the members of the class are expected to respond in thought and action. A haphazard presentation, obviously given because there seems to be nothing else to do, will start the work in the wrong direction and make a poor impression on the class. In some cases, where the teaching content provides for activity under larger coordinated units, or where a comprehensive lab program is involved, students may get into activity early through instruction sheets, through investigation of projects to be made, or through the help of advanced students in the laboratory.

Informational content is profitable and should be introduced as the progress of the work may allow. Through the industrial education class, character training and cooperative responses may be developed unconsciously to a great extent. However, without definite manipulative work at a very early stage, the program is not likely to develop as it should.

A word of caution against overanxiety to have students get into the work at once may be in place here, although it might seem like a contradiction of statements made in previous paragraphs. It is obviously just as bad to send students to work before they are ready as it is to hold them for extended preliminary instruction. Too many explanations, lectures, and demonstrations will certainly kill interest; too few may fail to arouse it. Inadequate directions may result in failure to maintain interest, because the student is at once faced with problems that seem to be insoluble.

If, after the class has been allowed to go to work, it becomes evident the student has no fundamental understanding of the problem, no knowledge of the procedure necessary, and no organized plan for action, the instructor has probably failed to provide the students with the proper information. It pays to sacrifice some time at the outset with the idea of gaining it back in subsequent sessions.

Fifteen minutes spent in giving information to the class may result in the saving of hours by the students, to say nothing of the time the teacher saves by not having to supply later that information which should have been given initially. Lack of understanding results in lack of cooperation. Both are directly caused by lack of painstaking effort on the part of the instructor to lay a foundation for intelligent student action.

The Special Student

There is a strong feeling possessed by many industrial education teachers that their programs have been made "dumping grounds" because they have been used to accommodate the misfits of the school system. Since resentment of this practice is usually most emphatic at enrollment time, a brief discussion of the problem might be appropriate.

If by "dumping ground" is meant the assignment to industrial education classes of those students who have been failures elsewhere, the statement accurately reflects what often takes place. But why register a complaint because such students are assigned to the laboratory? There are two probable reasons for this feeling. The first is that students of the type mentioned have been classified as inferior in their abilities to master language, mathematics, and other academic subjects. Because of this the lab teacher feels indignant that he or she should be called upon to care for those students who have failed in other courses. A second reason, and one which the teacher might not always wish to admit, is that he or she does not want to have to bother with special cases. The teacher has planned the work for the average student, and cannot take time to instruct those who are slow to learn or who present discipline problems.

A further investigation of the problem may reveal that it is not entirely justifiable to classify a student as being inferior merely because he or she has been transferred from academic subjects to those of the industrial education program. Certainly, there are qualities and abilities that a person must possess in order to progress as a student and attain success in later life. However, to judge a student's aptitude merely by evaluating his or her IQ is not a safe approach outside the traditional school program. Indeed, there is some question as to whether such an evaluation can be accurately employed even within the program.

CHAPTER 8—BEGINNING THE SCHOOL YEAR

Interest in the work is an important prerequisite for success in it. With some people, interest is dependent upon their awareness of the practicality or relevance of the subject being studied or the work being undertaken. Thousands of students have left school with the stigma that they could not "make the grade," and many of these have later achieved outstanding success in industry and business. This fact should serve as a reminder that a student who does not excel within the traditional school program is not necessarily in an inferior position to be an effective member of society.

The second reason given, that the instructor has no time for the student who has a reputation of not conforming to the program, has probably been shared by all other teachers in the school. However, many of the teachers who find themselves with a problem student in their classes do not take the time to learn anything about the problems of the individual. Thus, they are aware only of the fact that the student may ask too many questions, or fail to become interested, or misbehave.

There are two responses possible for the industrial educator who finds these special students in his or her program. The teacher can adopt the uncaring attitude of those teachers whose lack of attention may have forced the student to lose interest in their programs. Alternatively, the teacher may accept the challenge of attempting to educate these students. In adopting this approach, the teacher indicates awareness of the student's potential. The real problem becomes one of educational rehabilitation.

Even in cases where the student possesses no great talent, mechanical or otherwise, if interest can be established through manipulative work, there is an opportunity in the school lab for the teacher who is sympathetic to the problem.

However, in fairness to the teacher with an overcrowded schedule, it should be said that working conditions often make it relatively impossible to find all the time necessary for special attention to students of the type discussed here. Obviously, if good results are to be expected, there should be time for special work with those who need it. The industrial laboratory presents an excellent environment for rehabilitating students who have lost interest in school and lost confidence in education. However, without time available for personal attention, not much effective work can be done.

Perhaps a new type of educational laboratory should be provided in every large school. This laboratory should be made the most attractive in the building, for the purpose of interesting disinterested students. The teacher in this lab should be a good mechanic, but more than that, he or she should be a professional teacher, interested in the problems of students. A student-oriented educational philosophy should be the basis for his or her operation. The teacher should have wide knowledge of many occupations, but this knowledge should make him or her more humble and willing to let the students work out their own destiny. As a human relations expert, analysis of human nature will be the chief function of this teacher, and this special facility and program will be used as a laboratory for accomplishing it. As soon as students develop an interest in school, life, and vocation, they may be transferred elsewhere. Many may go back to the academic work from whence they came, but with new vision of the personal value of an education. Some may go into the shops for vocational training. Others, without stigma, may be guided into jobs that will lead them to their choice of occupation.

Possible Changes

The extent to which a new teacher should feel free to recommend or institute changes for the first year is a problem that troubles both beginning and experienced teachers. Every instructor who is interested in his or her work is likely to see opportunities for changing existing conditions to produce what he or she might consider to be a better teaching environment. How far to go in this direction will depend upon a number of factors. The following points may be given on the affirmative side:

• The instructor will be of more value to the school for the first year if allowed to use his or her own ideas or plan of organization. The instructor may be less effective if forced to conform to some less workable scheme originated by a predecessor.

• If the instructor's proposals are of value to the school system and to the students, it is unfair to wait a year to put them into effect. A year of the teacher's time as well as that of the school would be lost as far as these ideas and practices are concerned.

• Money may be saved immediately by making such changes. The previous teacher's pet schemes might have been tolerated in the presence of their champion but may appear unjustifiable in the teacher's absence.

• Teaching conditions may be bad and in need of immediate attention.

• Wise reorganization gives the teacher an opportunity to demonstrate ability and gain the administrator's confidence.

• Students may demand changes in order that they may feel justified in enrolling for further work in the department.

• Reorganization of the budget may call for changes in the work.

• The teacher may have been hired for the purpose of reorganizing the program.

• With the coming of a new teacher, the students expect a variation in the program.

• A teacher who has accepted a job within the field of his or her specialty has a right to assume that he or she is qualified to improve existing conditions, or they would not have been hired for the job.

On the negative side of the question, the following suggestions may be considered:

• The teacher should first prove ability and establish confidence on the part of the administration before proposing any changes.

CHAPTER 8—BEGINNING THE SCHOOL YEAR

- Lack of knowledge of local conditions will stand in the way of intelligent action at this time.
- The mood of the students and the level of their support must be ascertained before attempting any revolutionizing of the program.
- The confidence of the administration can best be established by following existing programs intelligently, rather than by appearing critical of them.
- Too rapid changes at this time tend to lead to criticism and suspicion on the part of administration and co-workers.
- There is danger that the teacher may be inclined to make changes only to attract attention.
- It is much better to initiate no action than to run up against unforeseen difficulties and leave the job unfinished.
- There is danger of overdeveloping the program, with subsequent damaging reaction from the administration and public.

Local conditions should, of course, be studied in order to determine whether the positive or negative arguments offered here should lend the most weight. No rule can be made to apply to all situations. It is probably just as bad to be totally lacking in a spirit of reform as it is to be over-progressive and have one's judgment questioned on future endeavors. No efficient teacher is likely to stay a year on any job without finding it desirable to make changes in content, in teaching procedure, and perhaps in the facility.

DISCUSSION QUESTIONS

1. Make a list of questions that a prospective teacher of industrial education might ask the superintendent before signing a contract.

2. What would you reply to the suggestion of a prospective employer that industrial education programs should pay for themselves in the school?

3. If an interview with a prospective employer provides the opportunity to explain the differences between industrial arts and vocational-industrial education, what would be your statement?

4. List all of the means by which a new teacher may get information regarding the number and character of students for various classes.

5. What activities may a teacher engage in before school begins to insure adequate enrollment in a new class or program?

6. What would be your reply to the statement by a prospective employer that "no one can teach industrial education well unless he or she has had extended practical experience?"

7. After he signs the contract, but before he arrives on the job, there are certain things a teacher might do to prepare himself for his new position. List some of these activities.

8. By what means can a new teacher learn what is his or her reasonable share of cocurricular and community activities.

9. Make a list of values that you, as a new teacher, would expect to realize from local in-service meetings before the start of the school year.

10. List all subjects that your teaching credentials entitle you to teach.

11. What may be done to secure a cooperative attitude at the outset from an uncooperative student in the class?

12. Make a sample of a special card which may be filled out by junior high school students the first day of school for the information of the teacher. Do the same for senior high school students.

13. Make a list of precautions an inexperienced teacher should observe the first day of school.

14. In what subjects or activities in industrial education do you think it feasible to start manipulative work the first day?

15. Do you think it would be a good idea to quiz students on the names of tool parts their first day in the laboratory?

16. If the instructor provided mimeographed copies of lab rules and regulations for distribution to the class, would there be need for discussing them? Why?

17. What should the new teacher do if the inventory of tools and equipment does not agree with that turned in by his or her predecessor?

18. What danger is there in attempting to make the course of study attractive to the students the first day?

19. What do you consider the best way to learn students' names quickly and help your class get acquainted?

20. During the first part of the work, to what extent should one show confidence in students by giving them custody of tools?

21. Give reasons why it is important to present the first demonstration with extra care.

22. In the teacher's mind, what should be more important for the students—"making something" or "learning something?" Why?

23. Under what conditions might the industrial education teacher justifiably complain that his or her laboratory is being used to accommodate those who are unable to perform well in other learning programs?

ADDITIONAL READINGS

Allen, Dwight W., and Seifman, Eli, eds. *The Teacher's Handbook.* Glenview, Illinois: Scott, Foresman, 1971.

Baird, Ronald J. *Contemporary Industrial Teaching.* South Holland, Illinois: Goodheart-Willcox, 1972.

Cenci, Louis, and Weaver, Gilbert G. *Teaching Occupational Skills.* 2nd ed. New York: Pitman, 1968.

Friese, John F., and Williams, William A. *Course Making in Industrial Education.* 3rd ed. Peoria, Illinois: Chas. A. Bennett, 1966.

Giachino, J. W., and Gallington, Ralph O. *Course Construction in Industrial Arts, Vocational, and Technical Education.* 3rd ed. Chicago: American Technical Society, 1967.

Jordan, Thomas E. *America's Children: An Introduction to Education.* New York: Rand McNally, 1973.

Leighbody, Gerald B., and Kidd, Donald M. *Methods of Teaching Shop and Technical Subjects.* Albany, New York: Delmar, 1966.

Pautler, Albert J. *Teaching Shop and Laboratory Subjects.* Columbus, Ohio: Charles E. Merrill, 1971.

Silvius, G. Harold, and Curry, Estell H. *Managing Multiple Activities in Industrial Education.* 2nd ed. Bloomington, Illinois: McKnight & McKnight, 1971.

Silvius, G. Harold, and Curry, Estell H. *Teaching Successfully in Industrial Education.* 2nd ed. Bloomington, Illinois: McKnight & McKnight, 1967.

Chapter 9
Class Organization and Discipline

Management and Discipline

The nature of industrial education in the school program is such that it offers superior opportunities for developing qualities of individual responsibility and group leadership. It should not be assumed, however, that these qualities will be developed to a high degree without careful planning and skillful management on the part of the instructor. Students are not in the position to take upon themselves more leadership responsibility than is delegated by the teacher, nor can they be expected to take the initiative in participating in class management. It thus becomes the teacher's responsibility to so organize the class that students may receive maximum benefits from assisting in problems of lab routine as well as from performing individual work projects. With this concept in mind, the teacher will plan for student participation in management in order to furnish experience in situations similar to those found in adult occupational life and in social groups. Whether the plan saves time for the teacher becomes unimportant if it promises to develop a sense of responsibility on the part of the student.

The interpretation of discipline in the school has changed remarkably in recent years. Rather than demanding blind obedience to rules and regulations, the modern teacher considers effective discipline to be connected with self-imposed personal and social adjustments on the part of the student—adjustments that will foster habits of thinking and conduct that will lead to social responsibility. Under this interpretation of discipline, rules and regulations lose much of their importance, except as they are understood and accepted by those who are affected by them. It is also implied that enforcement of rules will be approached from a new viewpoint, and the correction will not be blindly imposed, but will rather be administered after a consideration of the student's attitude.

For industrial education, successful class management of the type discussed here is largely dependent upon the following conditions: interest, understanding, and participation on the part of the student; careful planning by the instructor; and suitable working conditions.

Bases for Effective Management

The previous introduction points to the conclusion that good discipline is an outcome of proper organization and supervision, and is a direct by-product rather than a stated objective. Teachers who must constantly secure and maintain discipline through punishment are wasting much of the class time. It is much better to spend the time in preparation of interesting

CHAPTER 9—CLASS ORGANIZATION AND DISCIPLINE

and profitable activities, and let proper conduct and discipline come of their own accord. From the student's angle, the following factors should receive consideration:

Is the student interested? Students who are not interested soon become a problem for the teacher. If time is taken initially to organize a plan for motivating them, time will be saved later in enforcing discipline. Probably without exception, every class member can become interested in the work if properly encouraged.

Is the student definitely occupied? The statement, "An idle mind is the devil's workshop," applies here. Discipline problems and other difficulties arise when the class program is poorly organized. The instructor's responsibility is to plan educative and interesting work for everyone. The student who works quickly often becomes a problem when his or her work is completed, and when nothing more can be planned until the next class meeting. An unorganized program can lead to discipline problems and unproductive activities.

Does the student appreciate time values? One of the most difficult things in dealing with young and inexperienced students is to develop in them an appreciation of the value of time. Wasting time appears to be the principal occupation of some students, and where there are loafers present, the question of order and discipline soon becomes acute.

Does the student take pride in his or her work? Some discipline problems probably arise from the fact that the student has no pride in his or her own accomplishments. Be sure to give recognition to even the smallest degree of success. Habitual failure in work makes a student quit trying and begin to play, whereas success tends to encourage students to attempt other successful projects.

Does the student know what is required? Frequently, students who lack knowledge of requirements may appear to be uncooperative. It is the duty of the teacher to provide definite information regarding laboratory practices, reading assignments, standards of workmanship, care of equipment, and other requirements of the program.

Does the student have a purpose? Upon the answer to this question depends the solution to many problem cases. Lack of a purpose in the student's mind is the cause of their lack of interest in industrial, as well as academic, education. A method of acquainting students with values to be gained has been discussed in Chapter 8.

Does the student think well of the teacher? Once, the author heard a school superintendent say that the quality most necessary for success on the part of an elementary teacher is to be well-liked and respected by his or her students. This statement deserves consideration by teachers of all grades. Some teachers complain that students do not have the proper respect toward them. The reply might well be that there is just as much respect as the instructor has given the students. There is a difference between familiarity and friendliness when dealing with students. Aloofness on the part of the teacher for the purpose of preserving dignity is probably as bad as a total absence of reserve. After all, the teacher must be looked up to by the students. Some teachers can go further than others in meeting the students on an equal basis, but in most cases, a certain amount of reserve seems to be essential for successful discipline.

Does the student have aptitude? Total lack of aptitude for the work is justifiable cause for lack of interest in it. In extreme cases of ineptness, might it not be better to substitute other types of work, or change the routine in the manipulative work, rather than to run the risk of developing in the student undesirable habits and personality traits? At any rate, lack of aptitude should be recognized when dealing with discipline problems in industrial education.

Is the student compatible with the group? Differences in age, failure in other school subjects, differences in social and economic status, and similar conditions typical of adolescence must be understood by the teacher when dealing with problems of discipline and class routine. In respect to these problems, the teacher has superior opportunities to assist students because of the informal atmosphere that may be maintained and the close personal contacts possible in the laboratory situation.

Is the student properly dressed for work? When not properly dressed for work, the student is at a disadvantage from the outset. Lack of proper clothing may exempt the student from certain phases of the work. This places the student in a privileged position, which may cause the student to be criticized by classmates.

Student Participation in Management

In the contemporary approach to the problem of class management and discipline, the degree of student participation must be related to the age of the students, the types of work to be undertaken, and probably the ability of the teacher to organize and implement the plan. In general, adolescent students like organization, and will respond to a reasonable plan, in addition to carrying out responsibilities placed on them. It is true, however, that even in our day, numerous teachers of industrial education probably are centering their work on an emphasis other than that of active student participation.

In order to have the cooperation of the students in dealing with the question of class management, the instructor may take the position of industrial administrator, while the organization of the class is carried out extensively by student supervisors appointed for each of the following areas of responsibility:

- *Personnel.* Maintain attendance records. Instruct students in habits of cooperation, good personal attitudes, compliance with regulations.
- *Tools.* Check tools according to the system used. Might also study construction of tools and complete minor repairs.

CHAPTER 9—CLASS ORGANIZATION AND DISCIPLINE

- *Materials.* Issue materials and supplies. Maintain records of stock on hand.
- *Production.* Assist in routing work. Give technical assistance. Organize group work.
- *Library.* Maintain reference materials. Have charge of sample projects and instructional media.
- *Safety.* Call attention to safety rules and practices. Report and record all accidents.
- *Ventilation.* Have charge of windows, heaters, and ventilators for maintenance of comfortable working environment.
- *Finishing.* Check condition of finishing room at beginning and close of the class period.
- *Maintenance.* Oil and check machines. Inspect guards, and complete minor repairs.
- *Sanitation.* Check washbasins, lockers, workbenches, and machines at the end of the period.
- *Public Relations.* Contact persons in the school who request work from the laboratory classes, or who have work in progress in the lab.

Many other duties may be assigned, depending on prevailing conditions, but those listed will indicate the range of possibilities for giving practice in carrying out tasks in which the entire group is interested. Some of these jobs will usually involve more than one person, in which case a chairperson may be appointed for the group.

The procedure for making assignments may differ according to circumstances. Some teachers feel that nominations and elections by the class are preferable, since such a method gives practice in democratic living to the group. If a scheme of rotating these positions is followed, each student eventually will have experience in many of the assignments. Thus, it might not make a great deal of difference on which job the student begins. The practice of rotation has obvious advantages because it offers experience in a variety of responsibilities. It also furnishes new interest each time the job shift is made. Under this system, menial jobs and responsible assignments are divided more equally. The rotation system has its drawbacks, however, in that all students are not equally capable of assuming responsibility. Some students may not care for places of leadership. With this in mind, some teachers appoint the general supervisor, tool checker, and materials clerk for longer periods, while other appointments are made on a weekly basis.

The assignment of students to particular jobs will not provide the most beneficial social lessons unless the program is monitored by the instructor. If job appointments are to be a serious matter, the teacher must see to it that there is a job to do. A definite list of responsibilities should be worked out and posted before the class, showing in detail what is expected in each job. Definite evaluations of efficiency should be given each student at prescribed intervals. The lack of such evaluations renders the program less effective,

TEACHING INDUSTRIAL EDUCATION

with the result that habits of negligence and indifference are cultivated, rather than those of responsibility and leadership. Consideration of laboratory design factors, as discussed in Chapter 7, will provide further direction in the establishment of opportunities for student involvement.

The Disciplinary Role of the Teacher

The teacher and his attitudes have great bearing upon the responses that students will give. Too often it is felt that students are inferior in ability or irregular in their behavior, when in reality the instructor has failed to do his or her part. The questions directed toward the instructor in the following paragraphs may help to define those qualities necessary for the enforcement of good discipline.

Is the teacher interested in teaching? It is obvious that interest on the part of the teacher stimulates student interest. Teachers whose hearts are not in the work, who have no real concern for the youth under their care, or who may be in the teaching profession only as a temporary measure will soon be found out by their students. A disinterested teacher will soon have disinterested and unproductive classes.

Is the teacher interested in the subject? A teacher may be effective in certain subjects where his or her interest is strong, and not so effective in some other subject. Interest in the subject matter can be developed if one is interested in students. Sometimes teachers are requested or required to teach new subjects when they have no particular interest in such subjects. Unless the teacher soon develops an interest in such work, his or her lack of enthusiasm will have bad effects on the students.

Does the teacher know the subject matter? This question needs no elaboration. Many a teacher has lost control of the class because he or she has not had sufficient knowledge and teaching skill in the subject. Lack of respect develops from lack of confidence in the instructor. The instructor who lacks the knowledge or skill necessary for efficient teaching should improve without delay or leave the profession.

Does the teacher have aptitude for teaching? There are "square pegs in round holes" among industrial education teachers. The teacher without aptitude has difficulty enforcing discipline. He or she should go into some other occupation or develop a vigorous program for self-improvement. The pursuit of excellence in instructional delivery and learning activity contributes substantially to a positive and creative educational environment. Teaching aptitude can be developed through consideration and practice of many of the techniques discussed throughout this text.

Does the teacher speak plainly and convincingly? An instructor's manner of speaking can be a great asset. Extensive self-improvement can be exercised on this point. The manner in which directions are given and the tone of the instructor's voice are of great importance.

Can the teacher control his or her emotions? It may seem strange to question a teacher on this point, but the question is pertinent. No one who

CHAPTER 9—CLASS ORGANIZATION AND DISCIPLINE

lacks the ability to "keep cool" can expect to be successful in directing and controlling others. One display of temper will put the teacher at a disadvantage with the class. Humiliation, sarcasm, and threats only lessen student respect for the instructor. Whatever else a teacher may lack, he or she must be calm, sensible, and able to maintain a sense of humor.

Has the teacher a sense of fairness? The lack of ability or inclination to be fair may be unthinkable by some in connection with the attributes of a teacher. The instructor who does not check his or her attitudes and procedures closely and continually may find that students may have cause to consider some dealings unfair. Also, there are teachers who seem to lack the natural qualities of leadership and personality that enable them quickly to make just decisions that are acceptable to students. As an example, mass punishment given because of unidentified offenders provides the entire class with a reason to feel they have been unfairly treated. If the instructor is just, and reasonably tactful in his or her contact with students, such a feeling eventually will be replaced by respect and admiration.

Are learning difficulties appreciated? Discipline problems sometimes are created by lack of sympathy with the student in the early stages of his or her learning. Teachers are prone to forget the difficulties they experienced in learning those processes of thought and performance which have now become habitual with them. The more expert the teacher's mechanical skills, the more danger there is that he or she will underestimate and sometimes ridicule important problems of beginning students. Such an attitude on the part of the teacher leads to difficulties because young people—and older ones as well—will lose interest when that which is expected of them is far beyond what they are capable of producing. The inevitable outcome of such a condition is that the student gives up trying and becomes accustomed to failure.

Does the instructor support the administration? Apparent loyalty to the administration is necessary at all times if the morale of the students is to be high. Lukewarmness toward policies of the school, or what is worse, adverse suggestions to students, have no place in the teaching profession. If the instructor cannot be loyal and cooperative, he cannot expect to receive the loyalty and cooperation needed for effective work and good discipline. If a faculty member wishes to criticize a superior or employer, he or she should go directly to the person concerned.

Environmental Conditions Affecting Discipline

Interest in the educational activity is closely related to the conditions under which one works and studies. This is especially true in schools, because of the compulsory nature of student attendance. Consider the following questions in this connection.

Does each student have an assigned work area? Students who do not know where they belong cannot be expected to go to work in the regular manner and attend to their tasks. Continued interest cannot be maintained, and discipline problems may result. This does not mean that under some conditions such working places may not be assigned, but the student must know where he or she is expected to be, and that their laboratory work will not be interfered with.

Is there sufficient space between benches? Lack of space for doing work, and too close contact with other students, cause distractions that lead to poor morale and weak class organization. Even though playing may be prohibited in the laboratory, it is likely to occur when students are placed in close proximity to each other during work periods.

Is there adequate light? Working in poor light may help make a discipline case out of any type of student. Lighting conditions may be improved in many ways, among which are adding skylights, installing updated, artificial-lighting fixtures, repainting walls, or moving benches closer to available windows.

Are machines and common equipment well-located? The location of machines has an important bearing on this problem. Lack of success due to lack of accessibility to equipment is preliminary to lack of interest, and lack of interest leads to unproductive activities.

Are there special facilities for class teaching? A classroom where the students may be called together to sit down is a desirable feature in connection with all labs, but an absolute necessity where more than one class is at work in a single room. An orderly demonstration with proper attention can hardly be given in a laboratory where a large number of other students are at work. There should be facilities for instruction if students are expected to pay attention to the work and profit by it.

Are there adequate locker facilities? A place where the student can keep unfinished work is a valuable factor in maintaining student morale. To lose parts of a project upon which hours of patient effort have been expended leads to discouragement and dissatisfaction.

Is the equipment in good condition? Tools which do not serve their purpose and machines which are faulty or inoperative weaken student morale. Respect for equipment is as important as respect for the teacher in securing proper behavior in the lab. One should probably go a step further, and list it as a prerequisite for the proper respect toward the instructor. Unless the instructor is able to maintain the equipment in good conition, he or she will very likely not hold the students' respect.

Are the tools in the storage cabinets arranged in an orderly fashion? The condition of the tool storage cabinets is the key to the condition of the entire laboratory. The way in which tools are handled here, the system of checking tools, the language and manners allowed and practiced, can easily be taken as a sample of the tone of the entire program. No orderly lab can have a disorderly toolroom. The location of the tools also has a bearing upon this topic. An inconveniently located toolroom causes waste of students' time, and offers them a temptation to loaf.

Is there ample ventilation? Every experienced teacher knows how ventilation relates to the problem of attention and concentration upon the work. In the laboratory, where the working temperature should be lower than in the regular classroom, there is no reason for disregarding proper ventilation.

Is cleanliness practiced? This question can be asked with reference to washrooms, toilets, floors, tools and machines, and the clothing of the instructor and students. Proper clothing helps to establish a spirit of industry.

Is there a laboratory atmosphere? It is difficult for students to practice habits of mischief and idleness in a laboratory environment where a spirit of industry is evident. Once an atmosphere of earnest endeavor has been established, discipline problems will diminish or disappear. In an organization in which everyone has a job to do and is doing that job, there need be little time devoted to detecting and punishing offenders.

Maintaining Effective Discipline

Little has been said about specific practices in class management that would apply to maintaining good discipline. Practices vary with different teachers and different systems. The reason for not attempting here to define methods and procedures for teachers to follow is that there is no one set of rules that can be successfully used by all teachers and all students in all situations.

The best progress cannot be made in industrial education unless the student has the feeling that he or she is permitted to use initiative and take the responsibility for his or her own actions. There is also a need to provide students with the opportunity to observe each other's work, and to plan and learn together. The concept of discipline in schools should obviously go beyond the purpose of conforming student behavior to school regulations. The ultimate purpose is, of course, a self-discipline that is a result of students accepting principles of democratic living and individual adjustment. This means that the atmosphere of the school should, insofar as possible, be similar to that of real life. Here industrial education has a distinct advantage, in that it can offer the student freedom of action and a chance to participate in group life with a more natural opportunity to interact than is offered in most other types of class sessions.

Freedom turned into license, however, means that classwork will result in chaos. Whatever else might be expected from work in industrial education, it is reasonable to assume that some contribution should be made toward establishing habits of cooperation and orderly procedure in dealing with one's peers. Unless a systematic schedule is established for the conduct of each individual and followed to a reasonable degree, the students will be deprived of a fundamental training for life and work that the school laboratory can reasonably be expected to offer.

The criticism expressed by some administrators and academic teachers implies that, in the labs, students acquire poor habits and attitudes with reference to manners and conduct. The range of conduct permitted in the lab should be just as definite as that allowed anywhere else in the school. The fact that the class situation may differ does not mean that student understanding of standards of discipline will be altered.

The most important requirement in enforcing discipline is that the teacher be in control of the class situation. Students will quickly adjust themselves to any reasonable type of schedule, as long as the instructor is in control. The poor habits that may be developed will not arise from the types of rules and regulations that prevail, but from the reactions of the students to those rules.

Preparedness has previously been emphasized as an attribute of the effective teacher. Problems in discipline can best be avoided through anticipating them and making plans for their elimination. Close attention to certain details in the routine of teaching will go far toward removing the causes of disciplinary troubles. There are several points to consider.

1. *Begin the class promptly and with authority.* The seed of trouble is often sown before the class actually begins. Mark attendance quickly, or have it marked by a student, but let earnest work begin at the first possible moment.

2. *Start the class with definite instructions.* Calling the class together for a few words, directions, or a roll call will direct the students to the work at hand. The fact that there may be nothing new to demonstrate does not mean that such a meeting should not take place. Brief suggestions can always be made that will help to maintain student interest and increase efficiency in the work.

3. *Check closely and frequently on students' work.* The instructor who becomes involved in the problems of one student, and spends much of the period with that student, may neglect other students who need help. Needing help and not getting it, some of the students may become impatient. Interest is also lost when frequent attention and comments are not given by the instructor. Such comments may simply state approval of work already accomplished. They may also detail instructions for continued activity.

4. *Evaluate students' work often.* Grading of students' work is discussed in detail in Chapter 13. Periodic evaluation of student work will increase their interest, thus helping to eliminate discipline problems before they begin. The morale of a class can be greatly improved through frequent grading and constructive criticism.

5. *Stay in the laboratory.* Some teachers have the habit of leaving the laboratory during class hours. They leave for good reasons, such as turning in requisitions or going for mail or phone calls, but their absence is not without its effect on the class. The age of the students and the type of work being done have some bearing on this point. However, it should be emphasized that those teachers dealing with young students should stay in the

CHAPTER 9—CLASS ORGANIZATION AND DISCIPLINE

room. Remember, the teacher is always responsible and legally liable for all that happens in his or her classes, whether or not he or she is present.

6. *Limit the closing time of the period.* Too much time for putting away work and tools is as bad as too little. One should experiment to see how little time can be used for this purpose. Close teamwork and student cooperation can reduce the amount of time usually consumed. Five to ten minutes are usually required.

7. *Acquire habits of supervision.* The habit of supervising all students and all work at one time and at all times can be acquired by the instructor. The teacher should never become absorbed in any single project or the problems of one individual, but should constantly be aware of the problems of the entire group. This is an attribute desired of good teachers in every program, but most particularly of those in industrial education.

DISCUSSION QUESTIONS

1. In what ways might a teacher inadvertently create situations in which discipline problems might arise? Derive solutions for each problem.

2. List some problems of conduct that would necessitate referring the student to the principal for disciplinary action.

3. Make a layout of a laboratory for twenty students that is planned especially to facilitate ease in the instruction and class management.

4. Work out a detailed plan for self-government by a class of twenty ninth-grade students in industrial education.

5. What are the advantages and disadvantages of student self-government from the standpoint of discipline?

6. List twelve rules of conduct that you think would be reasonable for a beginning ninth-grade class.

7. Make a list of points for judging whether good order exists in an industrial education laboratory.

8. What are some ways of dealing with a student who has become a discipline case?

9. How might the lack of locker space for storing unfinished work affect discipline?

10. What do you think of the idea that modern methods of class organization and discipline tend to eliminate respect for the teacher, and for adults in general?

11. What degree of freedom can be given to high school seniors?

12. How would your procedure in class organization vary between the junior- and senior-high-school levels?

13. Should projects be compulsory for students who apparently have little mechanical ability or aptitude? Why, or why not?

14. Make a list of points and procedures that would increase respect for the instructor.

TEACHING INDUSTRIAL EDUCATION

15. In what way does appropriate dress, on the part of students and instructor, affect student conduct in the laboratory?

16. How does frequent evaluation of student work promote effective discipline?

ADDITIONAL READINGS

Allen, Dwight W., and Seifman, Eli, eds. *The Teacher's Handbook.* Glenview, Illinois: Scott, Foresman, 1971.

Baird, Ronald J. *Contemporary Industrial Teaching.* South Holland, Illinois: Goodheart-Willcox, 1972.

Jordan, Thomas E. *America's Children: An Introduction to Education.* New York: Rand McNally, 1973.

Littrell, Joseph J. *Guide to Industrial Teaching.* Peoria, Illinois: Chas. A. Bennett, 1970.

Lueck, William R., et. al. *Effective Secondary Education.* Minneapolis: Burgess, 1966.

Pautler, Albert J. *Teaching Shop and Laboratory Subjects.* Columbus, Ohio: Charles E. Merrill, 1971.

Silvius, G. Harold, and Curry, Estell H. *Managing Multiple Activities in Industrial Education.* 2nd ed. Bloomington, Illinois: McKnight & McKnight, 1971.

Silvius, G. Harold, and Curry, Estell H. *Teaching Successfully in Industrial Education.* 2nd ed. Bloomington, Illinois: McKnight & McKnight, 1967.

Chapter 10
Teaching and Learning

Teaching Methods in Common Use

A comprehensive study of available literature in the field of teaching will reveal extensive listings of teaching methods as conceived and classified by various authors and groups. As presented in this chapter, however, the discussion of teaching methods will be confined to the examination of a number of generally accepted teaching practices and procedures which appear most suitable for instruction in industrial education.

With this thought in mind, the fundamental teaching methods which will receive special consideration are the following:
- The *demonstration* method for operation lessons.
- The *lecture* method for information lessons.
- The *seminar* method for discussion.
- The *discovery* method for self-development.

It is evident that it would not be necessary or even desirable to confine a teaching situation to the use of only one method. Basic elements of several of these approaches may appropriately be combined for best results depending upon the age of students and type of subject matter being taught. The skillful teacher will use these methods in such rotation and combination as will be indicated by existing needs.

As discussed here, teaching techniques or strategies are integrated with teaching methods. The teaching methods listed are thought of as broad, basic, coordinated procedures, each one sufficient in scope to be used rather exclusively for teaching segregated learning units. Techniques are procedures used to give variety to the teaching process and to stimulate and maintain interest in it. Under this interpretation, the use of questions could be a teaching technique used in connection with the direct and filmed demonstration, the seminar, the lecture, or the discovery method.

Presenting a Demonstration

From the time that instruction in the manual arts was introduced as a school subject, the demonstration has stood out as the most definite and valuable means of instruction for operation-type lessons. It continues to be so whenever it is desirable to have students learn exact and acceptable procedures in mechanical operations. Its success is based upon the fact that imitation, the repetition of an operation, is an important factor in any learning experience.

Demonstrations can be performed directly. Films and still displays may also be utilized, although these cannot adequately provide for an unskilled teacher's ability to guide the student. However, the shop demonstration, when performed by the skillful teacher, is unsurpassed in developing and maintaining interest among students. Demonstrations appeal to many senses. Skillful performance in the use of tools always attracts attention. In a demonstration, students see immediate progress as a result of the effort. Consequently, their desire is aroused to emulate the work of the teacher, and others.

The demonstration, then, is probably the teacher's greatest aid in training students in fundamental skills and practices in the shortest possible time. It may well be said that, for the average school lab, the quality and quantity of work produced will depend greatly upon the instructor's use of the demonstration.

Ability to perform in industry, or expert craftsmanship on the part of the teacher, is not a sufficient guarantee of ability to demonstrate to others. Ability to demonstrate comes from analysis of the problem, from organization of teaching procedures, and from a knowledge and appropriate use of those media helpful in emphasizing the key steps of a demonstration. A knowledge of the level of student comprehension is also necessary. Demonstrations as used in this type of teaching may be divided into three classes: class demonstrations, group demonstrations, and individual demonstrations.

The Class Demonstration

In all groups where one subject is being taught, there are good reasons for presenting demonstrations to the entire class at one time. This is true particularly in the early stages of a course in which individual articles are being produced. Such a procedure applies to the entire course when production work is being done. Wherever class demonstrations can be used, several advantages may be noted. The instructor's time is utilized more efficiently. Also, the entire class receives at the same time the same instructions and suggestions. Thus, there is little chance that students will later discover that they have not been given certain basic information. Generally, demonstrations presented to a large number of individuals generate more enthusiasm and interest.

The need for efficiency in the demonstration has already been stressed. In addition, the following practices must be observed if the demonstration is to be successful.

1. *Make the class feel a need for the demonstration.* It may be the task of the teacher to use some artificial means to produce such an attitude. However, in most cases the need for information about work that students are eager to do can be the determining factor for the time of the demonstration. It is an error to present demonstrations primarily because they have been planned in advance for a certain date.

2. *Practice privately.* Every demonstration covering a new unit of work that has not been recently performed by the instructor should be practiced

CHAPTER 10—TEACHING AND LEARNING

beforehand. Book references, printed cards, electronic materials, and other materials should be examined and edited so that they are properly integrated with the program. If this is not done, their effectiveness is diminished. Often the instructor encounters some unforeseen difficulty when he or she relies only upon imagination and previous experience. Thus, the class loses confidence in the instructor, and interest in the work.

3. *Effectively explain the demonstration.* Many demonstrations that might have been successful have been weakened by the inclusion of too much information that the instructor believed to be relevant. Often, however, the material was unrelated to the subject. Information that is related to the topic may create interest, but too often the instructor is possessed by the urge to tell about his or her own experiences in school or industry, or is sidetracked by suggestions and questions of members of the class. To decide beforehand just what ground will be covered, and not to deviate too much, is good advice in this connection. There are cases, however, where teachers do not carry on sufficient conversation to maintain interest in the demonstration. Oral explanations and discussions are needed, but they must serve to focus and hold attention upon the work at hand.

4. *Confine the demonstration to a single unit of work.* Teachers often fail to analyze the instructional material into sufficiently small units. As a consequence, the demonstration becomes long, involved, and uninteresting. Emphasize a small unit and enable the class to go to work as quickly as possible after proper interest has been aroused in the work. This approach will also make the material more easily understood.

5. *Do not demonstrate on students' work.* It is unfair to give one individual student the benefit of the work done in the demonstration. The article used in the demonstration should belong to the instructor or to the lab when completed.

6. *Have equipment and material in readiness.* All devices to be used in a demonstration must be at hand. While the instructor sets up flash cards, electronic stills, films, or projectors, or goes to the toolroom or stockroom, attention is diverted, time is used foolishly, and the emphasis on the unit of instruction is weakened and possibly destroyed.

7. *Use common tools.* To reserve the newest and best-looking tools for the teacher's demonstration bench is a mistake. Such tools may not work better, but they appear as if they might. Give the new tools to the students and use older ones for demonstration. This will show that the outward appearance of tools has little to do with the work they perform if they are in proper condition. The tools used should be the same size as those given to students.

8. *Give an example in accuracy.* The instructor should take the time to do the job well. No greater accuracy or better technique can be demanded rightfully at any time, either in labs or drafting rooms, than is set as a standard by the instructor's work.

9. *Use accepted trade methods.* There may be a good reason why some teachers lack trade practice in some subject which they teach. There is no reason, however, why they should not learn accepted procedures used in industry. After knowing such methods, there may be good reasons for deviating from them because of differences in objectives, ability of students, lack of equipment, and so on, but that is a different matter.

10. *Make the demonstration accessible to learners.* The necessity for planning the demonstration so that all students can see it in detail and hear the explanation is not always considered by teachers. Even teachers with years of experience fail to present the demonstration so that it will appear normal to those who observe. Failure on the part of students to do the work demonstrated often has been due to the fact that the teacher was facing the group when presenting the demonstration. Therefore the students failed to follow the motions of the teacher and in turn were unable to imitate those motions when assigned to the work.

11. *Do not finish too quickly.* It is better as a rule to give a longer demonstration, carried to a satisfactory completion, than to stop short of the goal and attempt to cover the remainder through oral directions. In demonstrations that are completed too quickly, the proper confidence is not established, and the complete visual image is not received. This does not indicate that certain phases of the work cannot be carried to completion by the instructor after the class has been sent to work. But care should be taken to prevent the impression that the instructor is afraid to try to perform certain processes because of lack of skill.

12. *Check the success of the demonstration.* Learn, before sending the class to work, whether the demonstration has served its purpose. This is probably best done through student repetition of the demonstrated operation or process. To ask the class if there are any questions will seldom be helpful, for students may not know how to formulate them. It is easier at this point to correct wrong impressions than after material has been spoiled and time has been wasted by students. The success of a demonstration depends on diligent and patient checking to see that it is put into operation. At the best, there will be need for assisting in establishing correct habits and encouraging those who lack confidence to go on.

Small-Group Demonstrations

The small-group demonstration is presented to a portion of the class while the remaining members are at work. Such demonstrations are necessitated by one or more of the following conditions:

- A certain number of students in the class may not get sufficient value from the class demonstration, and some repetition may be necessary.
- In making individual projects, the processes covered may vary too much to be of use and interest to the entire class.
- Differences in ability and speed of students may have caused some to be too far ahead to make it profitable for all to follow a uniform demonstration.

• The organization of the comprehensive lab divides the class into sections doing entirely different work.

If there is a separate room where such groups may be taken aside, efficient demonstrations and the reshowing of film loops become much easier. If such instruction must be given in a noisy laboratory, the load on the teacher is increased. In planning and performance, such demonstrations have much in common with those given to the entire class. Since most group demonstrations must be repeated at some other time to other groups of the same class, it is very important to keep complete records of the points covered, in order to be able to present the same material and use the same basis for checking on the achievement of all groups. This suggestion applies to all teaching, for the instructor who organizes data and materials will soon find that much repetition of preparation of material can be eliminated, and the time so spent used to better advantage.

Demonstrating to the Individual

There are various reasons for the fact that, regardless of the efficiency of the general demonstrations, there is always need for teaching individuals one at a time in the lab. Variations in mechanical aptitude and in general learning ability, irregularity in attendance, differences in speed, and differences in problems attacked by the students are some of the outstanding reasons involved.

The teaching of the individual student through demonstration of work on the individual basis is stressed here because there is a tendency to be less thorough when instructing one individual than when dealing with a class or group. Individuals who need instruction at all need the right kind, and whether one or ten students are involved, the problem is the same, namely, that of showing in detail the procedure to be followed for a certain accomplishment in manipulative performance.

A conscientious follow-up of the general demonstration, as suggested previously, and close individual touch with students at all times will determine how much of this type of teaching is needed. If 50 percent of the class give evidence of lacking ability to attack the problem without further assistance, the general and group demonstrations have not been a success, and the instructor needs to revise the procedure. If 90 percent can go on with the work without special difficulty, the teacher may be proud of the job and hasten to assist the remaining 10 percent.

The use of expensive projectors, films, flash card assemblies, slides, and other forms of media may not be justified in some individual cases. By now, the individual should be able to complete the learning of a procedure by consulting with the instructor. Remember also that films, slides, and equipment may be damaged by an untrained individual.

The Lecture

Even a modern teacher who thinks he or she uses the "discovery" method may often lecture by making assertions that dispense information. The lecture is essentially the basic method of teaching outside of involving students in manipulative work, research, seminars, and discussions. In the lab it is useful, provided its place and function are known and appropriately used. Facts to be learned in connection with the work performed are as important as the tool operations involved in the performance. To tell facts to students may be the shortest way to their acquisition of such facts. And, while the argument has been advanced that "telling is not teaching," the lecture method at least offers opportunities for presenting useful and essential facts with a minimum expense of time. In many cases knowledge may be just as effectively assimilated as if students were to go to much trouble in finding it for themselves from reference material and other sources. Because a student takes much time to obtain certain facts is no guarantee of the increased value of such facts.

Whenever possible, the lecture should be augmented by electronic and other aids. They should be keyed to textbook statements and graphics, so that students may note all major points for review. In this way, the interest will be increased in the materials presented. Because various senses are involved, the learning experience may be more beneficial. The illustrated lecture is particularly valuable in presenting information relevant to the techniques and materials required by a work project.

This type of presentation of subject matter must not be confused with the demonstration nor substituted for it. Some teachers are in the habit of telling how to do things instead of actually showing the operations, using tools only to illustrate their lecture and failing to carry out the actual performance of the demonstration in detail. Of course, any good demonstration involves oral explanations, but these are used only as a means for emphasizing the manipulative processes.

A good policy to establish, particularly with students of junior high school ages, is to keep lecturing to a minimum and to confine oral presentations to very brief periods. Instructors who like to talk need to watch themselves on this point. Unless there is a definite need felt by the students, or unless such need can be established at the outset, such instructors should guard against giving vent to their constant desire to talk. Relevant topics related to vocational guidance, past industrial experiences of the instructor, integrated math and science, and industrial production methods provide exciting lecture information.

The following considerations are suggested for the organization of effective lectures.

1. *Scope.* Definite aims should be expressed for student outcomes, and the presentation should be limited to one topic.

2. *Opening.* An interesting introduction will capture the attention of most students and provide a need to want to know more about the topic.

3. *Body.* This is organized in two parts—the information and the method—both must be used simultaneously for presenting the sequential outline of facts in a clear, concise, expository manner.

CHAPTER 10—TEACHING AND LEARNING

4. *Closure.* Just as the introduction is important for the initial motivation of the students, so should the summary and conclusion bring the lesson to a meaningful close. This final portion of the lecture should also allow for questions by the students. If these are not quickly forthcoming, the teacher should take the initiative and address specific questions to individual students in order to evaluate and reinforce their acquisition of information.

Seminars and Discussions

Seminars and discussions are based upon extensive contributions of ideas and expressions by the members of the group participating. The discussion technique, which has been developed to a high degree in dealing with adult groups, is probably the most fully developed form of this method. The seminar is extensively used in training foremen and in training individuals for similar occupations, but it need not and should not be confined to adult programs. In various forms, the seminar is being used for all types of subjects for all ages. It was considered a vital part of the project method of teaching popularized in the 1920s and has been stressed to a similar extent in connection with the concepts of the "creative approach," "integration," "units of work," "student-oriented" teaching, and similar movements of more recent years toward more democratic and innovative teaching procedures.

Although student involvement is essential to the success of a discussion, the teacher's role is not diminished by it, but is only altered in its strategy. Teaching skills that develop motivation, questioning, reinforcement, and direction play an extremely important part in the effective use of the seminar approach.

For the promotion of effective discussion during a seminar, a certain sequence of events is most helpful:

1. *Teacher-class interaction.* This is the initial step in fostering meaningful discussion. The instructor begins by establishing the direction or aim of the seminar.

2. *Teacher-student interaction.* Following the general motivation of the entire group, the teacher proceeds to direct introductory remarks and questions to individual students. This personal involvement of the students in the discussion of the topic provides them with a keener awareness of the main points of the question being considered. Their interest stimulated, each student should contribute to the development of the topic.

3. *Student-student interaction.* The ultimate aim of the seminar is to involve students to the degree where they will interact with each other. Through verbal confrontation, questioning, and peer reinforcement, the students develop their own unstructured learning encounter. It is imperative, at this point, for the teacher to take a somewhat passive role in the seminar. This does not, however, free the teacher from providing necessary direction for the subject under discussion. If the interaction wanes, the instructor must then stimulate the participants by renewing their interest.

This may be accomplished by directing statements to the group and questions to individuals.

A summary of such a planned discussion can later be provided by the teacher or a designated student. This will provide students with the necessary review of the most important information shared during the seminar.

Obviously there should be opportunities for self-expression in the educational program of a democracy. Just how much this method may be used will depend upon the type of work engaged in, the objectives of courses taught, the students' ages, and the general organization of the entire school program.

The Discovery Method

As a method of problem-solving for self-development, the discovery method can be best exemplified by a situation in which the learner identifies an objective, plans for its fulfillment, and works toward it with only limited guidance from an instructor. Consider a student who spends hours alone deciphering blueprints for a project of interest in a magazine and who improvises ways for building it. Under instruction from an expert teacher, the chosen project might be built in half the time, yet the fact remains that the learner has used a method of inquiry not often possible in the more traditional methods of instruction and learning.

The steps to self-development or discovery are quite similar to those used in other problem situations. Recognition and clarification of the problem are of utmost importance in the initial stages of study. A method of solution must then be selected, followed by processing and testing. Finally, if the need is satisfied, self-development is complete. If, however, the problem remains unsolved, the learner will have to pursue another line of inquiry.

Three types of learning activities are usually included in the discovery method.

- *Expository teaching* presents a student with a problem and a method of solution. Some instruction sheets are designed in this way for use in project construction in industrial education.
- *Guided discovery* offers the learner the opportunity to solve a teacher-presented problem. The entire class can then concentrate on the solution of the same problem, with the teacher assisting in the applications and principles. However, each individual student is free to seek his or her own method of solution.
- *Unguided discovery* might be used if the instructor decides not to present a structured problem or suggest possible solutions. This method offers the more intellectually oriented student an opportunity to formulate a project or problem of his own interest and employ problem-solving methodology toward its solution. The question remains as to what extent it is justifiable to expect or allow students of junior and senior high school levels to attempt to discover their own methods of working or to solve their own problems of procedure in doing the work.

CHAPTER 10—TEACHING AND LEARNING

At this point, opinion among teachers is divided. Those stressing the need for the discovery method would say that older methods of teaching industrial education have been too dictatorial, since modern educational theory emphasizes individual thinking and self-expression. Also, industry and business are looking for persons with initiative and originality rather than those who blindly follow tradition and directions. For the majority of students, the development of traits leading to good character and employability is more important than the learning of traditional methods and perhaps even the acquiring of a skill.

Those opposed to the discovery method state that in most instances mechanical work techniques and methods of production have been established through a long period of trial and experimentation and to allow students to attempt to discover new and better ways is a waste of time. It is also suggested that for every person who will be in a position to plan and originate work there will be ten who must follow explicit directions. Many students are more interested in following directions than in discovering methods for themselves. These students may lose interest if made to do their own planning. Finally, following established methods is the best foundation for inventing new ones.

It is obvious, however, that more responsibility should be placed upon students for thinking out and solving a larger number of problems than is commonly the practice. To take the position, however, as some have done, that all assignments in the school laboratory should be solved by research and discovery is obviously a short-sighted viewpoint. In industrial education, there are many accepted ways of doing work, and many established facts that can be stated and accepted with the least expense of time and effort. On the other hand, there are many occasions for putting the students on their own in connection with applications and combinations of tool processes and factual information.

It appears likely that success in the use of this method is dependent to a large degree upon high initial interest on the part of the student in the activity undertaken. It is also necessary that the student possess a creative and inventive mind. Projects attempted should be within the basic experience and ability of the student, and a reasonable length of time should be allowed for concentrated work or the completion of the project. Student success should be recognized with positive reinforcement.

Planning for Instruction

A knowledge of available teaching methods is a valuable asset toward effective teaching. Such knowledge is only a foundation, however, upon which the daily work of the teacher may be built. In the last analysis, teaching success depends upon skillful application of teaching methods appropriately selected and applied in daily contacts between teacher and student. In order to make his or her teaching effective, the teacher must analyze the instructional content and plan the teaching procedure ahead of time for each teaching unit to be covered, regardless of the basic method used. Techniques for lesson planning are presented later in this chapter.

The preparation of the lesson is the final planning step prior to actual instruction. A properly structured and arranged planning sequence will be patterned on the following order.

1. *The curriculum plan.* The formulation of this plan is the initial step in the organization of instruction. Through the establishment of a foundation, the derivation of objectives, the specification of alternative learning activities, and the noting of procedures for evaluation, the overall industrial education curriculum takes form.

2. *The course plan.* This divides the total curriculum into convenient courses of study. These offerings to students are determined through the selection and organization of subject matter. These procedures are analyzed in Chapter 4.

3. *The unit plan.* This type of plan is based on an instructional unit, which may consist of a small area of subject matter, or a theme concerned with subjects such as construction, manufacturing, transportation, and communication.

4. *The project plan.* This type of plan may cover the work of several meetings of the class and several demonstrations or lessons. It is based on the article to be constructed or the job to be completed. In general it is very easy to plan the teaching in this way in that most teaching occurs in demonstration form, in the sequence of operations needed to construct a project. Unit and project planning are discussed in Chapter 6, Program Emphases.

5. *The weekly plan.* Convenient use of the calendar of school days provides the teacher with long-range visualization of course planning for preparation of daily lessons, demonstrations, discussions, and the use of printed and electronic aids. The preparation of a daily school calendar will enable the teacher to see immediately the work and themes that are to be covered during a certain week.

6. *The daily plan.* This plan is organized with reference to the work that is to be covered in one day or one teaching period. It is difficult to use in shopwork, because one cannot foresee with accuracy how much work can be accomplished in a particular work period. For planning of this type, a plan book seems quite appropriate. With this book, it is possible to list each period of the day and keep track of routine details concerning the progress of each individual class.

7. *The lesson plan.* As a preparation for demonstrations, lectures, and seminars, the lesson plan is a very useful tool. A detailed analysis of the necessary operations, or of the facts and principles that make up the individual lesson to be presented, is basic to successful teaching. If this concept is kept in mind, it will then become imperative that such an analysis be made before the teaching procedure is determined.

CHAPTER 10—TEACHING AND LEARNING

Let us assume that a basic demonstration on the use of the marking gauge is planned for a ninth-grade woodworking class. Obviously the teacher will expect to present in proper order all the necessary tool operations as well as a logical order of facts that must be kept in mind when learning these operations and applying them. However, before the teacher can list the instructional procedure for the lesson, he or she must have determined just what the learner must know and be able to do in order to accomplish the aim of the teaching presentation. The teacher decides this by analyzing the desired procedure. The analysis may be based on experimentation by the instructor prior to the presentation, on available analyses made by others as presented in printed material, or, when the teacher has had extensive craft and teaching experience, from memory and mental analysis. The source used is not important, provided the analysis is reliable so that important topics are not omitted, with consequent embarrassment to the instructor.

Not only is it essential to have an analysis of the operations and facts pertinent to the presentation, but these must also be arranged in instructional order before they can be presented.

The Lesson Plan

The lesson plan is essentially a treatment in detail of a small unit of subject matter for presentation to students. No teaching unit can be presented with the greatest measure of success unless the instructor has first developed a plan for his or her teaching procedure.

The course of study furnishes an outline of the major phases of the program to be followed. A comprehensive course may furnish a part of the teaching directions. Nevertheless, it falls upon the instructor to organize the material in complete form before presentation to the class. Only by making definite preparation for each teaching situation can the teacher hope to be successful. Just how detailed the written plan must be will depend upon several conditions, among which are the extent of the teacher's experience in teaching the subject, the particular age or grade of students, the extent to which the teacher is skilled in the correct procedure from the standpoint of mechanical performance, and the ability of the teacher to think through a series of steps without the use of written analysis and steps of procedure.

The beginner who is learning to instruct through directed teaching as a part of his or her professional training is usually required to make extensive plans. The person who goes into teaching without such a period of supervised internship should write out his or her objectives, analysis, and teaching procedure. This will help the teacher anticipate possible problems. Written lesson plans are valuable also in that they furnish a check on one's activities for later reference.

Instruction in any subject area of industrial education will normally be based upon three recognized steps in teaching: *introduction, presentation,* and *evaluation.*

Step 1, *introduction,* refers to the necessity of interesting the learner in the new material that is to be presented and assisting the learner in establishing connections between his or her previous experience and the projected new experience. Reduced to its simplest terms, this means that the teacher must be skillful and resourceful in making the new topic or activity appear necessary and valuable before proceeding to present it in detail. Eagerness to learn should be the normal result of a suitable introduction.

Step 2, *presentation,* deals with the actual teaching procedure in minute detail. Whether a demonstration of tool processes or a topic for discussion is involved, the fact will remain that this part requires most careful planning. The content here comes from the analysis of content previously discussed, but, of course, the technique of presentation must be organized and suited to individual needs. Usually, the easiest way to organize the content is through the use of key words in an outline format. In this way, the plan becomes a guide for presentation rather than something to be read. If a sheet of paper is ruled into two columns, the subject matter can be noted on the left, while the instructional method and/or media can be conveniently noted in the right-hand column. Often it is necessary to use many of these sheets, the number of which is dependent on the length of the presentation.

Step 3, *evaluation,* insures that the student is given the chance to apply what he or she has learned at the earliest possible moment. The student should have opportunity to practice what has been presented in order that the material presented may become a part of his or her own experience.

The practice of testing and observing as indicated in this step must be a definite part of every teacher's activity. It is not satisfied simply by giving examinations at infrequent intervals. Evaluation of every lesson, presentation, or assignment is necessary in order to see whether the students have attained the desired goal.

Review questions and concluding activities can also be listed on this final sheet of the plan. Class assignments and other pertinent details may be noted in the final section at the bottom.

This teaching plan can be used equally well with any one of the teaching methods discussed earlier in this chapter. If instruction sheets, or book instruction, furnish the main body of information or direction, it will be so indicated in making the plan.

It does not take much time to write a plan of this kind. The benefits will far outweigh the effort put forth. If such plans are filed by the instructor, they become equally useful when the work is repeated. They also furnish an opportunity for checking results of the teaching, in addition to being available at any time as an evidence to the principal or supervisor of teaching efficiency.

While it would, no doubt, be of benefit to experienced teachers to write a detailed plan to check their own ability to analyze and organize their work in complete detail, it is obvious that to make such a plan for every lesson or meeting with the class would cause an undue drain on the instructor's time. It should be kept in mind that some organized procedure must be thought out before the work is to be presented. This procedure should be based upon the needs as established through an analysis of the instruction. As has been suggested previously, after much practice the instructor is able to keep this procedure in mind and do much of the recalling and organizing in the presence of students.

It is also true, on the other hand, that teachers become habitually careless about the efficiency of their teaching. In such cases, the plan is omitted not because it is superfluous but because the instructor does not care to draw it up. Supervisors and principals often require plans of some sort. However, whether or not such plans are compulsory, the self-motivated teacher will consider it good professional practice to plan the work with regularity and concise, detailed accuracy.

Annoyances and Distractions

A number of suggestions were offered in Chapter 8 for developing an interest in the work at the beginning of the course or the school year. It is probably easier, however, to establish an attitude of enthusiasm than to maintain it.

Unfortunately, the average school has not yet recognized the student as the center of the school program. In theory, all would agree that the school is organized for the students; in practice, evidence would refute the theory to a great extent. By carelessness, more than by design on the part of teachers and administration, the student is often annoyed, interrupted, discouraged, and otherwise treated as if his or her time and effort were of no real consequence. Too many of these annoyances are allowed to exist in industrial education laboratories. While some of them may be unavoidable, most are caused by lack of planning and lack of understanding of adolescent psychology. The following checklist indicates some of the more obvious annoyances and distractions that tend to kill interest and retard learning in school labs.

Distractions and Annoyances:
- Tools dull or unavailable.
- Power equipment in poor condition.
- Insufficient materials.
- Instruction begun late.
- Oversized classes.
- Class time too brief.
- Inadequate demonstrations.
- Indefinite instructions.
- Too much lecturing.
- Extensive demonstrations.
- Overemphasis on theory.
- Too much related and technical information.

TEACHING INDUSTRIAL EDUCATION

- Repetition of information and toolwork.
- Difficult manipulative work.
- Obsolete projects.
- Teacher lacking mechanical skills.
- Mannerisms of teacher detract from instruction.
- Students required to work on too many school projects in lab.
- Instructor working on personal project in lab.
- Facility poorly arranged.
- Inadequate lighting.
- Lack of work stations for all students.
- Lack of locker space.
- Maintenance persons working in lab.
- Outside noises and distractions.
- Student inactivity.
- Problem students in class.
- Excessive number of rules.
- Teacher showing favoritism.

Special attention is directed toward the control of personal mannerisms. Such nervous habits as the frequent clearing of one's throat, the rubbing of the chin or nose, or rapid pacing back and forth at the front of the classroom can be very distracting to many students. Similarly, the fingering of coins, chalk, keys, small tools, or pencils is annoying during presentations. Detection and treatment of these behavioral habits are possible through self-awareness and instructional improvement clinics.

Techniques for Maintaining Effectiveness

The following suggestions are offered for maintaining teaching effectiveness and sustaining it at a high level over a long period of time:

- Have planned instruction ready for presentation to each class.
- Call class together at beginning of period.
- Make each presentation different from that of the day before. This can be done by varying the subject matter or its manner of presentation.
- Use chalkboard sketches to stimulate interest.
- Use a variety of teaching materials. (See Chapter 11 for a discussion of media.)
- Draw upon popular magazines, motion pictures, and newspapers for examples of applications to work that students are doing.
- Ask questions to stimulate thinking and sustain interest.
- Assign work so that each student can experience success.
- Present difficult, but interesting, problems for solution by the class.
- Encourage problem solving through independent study.
- Give recognition to student effort.
- Allow the work of the class to progress as quickly as possible.

Student interest in instructional delivery by the teacher is heightened through the initial removal of distractions in the area where the teaching is

CHAPTER 10—TEACHING AND LEARNING

to take place. The teacher is then in a better position to gain and hold all students' attention. The teacher should always try to look directly at students while speaking, and have a well-organized plan of instruction supported by information, media, and references as needed. The teacher should be ready to admit fallibility when asked a question to which he or she does not know the answer. The teacher's voice should retain a conversational tone and volume unless variations are desirable for emphasis. Note taking should be encouraged, since it prompts students to refer to textbooks outside of class. It also aids students in courses in which there are not enough textbooks for outside study.

Evaluation of Instruction

Whether the teacher is working directly under a supervisor or not, it is a good practice to use some means of checking at regular intervals upon the success in teaching the material outlined in the teaching plans. A more complete treatment of evaluating teaching efficiency appears in Chapter 15. It seems, however, that some type of checking and report sheet is a distinct complement to the teaching plan, and for this reason it is mentioned here. A form for this purpose which has been used with apparent success in evaluating student teachers under the author's supervision is furnished in this connection and is illustrated in Fig. 10-1.

Similar formats are used in many school systems for evaluation by curriculum coordinators, department chairmen, principals, and superintendents. Self-evaluation of instruction is also quite possible when this form is used in conjunction with videotape recordings of lectures, demonstrations, and seminars. The most important portion of the evaluation sheet and process can be the comments. For this reason, the right half of the sheet provides the supervisor ample room for suggestions for improvement to be referred to during the lesson critique. Depending on individual preference, plus, check, or minus signs can be used in place of the 5-, 3-, and 1-point system of evaluation. Final evaluation is still possible when the signs are keyed to numbers.

DISCUSSION QUESTIONS

1. What additions would you make to the suggestions for a successful demonstration presented in this chapter?

2. Under what conditions should the teacher call upon students to make demonstrations before the class?

3. Are demonstrations of trade methods always feasible or desirable in the school lab? Why?

4. A student begins four weeks late in a class in electrical work. Is it better to start the student from the beginning or to let the student go with the class as far as possible? Why?

5. List topics which you think can best be taught by the lecture method.

6. How could industry and technology be used for the core in the junior high school curriculum?

TEACHING INDUSTRIAL EDUCATION

EVALUATION OF INSTRUCTION

Topic _____

Teacher _____ Class _____

Criteria	Appraisal			Comment
I. The Teacher:				
Appearance	1	3	5	
Enthusiasm	1	3	5	
Voice	1	3	5	
Actions	1	3	5	
Organization	1	3	5	
II. The Presentation:				
Objectives	1	3	5	
Introduction	1	3	5	
Content	1	3	5	
Method	1	3	5	
Media	1	3	5	
Summary	1	3	5	
III. The Class:				
Arrangement	1	3	5	
Control	1	3	5	
Enthusiasm	1	3	5	
Involvement	1	3	5	
Evaluation Key	DEFICIENT	ACCEPTABLE	OUTSTANDING	Total Supervisor
65–75 Outstanding				
40–65 Acceptable				
15–40 Deficient				Grade Date

10-1. Instructional evaluation format.

CHAPTER 10—TEACHING AND LEARNING

7. Discuss teaching methods other than those mentioned in this chapter.

8. Explain what is meant by the "student-oriented school."

9. To what extent do you feel that integration of courses may be carried out in teaching industrial education?

10. How should one deal with the student who always wants to do things in a way different from that shown in the demonstration?

11. What method or methods of teaching will best promote problem solving and discovery on the part of the students?

12. In planning a lesson for a new group, what means would one have for determining what the group already knows.

13. Why should students be allowed to make up their own procedure sheets?

14. Write a teaching plan on some topic involving the seminar method. Follow the style of the comprehensive plan presented in this chapter.

15. Compare the relative length of discussion with the time typically allowed for manipulative work in industrial education.

16. Name five magazines in which the teacher would expect to find suggestions for industrial education projects.

17. List ten teaching topics which would lend themselves to the use of the seminar method.

18. How much time should a lab teacher have for preparation as compared to a teacher of mathematics?

19. What can industrial educators do to impress upon principals the need for scheduled time for preparation of daily work?

ADDITIONAL READINGS

Allen, Dwight W., and Seifman, Eli, eds. *The Teacher's Handbook.* Glenview, Illinois: Scott, Foresman, 1971.

Baird, Ronald J. *Contemporary Industrial Teaching.* South Holland, Illinois: Goodheart-Willcox, 1972.

Cenci, Louis, and Weaver, Gilbert G. *Teaching Occupational Skills.* 2nd ed. New York: Pitman, 1968.

Larson, Milton E. *Teaching Related Subjects in Trade, Industrial and Technical Education.* Columbus, Ohio: Charles E. Merrill, 1972.

Littrell, Joseph J. *Guide to Industrial Teaching.* Peoria, Illinois: Chas. A. Bennett, 1970.

Pautler, Albert J. *Teaching Shop and Laboratory Subjects.* Columbus, Ohio: Charles E. Merrill, 1971.

Silvius, G. Harold, and Curry, Estell H. *Managing Multiple Activities in Industrial Education.* 2nd ed. Bloomington, Illinois: McKnight & McKnight, 1971.

Silvius, G. Harold, and Curry, Estell H. *Teaching Successfully in Industrial Education.* 2nd ed. Bloomington, Illinois: McKnight & McKnight 1967.

Chapter 11
Media and Technology

Emphasis on Learning

The teacher's role is in a period of transition. Since the teacher is now to be a facilitator of learning, it is important that he or she plan and provide opportunities and activities relevant to student involvement. These opportunities and activities should stress student participation, and hold formal supervision and control of the ongoing educational experience to a minimum.

The "open-concept" philosophy of school organization promotes the self-development of the learner under the guidance, but not the explicit direction, of a teacher. The teacher becomes a learner also, and discoveries are made as a cooperative venture.

Generally, it is possible to increase the effectiveness of teaching and learning through the incorporation of many types of media. Often, teachers feel there are many positive contributions that can be realized since media tend to:

- *Reduce verbalism*—by taking advantage of multiple approaches to sensory involvement.
- *Provide perceptual uniformity*—by including samples, photographs, and diagrams of the object being described.
- *Provide realism*—through experiences with actual materials.
- *Add interest*—since the student visualizes the topic under discussion.
- *Improve comprehension*—as a result of multi-sensory experiences.
- *Motivate activity*—through the use of instructional devices.
- *Reduce failure*—by presenting an interesting and informative learning opportunity.

Regardless of the above, many teachers feel justified in failing to make use of media in their instruction. Reasons for such action can be attributed to:

- *Excessive time*—wasted in the ordering, setup, administration, and scheduling of media.
- *Technical assistance usually unavailable*—especially when the equipment breaks down.
- *Inconvenience in use*—for it takes a great deal of time and effort to plan, order, and prepare materials and equipment. Often films do not arrive on time. Sometimes the efforts are not worthy of the educational outcomes.
- *Depersonalization of instruction*—contributed to by the use of media devices and materials.

CHAPTER 11—MEDIA AND TECHNOLOGY

While it is true that the use of media usually requires more work on the part of the instructor, students often find the results more interesting and enjoyable. The main reason for systematic education is student learning. The main concerns of the professional industrial educator should be how, when, and where that learning can better be facilitated.

The history of teaching and learning has been marked by an emphasis on the acquisition of facts. This stress on information retention necessitated the use of written materials. During the early 1800s, the chalkboard became a permanent fixture in most school rooms. Later, such additions as bulletin boards, projects, and exhibits extended the environment of the learner, and "teaching aids" came into common use.

Not until recent years, however, has there been a decided expansion in the concept and outlook toward this area of education. The research findings of learning theorists, combined with current developments in electronic and photographic instrumentation, have broadened the horizons of the student through a variety of more meaningful sources of sensory involvement in the teaching-learning situation. Contemporary instructional practice emphasizes the act of communication as an exercise in dialogue between the learner and the environment. To foster such conversational interaction, many forms of instructional media have been developed as the "communication tools" of the classroom. Because of the proliferation of these tools, they have been organized for study into the categories of *printed, display, projected,* and *recorded* types of media. Before proceeding to a discussion of each of these categories, it is important for the teacher to become aware of the following principles of use for all types of media.

1. *Selection.* Instrumental aids to classroom communication should only be used when appropriate to the specific situation. During seminars, for instance, samples will usually enhance conversation, while a full-length film may inhibit dialogue. Lectures, on the other hand, can be improved when the instructor incorporates projected and recorded materials to fortify the basic monologue.

2. *Preview.* Whether the materials are commercially or personally produced has little bearing on the fact that all should be viewed prior to use in order to determine their capacity to clarify or amplify the subject under study. Once this quality has been established, timing should be considered. The inclusion of media, scheduled throughout a lesson, should be an organized activity. Just as planning and rehearsal are essential to drama, so too are they essential to effective teaching.

3. *Utilization.* If the first two steps have been taken into consideration, successful use of the media is usually assured. However, it should be remembered that each type of medium necessitates special room and class arrangements. Window light, for example, can impair the students' ability to see a film. Students may have to be placed in certain seating patterns to assist the teaching-media strategy. The effective use of instructional ma-

terials, the tools of communication, can assist both the teacher and the student in the learning activity.

4. *Evaluation.* Following the lesson, it is important for the industrial educator to determine the contribution made by the instructional device. Whether or not the materials improved the teaching and the learning should be assessed and appropriate action taken as a result. Either the media should be retained, altered, replaced, or discarded. This evaluation is most efficient if carried out soon after the lesson. If materials that have been used in a learning activity are filed without recommendations, errors in content, composition, or use may occur.

Printed Media

Learning is a continuous process. Activities, activity guides, and materials to aid in continuous intellectual growth of the student beyond the teacher have been devised throughout the history of education. One of the earliest was the textbook, long considered functional, supportive, and preparatory to the in-class activity. Since books were generally unavailable in the early years of industrial education, many teachers authored their own instruction sheets. Even with the current proliferation of texts, visuals, and media of all types, students still find "handouts" invaluable aids to achievement in class, laboratory, and home study.

In more recent years, programmed materials have provided a method of self-instruction for intrinsically motivated students. Such materials are available in many subject areas. Learning activity packets, or "LAPs," also offer the student another opportunity for independent study and work. Each of the previously mentioned materials and methods is discussed in detail in this section. In addition, descriptions of the most common duplication processes are presented for general knowledge.

If an entire class has low reading ability, graphic materials can be used to increase student understanding. Industrial educators have the opportunity to introduce these students to interesting magazines and pamphlets designed to motivate them to read. Many corporations have developed pictorial pamphlets concerned with contemporary developments in industrial materials, processes, and products. Whereas textbooks provide a structure for curriculum development and implementation, instructor-prepared sheets and commercially developed booklets also help to meet the relevant needs of individual students.

Books for Industrial Education

A dependence on the printed, illustrated page as the chief means of offering classroom instruction has historically been the standard method of teachers. Recently, however, the value of the use of only the textbook has been seriously questioned. In the fields of industrial education, the method of teaching by means of a textbook has been less practiced than in some other subjects, yet there are many valuable uses for book assignments in laboratory-oriented instruction.

CHAPTER 11—MEDIA AND TECHNOLOGY

Books are of value in the classroom because they:
- *Encourage the covering of a definite scope of work* with the most important subject matter enclosed in one handy volume.
- *Check the instructor* and his or her methods and practices with those suggested in the text.
- *Fix the responsibility on the students* for the acquisition of a minimum amount of information and knowledge.
- *Provide practice in reading,* so necessary as students read and interpret technical materials in all phases of their careers in later life.
- *Specify standards,* methods of procedure and design, insure accuracy of terms, and identification of long-range trends and concepts.
- *Assist in teaching* by enabling the instructor to give more attention to the auxiliary details, thereby relieving the teacher of the responsibility for imparting routine information.
- *Become an economical investment,* as there is never sufficient time for doing all the work that the willing teacher sees. A book of moderate cost will save time for the teacher to the actual value of many times that sum.

Books for industrial education should not be used to take the place of personal instruction. When the use of a book causes the industrial educator to withdraw to the desk or office, such a book has probably caused more harm than good. Effective and efficient use is essential. All the published materials available in the field may be classified as *textbooks, project books, laboratory manuals,* or *reference books.* Each type has its own unique place for assisting in teaching, learning, and making a particular contribution to student development.

Textbooks. These books usually furnish the fundamental information regarding the subject matter to be covered. In them should be found general information pertinent to the subject as well as detailed explanations covering mechanical operations. This information is often supplemented with examples of activities and laboratory projects and problems. In addition to presenting technical information, some textbooks are fully illustrated, often in color, and are as attractive as any visual aid.

Project books. These are books that illustrate projects for construction in the laboratory. Drawings are usually accompanied by photographs and specifications. Often the author also uses a convenient worksheet format to indicate directions for processing. Books of this type are most popular with industrial educators who lack a variety of project ideas or who feel unsure of their ability, training, or aptitude for making original designs.

Laboratory manuals. A manual usually furnishes detailed instructions, directions, or procedural steps for the work to be done and makes these directions apply to specific, prescribed projects or processes. Such books may also include bills of material, drawings, lists of necessary tools, and other pertinent data. Series of job sheets covering an established set of problems or projects are sometimes expanded into this type of book so that the student receives working directions at the same time the scope of the work is prescribed. In many respects, the organization of these manuals is similar to that of the well-known physics and chemistry manuals used in schools. Lab manuals, or "workbooks," have found increased popularity in electricity, electronics, and power mechanics classes.

Reference books. Reference books fall in a different classification from any of those mentioned so far. Their place is in the department or laboratory library, and their principal usefulness is in connection with immediate needs for information. They are valuable to students and teacher alike for obtaining data of the related-information type, or for solving problems or determining methods of procedure. Within this category are included catalogues and manufacturers' instructions regarding scope of work and special uses of machines and equipment.

Instruction Sheets

Instruction sheets were originally developed and used in connection with vocational classes under the title of "job sheets." The content of these sheets was organized for the purpose of analyzing and presenting instruction in printed form, thereby enabling the learner to proceed with less personal attention from the teacher.

The introduction of instruction sheets into the junior-high industrial education program was probably stimulated by the organization of the comprehensive industrial laboratory and the increased emphasis upon a larger variety of experiences to be offered. They have also been accepted as a teaching device in practically all other types of industrial education classes, including many evening adult programs in trade and technical work.

It should be kept in mind, however, that teaching through the use of instruction sheets has its limitations. While such sheets constitute a valuable teaching device, it is not intended that they should supersede other forms of instruction. The instructions must be prepared and the work organized with this specific method of teaching in mind. Difficulties and disappointments are sure to follow the attempt to make instruction sheets replace lectures, seminars, and demonstrations, or to use them without corresponding adjustments in class organization.

When instruction sheets are properly written and effectively used, they offer a number of advantages as a method of instruction.

- *They offer a greater variety of work,* usually not possible by individual, personal instruction.
- *They save the time of the teacher,* which can then be used to perfect other phases of program management.
- *They save the students' time,* that would otherwise be used in waiting for the instructor's attention.
- *They maintain student interest,* since students are able to proceed with work without waiting for demonstrations and instructions.

CHAPTER 11—MEDIA AND TECHNOLOGY

- *They furnish printed directions,* which, if followed, should insure success.
- *They leave students largely on their own resources,* a means of emphasizing initiative and self-reliance.
- *They provide a means of review* concerning lectures and demonstrations.
- *They furnish uniform instructions* for the progress of all students.
- *They emphasize a single unit of work,* providing concentrated activity toward fulfilling a specific goal or small number of objectives.

If the instructional materials are not well-written, or if the instructor does not have the work properly organized, he or she has failed to appreciate the real uses and purposes underlying this method of teaching. Experience in organizing material for instruction sheets and using instruction sheets in the teaching process has resulted in the development of *job sheets, operation sheets, information sheets,* and *assignment sheets.*

Job sheets. Job sheets are designed to give detailed instruction and steps of procedure for doing a complete piece of work or performing a job which would normally require a variety of operations. If written for persons with limited background, they may include the following:

- A brief description of the job to be done.
- A list of tools and materials needed.
- A list of steps of procedure.
- Drawings and illustrations needed to clarify the job.
- References to other instruction sheets for other sources of information.
- Questions that will measure and add to the student's understanding.

The job sheet is usually constructed on the supposition that the worker has basic knowledge of the use of tools or will get it elsewhere. The job sheet approach is widely used in presentations of "do-it-yourself" projects in popular magazines. Such projects may be simple, such as repairing your kitchen faucet. Other projects may be difficult, such as building a new addition for your house.

Operation sheets. The operation sheet differs from other instruction sheets in that it is based upon an operation, or manipulative performance, and not on a job. It can be used in all types of teaching where the instructional area to be covered can be analyzed into units of performance such as "how to cut a miter," rather than "how to make a picture frame;" or "wiring an edge," instead of "making a drinking cup." The following are typical items appearing on an operation sheet:

- A statement of purpose for the operation.
- Illustrations to clarify procedures.
- Detailed steps of procedure.
- Questions to provoke thought and to clarify understanding.

Information sheets. This type of sheet is made to cover some topic of information, and does not usually deal with performance or manipulative procedures. Information sheets include:

TEACHING INDUSTRIAL EDUCATION

- Textbook and reference material, organized in small units and arranged to deal with the needs of certain age and ability levels.
- Related information.
- Occupational information.

Any of the facts to be learned in connection with industry and technology offer opportunities for the use of this type of sheet. One of its values lies in the fact that it may be made up in such a way that it serves the needs of an individual class better than would a standard textbook. The information sheet also presents a small unit of information segregated from the text or reference book.

Assignment sheets. The purpose of assignment sheets is to give directions for specified work and procedures to be undertaken by the student. Involved here are:

- Assignments for investigations and written or oral reports.
- Directions for procedure in selection, planning, and construction of projects.
- Directions for making up procedure arrangement cards or charts.
- Assignment of personnel in cooperative and group projects or the establishment of a problem for individual research.

The use of this type of written instruction is more valuable than oral instruction in that both teacher and student have a record of the assignment, and repeated reference can be made to the instructions.

Programmed Materials

Industrial educators have used programmed, or "self-instruction," materials for many years. Many instruction sheets were designed with self-study in mind, to further learning without the direct influence of the teacher. Programming is based on the tutorial system of instruction, or a "one-student-to-one-teacher" learning team. Although there are values inherent in the tutorial method, an actual one-to-one student-teacher ratio is unrealistic, due to the expanding student population. As an alternative, much programming has been done to promote a simulated tutor-student relationship.

Programmed materials should be considered for inclusion in the industrial education program for the following reasons:

- *They provide for more individualized instruction.*
- *They actively involve students in learning through reading, answering, and interacting.*
- *An individual rate of speed characterizes student progress.*
- *Only essential subject matter is included in the program.*
- *Information is sequenced for steady progress.*
- *Repetition can be designed into the format for spaced review.*
- *Knowledge of results is provided by immediate feedback through a self-evaluation of responses.*

CHAPTER 11—MEDIA AND TECHNOLOGY

Most materials are based on a four-step design providing:
1. *Subject matter*—the information to be learned.
2. *Questions*—a stimulus necessitating immediate recall of facts along with some provision for writing an answer.
3. *Knowledge of results*—the correct response to the question providing immediate feedback.
4. *Reinforcement*—encouragement to progress to new material, or remediation and review, depending on the correctness of the answer given by the student. This sequence is used in both linear and branched programming formats.

Linear format. In this arrangement, the student reads a short presentation of subject matter. Immediately following the paragraph or two, a question is asked regarding the information. Usually, only one or two words are required in the answer to be written in the blank provided. The student is then allowed to check his or her answer with the correct one marked below or printed elsewhere. The student is promptly notified of the correctness of the response. If the answer is correct, the student may be congratulated in the text and encouraged to proceed to the next paragraph of information. Should the answer be incorrect, the student is instructed to review the material until he or she can derive the correct answer. See Fig. 11-1.

The linear format is the most convenient for teachers to construct. Often, well-written instruction sheets (as described previously) form the basis for a teacher-made program. The following is a sample of a linear program dealing with terms commonly used in architectural design and construction. Only a few frames of subject matter are shown. These would be part of a larger programmed sequence. See Fig. 11-2.

Branched format. In the branched, or intrinsic, program design there is a similar presentation of material to be learned by the student. A question with a multiple choice of answers usually follows. Should the student select a correct response, he or she is rewarded and directed to go on to further learning. An incorrect response usually provides an explanation of the student's error along with remedial information designed to alter the misunderstanding. Eventually, the student will be routed into returning to basically the same information for relearning. See Fig. 11-3.

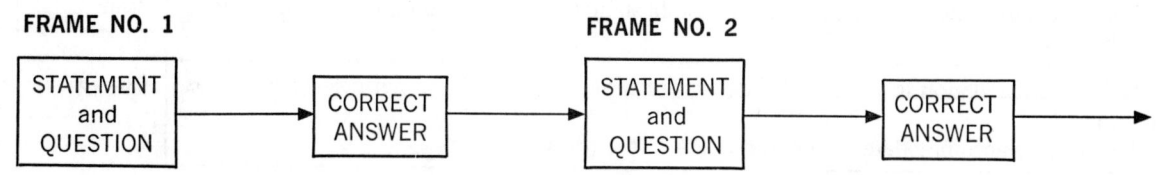

11-1. Linear program format. With each statement of information, a related question is asked. From all the possible answers a student might provide, only one is correct. This response will allow the student to proceed to the next frame in the program.

TEACHING INDUSTRIAL EDUCATION

Mathematical computations can be conveniently learned through the use of branched programs. Following is one frame from a woodworking program. See Fig. 11-4.

The most likely, or most common, incorrect responses must be presented as alternate answers. In this way, student errors can be corrected through an explanation of the misunderstood information.

Programmed materials come in a variety of formats. Books and machines may be purchased or pamphlets and loose-leaf sheet lessons may be written by the instructor or a group for a particular unit of instruction and duplicated for use by the students.

In order to prepare a beneficial learning program, you should follow certain steps.

1. *Analyze the subject matter* to determine the amount of information to be included.

2. *Specify the behavioral objectives* expected of the students.

3. *Plan the sequential program outline* with material arranged in an order of increasing difficulty.

4. *Compose the final test,* keeping in mind the originally stated objectives.

5. *Construct the individual frames,* introducing new material and asking related questions in each.

6. *Attempt to revise the program* with students, in order to eliminate imperfections.

7. *Complete the tested program by duplicating it* for general utilization in the instructional program.

When considering the many factors involved in relating a house to the land, the architect must draw a plot plan. This carefully locates the house on the site. The builder is then responsible for laying out the exact location of the foundation hole (excavation) by using the _____ plan.	plot
The foundation is the entire below-ground concrete structure used as a support for the house. The house rests on the _____, which must be large enough for its support.	foundation
Telescopic transits are sometimes used to lay out foundation limits. The builder uses the _____ for establishing the building's outline in place of batter boards and strings.	transit
When the foundation is laid out, the digging of the _____, or cellar hole, takes place. This usually accommodates the entire limits of the house.	excavation

11-2. *Linear program sample. While reading such a program, the student covers the answers with a piece of paper. Once the student has written the answer, he or she then moves the paper to reveal the correct answer, providing an immediate evaluation of the response.*

CHAPTER 11—MEDIA AND TECHNOLOGY

Programmed materials can be used for total teaching in some situations. This is especially appropriate in independent study and correspondence coursework. More commonly, programmed learning is used for enrichment activities, remedial instruction, or for making up work missed through excessive absence. In the traditional teaching-learning situation, time is a constant with performance by individual students as the variable. In programmed learning, however, time becomes the variable with performance as the constant. All students will learn the same material. Some will simply take longer than others.

Learning Activity Packets

The transition from general to individualized instruction necessitates consideration of many fundamental alterations in the planning and operation of traditional class and laboratory activities. Programmed materials, as previously discussed, offer one method of self-instruction. Another method is commonly known as the "LAP," or *learning activity packet.* The LAP is a packaged combination of instruction sheets, lesson plans, text references, and testing instruments.

Before the LAP can be used to the best advantage, however, the subject matter must be organized into a series of small units, limited in scope, and sequenced for continuous mastery. Basically, it provides a student-oriented plan of action, including (1) a rationale, (2) behavioral objectives, (3) a performance contract, (4) a self-administered pre-test, (5) activity guides, and (6) a teacher-directed post-test.

1. *Rationale.* Included in this introductory statement are the scope of the LAP and the reasons for studying the material or participating in the

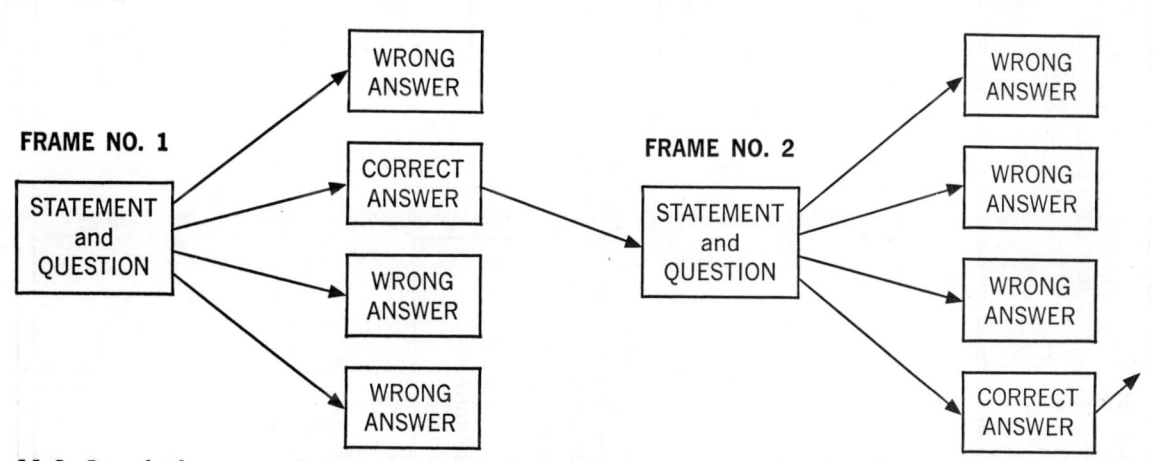

11-3. *Branched program format. Following each statement and question, a series of possible answers are presented to the student. Each wrong answer provides a reason and remedial work before directing the student to the original information. After each correct answer, the student is reinforced by encouragement to proceed to new information.*

BOARD MEASURE

Now that you know how to use the parts of the board-footage formula, solve the following problems using either $\frac{T'' \times W'' \times L''}{144}$ or $\frac{T'' \times W'' \times L'}{12}$.

Calculate the total board footage for a desk top that measures 22" wide, ⅞" thick, and 3' long.

A. 0.40 b.f. → Wood that is less than one inch thick should be figured as one inch in calculation. You also used the wrong denominator in the formula. Try the problem again.

B. 0.45 b.f. → When dividing by 144, all figures in the numerator must be in inches. Try again.

C. 4.8 b.f. → Board thicknesses of less than one inch should be considered as one inch in computation. Try again.

D. 5.5 b.f. → Very good. You came out with the correct answer. Now go on to the second problem.

E. 66.0 b.f. → When you use all measurements in the numerator in inches, the denominator should be 144, not 12. Try it again.

11-4. Branched program sample.

CHAPTER 11—MEDIA AND TECHNOLOGY

prescribed activities. As an example, a basic drafting course could be introduced with the statement:

> Hi . . . and welcome to your first course in drafting. Drafting has been used for many years to communicate pictorial messages in business and industry. This first LAP will be concerned with "graphic communication." As you proceed through it, you will learn to sketch maps, signs, symbols, and other designs to convey messages without the use of words.

2. *Objectives.* Behavioral objectives are employed to establish the direction toward which a student should work. The method of composition for such statements of intent is presented in Chapter 5. Since the LAP is designed for student use, all statements should be directed to them, as:

> Upon completion of the activities described in this learning packet concerned with wood-frame house construction, you will be able to:
> - Graphically describe two types of sill construction.
> - Identify (by name and common size) twelve framing members of the wood-framed house.
> - Name and describe five occupations associated with house construction (building trades).
> - Build a corner section of a house (¼ size).

By placing these desirable terminal outcomes at the beginning of the learning activity, the student is able to focus on "where they are going" and therefore can plan the most satisfactory route to completion or fulfillment of the task.

3. *Contract.* At the bottom of the page expressing the behavioral objectives there is usually a place where the student is asked to make a decision. Such a choice is offered to the student so that he or she may select the most desirable and appropriate personal course of action. The statements of a performance contract often follow a pattern similar to:

> If you already feel confident of being able to fulfill the objectives without further study, turn to the pre-test on page 4 and read the instructions.

> Should you feel unable to complete everything described in the objectives at this time, turn to page 5 and begin the series of activities. These have been designed to assist you in fulfilling the objectives.

4. *Pre-test.* Designed as an evaluative instrument for self-diagnosis, this test provides a series of questions that are directly related to previous learning and the specified objectives. Should the student take the test and not complete it satisfactorily, there is no failing grade. The student simply proceeds with the activities. After taking the test, the student can check the

answers with a key provided at the end of the LAP. In this way, the student decides when he or she is ready for the final examination.

5. *Activity.* The design of this section is often quite similar to the design of an assignment sheet as previously described in this chapter. The student is directed to textbook references, filmstrips and loops, slides, transparencies, instruction sheets, and other similar sources to assist with the experience and to develop mastery of the information and skills required in the behavioral objectives. Following the completion of some or all of these learning activities, the student returns to the self-test to check his or her achievement.

6. *Post-test.* Once the self-administered and self-corrected tests have been successfully taken, the student requests the post-test from the teacher. Although quite similar in format to the pre-test, this instrument is taken without any references at hand. It is subsequently corrected by the teacher and used to establish the level of achievement. After an acceptable fulfillment of the objectives, the student is encouraged to continue to new material. In the event that the student is unable to attain an acceptable level of performance, the teacher and the student, through a conference, attempt to diagnose the difficulty and select remedial activities.

Learning activity packets are a method of individualizing the learning process. Rather than forcing an entire class of students to progress at the same rate, they allow each student to master information and skills within his or her own time limitations and capabilities. One student may take an entire year to complete a standard course of instruction, while another may finish in half the time and either take advanced work or change to another course. Mastery of the subject matter and skills is the main outcome of the LAP system.

Individualized learning offers many advantages to students. However, it is not a panacea for all the educational ills of the contemporary classroom. Planning and organization of instructional materials takes a great deal of teacher time, perhaps more than with traditional teaching methods. Minimum reading ability is also an absolute necessity for student comprehension of the written materials. Remember, "variety is the spice of life" for students and teachers. If learning is to be a pleasurable experience for both, a multitude of instructional modes and materials is essential.

Duplication Processes

In order to provide a sufficient amount of written or printed material for all class members, various means of duplication must be employed. Of all the available processes, the two most common are the *spirit* and the *mimeograph.* These methods are most common because of ease in use, comparative low cost of multiple copies, and the potential for volume reproduction. The *electrostatic, thermographic,* and *diazo* processes also have the potential of volume reproduction, but the relative per-copy cost usually limits their use to single copy or short-run duplication.

CHAPTER 11—MEDIA AND TECHNOLOGY

Spirit Process. Spirit duplicating is probably the most used of all available processes in the contemporary school system. Masters can easily be drawn or typed. Corrections are easily made, and the resulting copy is sufficiently legible for short-run instructional materials. The master is composed of two sheets—a front sheet of heavy coated paper, and a backing sheet with a coating of alcohol-base ink dried on the surface. When an impression is made on the front sheet, the ink is transferred from the backing sheet onto the reverse side of the master. Upon completion of the intended design, the master is placed in the duplicator and the copy is transferred by subjecting the master to an alcohol-saturated pad. Usually, masters are only able to produce around one hundred good copies. With careful adjustment of pressure and alcohol flow, more than two hundred copies can be made.

Mimeograph. In the mimeograph process, a stencil-type of master is utilized. The image is cut into the master with either a typewriter (for written material) or an etching tool (for freehand illustrations). After being placed on the mimeograph machine, ink will flow through the etched portions of the master and be picked up by the paper. The resulting copy will be very satisfactory if the stencil was cut carefully. Sheets duplicated in this manner will retain the permanent image due to the use of ink, whereas in the spirit process continuous exposure to light will fade the image from the sheet.

Electrostatic Reproduction. When single copies are desired of illustrations, letters, or any written materials, electrostatic copying is often employed. Most users of the electrostatic process are familiar with the trade names of "Xerox," which employs a transfer method, and "Electrofax," which utilizes a direct method. Both are described below.

The *transfer method* takes place through a sequence of giving a positive charge to a selenium-coated drum within the machine and exposing the drum to the document's image as it is projected through a lens system. Where the light hits the drum, the charge flows to ground. However, the electrostatic charge remains in the image area. A pigmented powder is passed over the surface of the drum and clings to the charged portion, forming a powder image on the drum. Ordinary, untreated paper is placed over the drum and subjected to a charge that is the opposite of that held by the drum. As a result, the charged powder is attracted, or transferred, to the paper. The paper is then heated to approximately 200 °Celsius; this melts the powder and bonds it to the paper. Finally, the drum is wiped clean, ready for the next image transfer. The foremost advantages of this process are that no liquid chemicals are needed, it will copy all colors of ink, ordinary paper can be used for copies, and the duplicates are excellent reproductions of the originals. Major disadvantages of the method are that the machine is very expensive for the low volume user; it does a poor job of copying photographs and halftones from newspapers; the machine is quite complex, necessitating qualified maintenance personnel; and the drum usually requires replacement after fifty thousand copies.

The *direct method* of electrostatic copying has the advantages inherent in a dry process and will also copy all colors of originals. Photographs find much more satisfactory reproduction in this process. The speed is greater, yet the copies are still permanent. A few disadvantages to the direct method lie in its requirement of a coated paper that is heavier than the ordinary type. Thus, the resulting copies can be marred when scratched. The direct method is quite similar to the transfer method, except that the image is formed directly on the paper and does not require the transfer process. The coated paper, treated with dyes that are sensitive to light, is subjected to a negative charge. Next, the paper is exposed to the image through the lens. The light from the non-image area causes the charge on the corresponding areas to be dissipated to ground. This leaves an electrostatic pattern on the paper that matches the original image. For development, resin particles are applied to the paper with a brush. They cling to the charged image areas, are heated, and fuse in that position.

Thermographic reproduction. This method of duplication is best-known for its ease in copying from all inks except those that do not have a carbon or metallic base. New machines are being developed, however, that have the capability of copying inks of every color. Treated paper is used so that, when it is exposed to infrared light, a colored substance results in the image area. The process occurs when the heat-sensitive paper is placed face-up over the side of the original to be copied. Infrared radiation is passed through the treated paper to strike the surface of the original. The rays are not absorbed by the treated copy paper, but instead are accepted by the image on the original (providing the ink has a carbon or metal base), causing the printed area to generate heat and effect a transfer of the image to the heat-sensitive paper. The final result takes place when the treated paper forms a colored compound, completing the duplication process. Some advantages of the process are that it requires no liquids, the copies are quickly and easily made, and the equipment requires little maintenance. The main disadvantage lies in the fact that copies are best made from originals with only certain types of inks, and some of the papers become brittle with age. It is important to note that spirit duplicator masters and overhead transparencies are also conveniently made with this process.

Diazo reproduction. In diazo reproduction, the original to be copied must be printed on a transparent or translucent sheet. It is placed face-up over a sensitized paper. Exposure is accomplished by passing ultraviolet light through the original to decompose the sensitizing agent on the copy paper. An ammonia vapor is used to neutralize the exposed areas and produce a dye in the image areas. This process is used extensively in drafting rooms for "white prints" and "sepia intermediates." The process has also found wide acceptance in the production of multi-colored acetate transparencies for overhead projection. For producing individual paper copies, the diazo duplication method has the lowest cost. Inasmuch as the original must be

CHAPTER 11—MEDIA AND TECHNOLOGY

printed on translucent paper, and ammonia development is involved, the process is somewhat less desirable than others previously mentioned.

Duplication of materials is important to all teachers desiring to use multiple copies in class and laboratory instruction. Before any materials are copied, however, one should be aware of the copyright laws and restrictions placed on such activities.

Display Media

Many types of illustrative materials can be used along with printed materials to assist in conveying the meaning of the message. If the student is given only a verbal description of an article, a mental picture is possible which may, or may not, match the actual object being described. The use of a picture, sample, or illustration of the article may prove helpful. Display media include *chalkboards, bulletin or exhibit boards, posters and charts,* and *models, mock-ups, and samples.* Before proceeding to a discussion of the construction and utilization of these materials, the industrial educator should consider the importance of each of the following five principles.

1. *Simplicity.* This is perhaps the most important principle governing the construction of displays and exhibits. Quality and quantity are inversely related when considering such materials.

2. *Realism.* Display materials are mainly used to help communicate a message. Selection should be made because of the realism and visual accuracy they add.

3. *Attractiveness.* The use of color displays adds greatly to their interest-evoking capabilities. Although two- and three-dimensional materials take considerable time to prepare, the reward for the effort will usually show in the students' attentiveness and achievement. Tasteful use of the principles of design is an absolute necessity.

4. *Readability.* Most display materials are designed to provide a message through visual means, yet the accompanying written explanation must be legible. Selection of bold, plain, type styles is important, as is the selection of the proper type size. Only necessary titles and descriptions need be included, for an overabundance of printed material can detract from the subject.

5. *Appropriateness.* Whenever it is possible, the real or actual article should be used for the display. A photograph, slide, illustration, or model finds considerable use on those occasions when it is impossible to bring the object to the class.

A description of each type of display media follows. Each is considered in relation to the forementioned five principles.

Chalkboard

One of the oldest display devices is the chalkboard. However, because of its inclusion in almost all educational settings, its use has been taken for granted, and misuse often occurs.

Legibility is of utmost importance. Hand pressure must be firm if the information is to be read by the students at the back of the classroom. Clear chalkboard space increases the readability of the written message. All unnecessary writing should be promptly erased. Whenever possible, multi-colored illustrations should be used for clarity and interest.

The position of the teacher is also to be considered when using the chalkboard. If the instructor stands directly in front of the illustration, students will be unable to see the material. In addition, the teacher should write on the top half of the chalkboard so that students in the back of the room can see the material.

Simplicity, as mentioned in the introduction to display media, is also of utmost importance for the chalkboard's effective use. The drawing of difficult illustrations on the chalkboard wastes time, for the drawings will soon be erased and replaced. Many types of projected or printed media would better serve the purpose. However, if it is absolutely necessary for involved drawings to be placed on the chalkboard, they should be drawn before the students come into the classroom. Students tend to become quite restless while waiting for the teacher to complete an intricate illustration.

The chalkboard is especially suited to the display of developmental processes. Applied geometry in technical drawing, for instance, can be constructed in a step-by-step sequence for student comprehension. The solving of mathematical problems by the teacher or the students is also easily carried out on the chalkboard.

Many other types of media can be used in combination with the chalkboard to assist the instructor in the presentation of illustrations and problems. Partially completed drawing problems can be projected on the chalkboard through the use of the overhead projector. The student or teacher completes the missing material with chalk on the board. Perforated patterns, templates, and stencils prove to be invaluable as aids to assist in illustrations which must be repeated in successive classes. Some metal-backed chalkboards have built-in magnets. The magnetic aids will hold items in position on the chalkboard.

Bulletin or Exhibit Boards

The bulletin board also is taken for granted. Rather than being used as a convenient tackboard for hanging everything from fire-exit directions to the weekly hot-lunch menu, the bulletin board can be used as an effective and stimulating addition to the learning environment. Such use is the prerogative of an enthusiastic teacher bent on the development of exciting surroundings as an alternative to instructional routine.

Simplicity should govern the construction of an effective bulletin-board display. Only one idea or topic should be introduced with each exhibit.

The layout design should employ the principles of good design. Unity, clarity, center of interest, direction of reading order, and balance all contribute to good composition.

CHAPTER 11—MEDIA AND TECHNOLOGY

The use of two or three colors in a display usually increases its effectiveness. However, certain effects can be projected quite well with a monochromatic color scheme. More than this number of colors provides a gawdy effect that makes it difficult to identify the center of interest.

Short, bold headings and explanations are considered most instructive. A spontaneous interaction between the student and the exhibit can be elicited through the use of a question mark in place of a period. The lettering style chosen can also contribute to the presentation.

Fundamentally, the bulletin board is a means of advertising. Moving parts and other objects can be included on the bulletin board to increase its effectiveness by attracting the students' interest and curiosity. To foster such stimulation, however, the exhibit must be changed frequently. When the instructor has a new presentation to relate to each instructional topic, the change becomes a natural occurrence. Each new unit of study can be introduced to the class through casual reference to the bulletin board presentation. Often, student interest can be heightened through enlisting their contributions for future exhibits. Many ideas, illustrations, and objects from the students' surroundings will relate to the topic under study.

Posters and Charts

The structuring of one idea into pictorial form on a single sheet (approximately 2' x 3') constitutes a poster or chart. Information on tools, materials, projects, and especially safety, is appropriate to this type of media.

Posters are usually designed to be attached in one position in a lab or classroom for repeated reference. Some bulletin board exhibits can be easily stored when attached to a series of poster cards.

Charts, on the other hand, are portable when arranged in a series and mounted on a stand. Each chart presents an illustrated portion of a lesson, requiring the instructor to turn from the first in a series to subsequent illustrations. Even when a demonstration is at a machine located in the far corner of the lab, visual expression can be provided through the use of charts on a portable stand.

The same construction principles as those considered in other types of display media are also important to the development of effective posters and charts. Composition is important, as is the size of the illustration. Since felt-tipped pens offer a variety of colors, their use will help to make the illustrations more attractive.

Models, Mock-ups, and Samples

In addition to the two-dimensional illustrative types of exhibit materials, many solid objects can be used to assist in the communication of ideas and information. Most of these three-dimensional materials are classified as *models, mock-ups,* or *samples.*

Models. Models are objects that look like the thing they represent. A plastic or wooden representation of a house is termed a model. It looks like the real thing, but is reduced in scale in order to render it of a size practical to be used in the classroom for instructional purposes. Often, extremely small objects can be enlarged in a model for the same visual practicality.

All models should be realistic and accurate. The following sequence of activities should provide the necessary realism:

1. Collect all pertinent reference materials.
2. Determine a convenient scale for proportional accuracy.
3. Make a working drawing.
4. Select appropriate materials such as clay, soft wood, styrene, wire, and plexiglas.
5. Construct the model.

Mock-ups. Although often used interchangeably with models, mock-ups are simply a combination of parts which act like the object represented. Often they have moving parts made from available materials. A mock-up is used to illustrate action or motion only, and is not an accurate scaled model. However, should the instructor choose to combine the realism of a model with the action of a mock-up, the resultant is usually called a "working model."

Samples. Samples, or specimens, are real objects that can easily be brought into the classroom for presentation. Small animals are useful in biology or agriculture. Automobiles are a necessity for effective instruction in power mechanics. In home economics, foods and clothing constitute realistic articles, while minerals and plants contribute to learning in geology and botany. Tools, machines, materials, projects, and plans are typical samples in industrial education laboratories.

Projected Media

Often it is quite difficult to schedule field trips for students and faculty because of transportation problems, the necessity of obtaining parental permission slips, and other administrative details. Should this be the case, the industrial educator would do well to acquaint students with people, places, objects, and activities via the many types of projected media.

Although many types of *slides, transparencies, opaque illustrations, filmstrips,* and *films* are commercially available, it is possible for the instructor to prepare, process, and present many of these materials through his or her own initiative, expertise, and the use of school equipment. Each visual medium should deal with one idea at a time, for an overabundance of extraneous material often confuses the student. All of these materials offer visual identification along with verbal descriptions, either written in the projected image, recorded on tape or discs, or expressed by the teacher. Whenever printing is to be projected, letters should be at least ¼" high to afford visual legibility in the screen image. Just as with most other types of media, imaginative design characteristics employing simplicity, color, composition, and accuracy are of the utmost importance.

CHAPTER 11—MEDIA AND TECHNOLOGY

Since it is easier for students to remember what they see than what they hear, projected materials are perhaps most effectively employed when the teacher speaks only as often as is necessary. Along with this premise, however, is the necessity that the visual medium should not stand alone. In the final analysis, a multisensory system of media utilization will deliver a message much more effectively than any one approach used by itself.

Slides

Perhaps the most popular means of bringing outside scenes, events, and objects into the classroom, slides are easily made and provide a realistic presentation. They can be used for large group instruction with a projector and screen or for small groups and individual study through the use of projection boxes. Flexibility of use is possible in the sequential arrangement of the individual slides.

The most popular of all the available sizes is the 35 mm slide, as projectors are usually made for this 2" x 2" frame format. Also having a frame of the same size are the 127 size super-slide, and 126 or 110 cartridge films. This makes it possible to use these slides in the same projector. Many professional photographers prefer the jumbo slides (2¼" square) produced by 120 size film. It should be noted, however, that these slides require special projectors, storage trays, and accessories, since they will not fit into the standard (universal) 35 mm slide trays.

Many school systems have a great deal of difficulty in scheduling field trips to local industries due to parental pressures, insurance, bus availability, and security measures placed on defense-oriented industries. Industrial administrators often dislike the general inconvenience of large groups of students passing through production areas in their facilities. Rather than having the entire class go to the plant, it is often possible for the instructor to tour the facility alone. With a good camera, the instructor might take the slides necessary for a complete photographic presentation. After developing and mounting the slides, the instructor can acquaint students in the classroom and laboratory with those scenes and activities they would otherwise have seen only on a field trip. The use of videotape recordings, as discussed later in this chapter, offers other suggestions concerning field-trip substitution through media.

Sometimes it is desirable to incorporate charts, diagrams, and other illustrations into a slide presentation. This is possible through the use of a copy stand, which holds the camera in a fixed position, has lights attached, and also has a mounting board for the visual material to be photographed. In this way, illustrations on rather cumbersome poster paper can be photographed and conveniently carried and stored as slides.

Slides are also available from commercial vendors. Topics concerned with industrial organization, tool use, laboratory safety, material identification, production planning, and assembly work can be purchased from textbook publishers, professional organizations, and their affiliates. In many cases, a tape recording or record disc accompanies the slides and provides the audio portion of the presentation.

Transparencies

Having basically the same applications as charts, exhibits, and the chalkboard, the overhead projector with its accompanying transparencies has become one of the most popular types of visual devices in the classroom. Although it takes more time to prepare illustrative materials on transparencies than on the chalkboard, many advantages can be found in the use of transparencies.

Difficult charts, graphs, and sketches can be permanently printed on the transparent acetates in full color, alleviating the necessity of continuous redrawing on the chalkboard. Storage of the transparencies is convenient in a standard file cabinet, and retrieval is easy.

Both the instructor and the projector are at the front of the class. Eye contact is maintained throughout the presentation since the teacher faces the class in dialogue. Most projectors need to be placed only a short distance from the screen to provide a full-screen image. The resultant bright image does not necessitate a darkened classroom, and note-taking and sketching are carried out with ease. While it is quite difficult to mask portions of the chalkboard, information on transparencies can be disclosed as needed through the use of pieces of paper over portions of the image. In addition, should the material necessitate ordering, a separate transparency can be used for each sequential step. These multiple overlays can then be hinged to a transparency frame for presentation in the desired order.

Four processes for making transparencies are the *direct image, thermal, diazo,* and *color lift*.

In *direct image,* the illustration can be drawn directly on the glass stage of the overhead projector with a grease pencil or felt-tipped pen. Erasure is effected with a dampened cloth or tissue. For convenience, a clear acetate sheet can be placed over the stage so that it remains clean throughout the presentation. Tools and materials can also be placed directly on the stage for an enlarged, silhouetted image on the screen.

The *thermal process* may be used to reproduce on acetate illustrations that have been drawn in pencil on clear paper. The master drawing must be made with a carbon-based instrument in order for the thermal process to work (see *thermographic reproduction,* discussed earlier in this chapter). These black-and-white transparencies can be colored with the special felt-tipped pens used in the direct image process. Because of the ease in making this type of transparency, it is the most popular of all the available processes. A variety of colors is also available.

The *diazo process* requires that the master image be opaque on a translucent paper, since the light must pass through the paper to produce an image on the acetate film. An ammonia development is usually required

CHAPTER 11—MEDIA AND TECHNOLOGY

for this material (*diazo reproduction* is also discussed in other portions of this chapter). Many colors are possible and multiple overlays can be constructed for sequenced operations. Many of the commercially produced transparencies are made with this process, although some are now printed on an offset press with translucent inks, which allows for volume reproduction.

Color lift can take place in a variety of forms. First, the magazine illustration to be "lifted" must be printed on a clay-glazed (glossy) page. One way to effect color lift is to spread a coat of rubber cement on one side of a clear sheet of acetate. Lay this side over the picture to be transferred and apply rubbing pressure to force all air bubbles out from between the acetate and the page. When the contact is even, the combination can be soaked in a warm water bath. The paper page will eventually become very soft and separate from the plastic, leaving the ink illustration attached to the acetate. In another similar method, transparent contact paper is used in place of the acetate and rubber cement. Once the contact is made between the two sheets, the remainder of the process is the same. A third way uses a plastic laminating device to firmly attach the magazine illustration to the plastic sheet. Separation of the paper page in the same warm water bath will provide a very good transparency.

The overhead projector can often be used with other forms of media to produce effective channels of communication. For instance, incomplete illustrations can be projected onto the chalkboard, necessitating student involvement in that students may be called upon to complete the drawings with chalk.

Although cardboard mounts (frames) may be purchased, many instructors find file folders very convenient. The image "hole" can be cut from one side of the folder while the other side serves to hold teaching notes related to the particular illustration. Sheets of poster-card stock can also be used. With either of these materials, the cutouts for the image may be fashioned in all types of free-form and geometric shapes, thereby avoiding a "framed" look, which makes some presentations so static.

Opaques   Whenever the instructor wishes to project an illustration from a magazine or book without the bother of processing a slide or transparency, the opaque projector is the most appropriate instrument. By simply taking the magazine or book, and inserting it into the projector, a full-color, large-screen image can be projected for class instruction.

Major advantages of opaque projection are its acceptance of any comparatively flat material or object for projection, full-color realism, and the ability to project an image of an object without the necessity of specially processing or preparing that object.

The necessity of a darkened room is a major disadvantage, along with the awkwardness of the bulky projector.

Because of its inherent capacity to project opaque images, the machine is often used by teachers for assistance in the drawing of large chalkboard and poster illustrations. Although one of the older types of projection devices for instruction, the opaque projector still finds adequate acceptance and utilization in the contemporary classroom and laboratory.

Filmstrips

The use of filmstrips has found increasing favor as a teaching aid. Filmstrips have a definite place in industrial education, provided that the instructor appreciates their proper use. First, the idea of showing pictures for pure diversion and entertainment should be ruled out. After that is done there are at least three classes of pictures that will be found valuable: (1) those that illustrate mechanical operations and processes directly applicable to the manipulative work in the school lab; (2) those that relate technical data and knowledge about materials and manufacturing operations; and (3) those that will enlarge the students' vision with reference to occupational opportunities and employment conditions in specified areas of occupational life.

For many years, filmstrips were made with black-and-white film. However, some of the newest filmstrips employ full-color illustrations and photographs with captions and titles. Many come with records or tapes for the audio portion of the program. Realism is obtained through the use of background music when appropriate, or industrial "noise" in industry-related filmstrips. Although 35 mm film is used for filmstrips, it is difficult for the teacher to prepare them, since standard 35 mm cameras take pictures in the wrong size and direction on the film, and therefore cannot be used in filmstrip projectors. However, special cameras can be purchased for the taking of filmstrip photographs. The standard 35 mm camera is best used for the taking of slides.

There are many reasons for incorporating the use of filmstrips into the instructional program. The projection equipment necessary is easy to position and use. It is also relatively silent, due to the low noise level of the blower motors that cool the high-intensity light sources. When used with audio recordings, the program order is predetermined; and there is a light "beep" that signals the advance to the next frame. Finally, the projection of a filmstrip is a comparatively inexpensive method of informing students in the classroom or laboratory of the activities of industry and technology.

There are some disadvantages in the use of filmstrips, in that they cannot show action or motion, Also, effective projection necessitates a darkened room. Unless the school owns a special 35 mm camera, the teacher who attempts to produce his or her own filmstrips will encounter difficulties. Films are being increasingly used in individual study. They can be placed in a library or media center to be used by the student for completion or review of assignments.

CHAPTER 11—MEDIA AND TECHNOLOGY

Films   Many good films have recently become available for industrial education. Intricate parts of classroom demonstrations may now in many cases be shown more effectively on film than they can by demonstrations on the part of the teacher. Films possess advantages in that distractions from outside sources are eliminated in pictures, and "close-up" photographs can be shown large on the screen. Care must be taken in the selection of films showing work operations and techniques, however. Not all films advertised are likely to satisfy the instructor in regard to methods of working, safety, and other details.

Films giving technical information through depictions of industrial tours are available in greater number and variety than those showing work processes. Here again, selection must be made carefully because often the film is produced largely for the purpose of advertising rather than for giving technical information. The field here has become so rich that it should not be difficult for the teacher to find appropriate selections.

Knowledge of occupational opportunities, an essential part of the education of every student in secondary schools, can be largely acquired through suitable films. In this respect, films with sound tracks are especially valuable, since they can more effectively represent the sounds and activities relevant to certain job situations.

As suggested previously, just to show a few films does not insure that students are realizing significant values from the performance. The following suggestions for using films will indicate accepted procedures:

1. The teacher should make himself or herself thoroughly familiar with the content of the film by studying catalogue descriptions and previews.

2. The film should be evaluated for its contribution to the area of learning under consideration. Here the question should be asked whether the contribution is specific and applies to a single fact or process such as cutting gears, or whether it will contribute to a broad understanding of a subject such as the Bessemer steel process.

3. After the film has been analyzed and its specific value has been determined, the next step is to motivate the students and assist them to obtain maximum benefits from the film. This may be done either by discussion or by preparing outlines and questions.

4. The method of presentation of the film is important. Having selected the film carefully and prepared the students for an educational experience, give the necessary time to make the showing effective. To do this, it is often necessary to discuss the film after the first showing and then show it again either partially or in full.

5. A final check of values received by students is an essential feature in the effective use of films. This checking, which may be either oral or written, will help to correct wrong impressions received from the film and will emphasize the objectives for which the film was shown.

Films may be borrowed from various sources without cost. They may also be produced by the teacher, rented, or purchased. For small school systems, it will be found more economical to rent most motion-picture films of the type that would be used in industrial arts classes. Filmstrips and slides which are to be used in the instructional program will be found more useful if they depict conditions in local industry. This, of course, implies that the subject is such that the processes and facts to be shown are not likely to be changed and made obsolete until a reasonable period of time has elapsed.

Although teachers can make their own films, it is advisable for them not to attempt to produce functional motion pictures without a background of technical experience. Some experimentation, however, will help to stimulate interest because of the "local color," even if the results are imperfect from a technical standpoint.

Many valuable films are available without rental charge from industrial or other firms who offer them as a part of their publicity programs. In using these, care should be taken that the time of students is not wasted because the film is free. The tendency to use films that furnish principally entertainment, with little or no application to the subject or curriculum of industrial education, or to the broader field of industry in general, should be discouraged.

In addition to the standard 16 mm "open reel" types of films, many 8 mm cartridge films have recently become available. These find wide application in explaining a single concept or in making short presentations of ideas and operations. In industrial education, for instance, many of these cartridges provide individual instruction in the use of tools and machines, thus providing more time for personal contact within the class and laboratory.

Recorded Media

For years, background music has provided a relaxed atmosphere in supermarkets and merchandise marts. The educational environment of contemporary schools can similarly be enhanced through the discretionary addition of audio reproduction using radio, records, and tapes. In many schools, broadcasting over the public address system has progressed from scant use during lunch and activity periods to continuous transmission throughout the day in the corridors, lavatories, offices, lounges, and laboratories. Television is also enjoying wide acceptance as an integral part of the total instructional program. Satellites have provided an instantaneous visual link with distant lands and peoples, while videotape has the capacity for recording, storing, and replaying information whenever the instructor desires.

The use of audio and video devices and recordings has expanded considerably with the development of computer-assisted instructional systems (CAI). Growth is continuing at an increasing rate. Similarly, information retrieval systems (IRS) provide the opportunity for school systems to

CHAPTER 11—MEDIA AND TECHNOLOGY

centralize most of the projected and recorded information in one location. Simply by dialing a telephone in the classroom, a teacher can actuate playback equipment in the IRS facility to transmit the desired audio or video recorded message over a closed-circuit network. Home-based handicapped students find it possible to attend classes through similar electronic systems. The advantages of such centralized operations relate mainly to storage, control of inventory, and the lessening of transfer, breakage, and service of equipment and materials. However, for most educational settings, the high cost of equipping and operating such a facility makes it relatively impractical when compared with the cost of projectors, screens, and tote carts.

Audio Records and Tapes   Music, voice, and sound recordings are finding increasing acceptance in the industrial education program. As previously mentioned, background music provides a relaxed setting in the drafting room and laboratory. Programs are available through the public address system if there is provision for FM reception. Otherwise, portable tape players and record turntables can easily be brought to the classroom.

The teacher usually provides the monologue while showing his or her own sets of slides. However, commercially produced filmstrips and slide sets can often be purchased with records or tapes provided for sound track realism. In addition to the oral message, the recorded sounds of the industrial operations and machine processes can be used to enliven slides or filmstrips. With the use of these packaged systems, it is possible to eliminate the captions that were necessary at the bottom of older slides and filmstrips. Since a sound track is provided, the entire film area can be used for the photographed subject and the students can look while listening, rather than spending much of the viewing time reading the captions. Students' attention is focused on one area.

Some industrial educators have found unique applications for the newer, easily operated tape recorders in their instructional practices. Machines and tools produce individually peculiar noises. In the training of auto mechanics, for instance, recordings of untuned engines offer the opportunity for developing the listening skills necessary for the correct diagnosis of faulty conditions in transportation vehicles. Many similar applications are possible in other technological areas.

Records and tapes come in a variety of sizes, materials, and speeds. For instructional media uses, records commonly are available as 12" LP's, in order to include all information necessary for an entire slide series or filmstrip. The specified turntable speed is usually 33⅓ RPM. Tapes are supplied in two formats for classroom use. The older type, called "open reel," is similar to movie film and has to be threaded through the recorder onto a separate empty reel. The newer, compact type comes in self-contained cassettes, eliminating the need for threading the tape in the machine. These cassettes are made with two small reels enclosed within a plastic case. When the program is finished on one side of the tape, the operator must turn it over in the recorder to continue the message.

Industrial educators would do well to develop audio tape recordings to accompany their set of slides. Students could then use the material when the instructor is not present. Also, the entire package could be made available in the library, learning resource center, or information retrieval system of the school.

Videotape Recordings

Since the late forties and early fifties, when television was introduced to the consumer on a wide scale, this communication medium has followed a steady pattern of growth in programming and utilization. Soon after the establishment of the commercial networks and local stations, educators saw innovative applications for the medium in the teaching-learning environment.

Federal legislation in the sixties provided for the development and growth of educational television (ETV). The Magnuson Bill of 1963 underwrote 50 percent of the cost for transmitting equipment for stations employing an "educational" format. Other legislation soon followed, mandating that all television receivers have the capability for tuning UHF and VHF. In 1967, the Public Broadcasting Act provided funds for erecting facilities and transmitting programs of a noncommercial, educational nature.

During this same period, school systems were establishing closed-circuit television systems (CCTV) with the capability of transmitting over cable within a school building or extensively throughout an entire school system. Initially, programs related mainly to providing master teachers and subject matter specialists for all similar classes during the same time period. Whereas it had formerly been necessary for a music, art, or other special subject supervisor to travel throughout a system repeating a major lesson, it became possible to videotape the same presentation for simultaneous viewing. The resultant saving of time could be spent in preparation, consultation, coordination, evaluation, and curriculum development.

The following are some inherent limitations to the instructional incorporation of the television medium:

- *Face to face contact and interaction with students is practically impossible.*
- *Abstract ideas are difficult to present.*
- *The total program usually becomes a vicarious experience lacking physical involvement.*
- *The lack of color lessens realism.* However, color capability in equipment is available at a higher cost.
- *The relatively small picture size necessitates the use of many monitors when addressing a series of classes.* However, for large groups in an

CHAPTER 11—MEDIA AND TECHNOLOGY

auditorium, television projectors have been developed, making it possible to project the image onto the same relatively large screen used for film projection.

The positive aspects of this newer medium far outweigh the problems. Numerous advantages of using television and videotape in industrial education include:

- *The ability to magnify small objects used in a demonstration.*
- *The elimination of distractions since the small field of vision provided by the monitor focuses attention on the presentation.*
- *An unobstructed view of a demonstration for all students.*
- *The possible demonstration of dangerous processes and operations without subjecting students to the hazardous environment.*
- *Bringing the outside world into the classroom or laboratory.* Speakers and industrial demonstrators (who would normally have to come into the school) can tape their presentation at their convenience for repetition according to the class schedule.
- *Providing field trips, via videotape, to inaccessible industries.*
- *The capility for incorporating many other forms of media.* The instructor finds ease in using the overhead projector, chalkboard, charts, slides, models, illustrations, and even book pages in the program format.

Videotape recording equipment (VTR) is presently available in manageable sizes made possible through the miniaturization of electronic components. Capable of showing pictures in either black and white or color, the relatively small cameras and recorders have become almost universally accepted as the best means for bringing the outside world into the classroom. Some cameras operate with battery power and are considered "portable." Those necessitating standard electric current, even though often as small as portable equipment, are considered "studio" or "mobile" models. Most recently, videocassettes have been developed for the recording and playback of color videotapes. Such videocassettes can be played and rewound more quickly than open-reel tapes.

While it is possible for all well-planned programs to take on a professional appearance, portable presentations usually offer a more candid show. Studio productions should be developed with a script, cue cards, directors, technicians, and camera operators. These positions are often filled by students in industrial education. Regardless of the format, it is recommended that instructors always rehearse the program in detail prior to taping. The resultant presentation must be ordered and smooth, since videotape is difficult to edit and splice.

As with all other forms of media discussed in this chapter, videotaping should only be used when appropriate. Media should enhance the learning activity, not detract from it.

DISCUSSION QUESTIONS

1. Would the fact that textbooks are used in all academic subjects be a good reason for using them in industrial education?
2. From what sources may inexpensive material other than books be obtained for industrial education?
3. Make a list of points under which any textbook may be evaluated.
4. How much reading outside of class time would you expect from ninth-grade students?
5. List fifteen books that would be appropriate for a shop library. Choose them from your particular area of industrial education.
6. Show by a concrete example how a textbook may be used to prepare students for a demonstration.
7. What proportion of time would you consider legitimate to take for reading during class hours?
8. Make a list of ten books for either woodwork, metalwork, drawing, or automotive work that have been published in the past ten years.
9. Name some disadvantages in making assignments before the material has been covered in class.
10. Name and describe the two types of formats used in the design of programmed materials.
11. How is it possible for a student to receive positive reinforcement from programmed materials?
12. Describe the usual sequence of events in writing a program.
13. List ten lessons or demonstrations which might be suited to programming. Explain your choices.
14. Compare the composition of a LAP to the parts of a course of study, a unit, and a lesson plan.
15. If a LAP takes a great deal of time to plan and duplicate for class use, how is it possible for there to be more time for student-teacher interaction?
16. Can a complete set of LAP's ever replace all teacher-directed activities in a course? Explain.
17. In the traditional teacher-directed type of instruction, on what criterion is achievement evaluated?
18. On what basis is achievement evaluated in individualized learning?
19. When is it impossible to use the various types of written materials? What possible substitutes might be incorporated into such situations?
20. Describe the uses of the job sheet and the operation sheet. How do they compare? Are they both necessary and interrelated?
21. What are some of the greatest advantages in using written materials for individualized learning?
22. Relate the materials described herein to "discovery learning" as described in the last chapter.
23. Compile a list of industrial firms or sources from which valuable free instructional materials may be obtained for use in the industrial education

program. Cite the type of materials that would be expected from each source.

24. Name and describe five subjects in which mock-ups may be used to advantage.

25. What pieces of equipment can most profitably be "cut away" or sectioned for instructional purposes?

26. With extensive use of overhead projector transparencies, is it now possible to eliminate the chalkboard and bulletin board from the contemporary classroom? Defend your answer.

27. Why are slides the most popular means of bringing the outside world into the classroom? Should every industrial educator develop a slide series of his or her work?

28. What are the advantages of incorporating audio recordings into slide and filmstrip shows in instruction? Are they necessary when the instructor is present?

29. When should media be used in the classroom and laboratory? Describe situations where the incorporation of media will do little to enhance the learning environment.

30. Is it possible to use too many types of media simultaneously? Explain your answer.

31. Compare the advantages and disadvantages of film and videotape recordings. How can each be used for their unique contributions to the industrial education program?

32. Using a course of study with a listing of activities, describe how the various types of media can be used in each situation. Provide a rationale for the appropriateness of the material to the activity.

33. Is the opaque projector still helpful with so many other types of projection devices available today? What types of activities are most appropriate to its use?

34. Describe how exhibit boards and displays can be used to "sell" the industrial education program within the school. How can they be used in the community?

ADDITIONAL READINGS

Brown, James W.; Lewis, Richard B.; Harcleroad, Fred F. *A-V Instruction: Materials and Methods.* 2nd ed. New York: McGraw-Hill, 1964.

Burke, Richard C., ed. *Instructional Television: Bold New Venture.* Bloomington, Indiana: Indiana University Press, 1971.

Calvin, Allen D., ed. *Programmed Instruction: Bold New Venture.* Bloomington, Indiana: Indiana University Press, 1969.

Cram, David. *Explaining Teaching Machines and Programming.* Belmont, California: Fearon, 1961.

Erickson, Carlton W. H., and Curl, David H. *Fundamentals of Teaching with Audiovisual Technology.* 2nd ed. New York: Macmillan, 1972.

Espich, James E., and Williams, Bill. *Developing Programmed Instructional Materials.* Palo Alto, California: Fearon, 1967.

Fine, Benjamin. *Teaching Machines.* New York: Sterling, Bold Face Books, 1962.

Gerard, R. W., ed. *Computers and Education.* New York: McGraw-Hill, 1967.

Goodland, John I.; O'Toole, John F., Jr.; and Tyler, Louise L. *Computers and Information Systems in Education.* New York: Harcourt, Brace & World, 1966.

Haney, John B., and Ullmer, Eldon J. *Educational Media and the Teacher.* Dubuque, Iowa: Wm. C. Brown, 1970.

Horn, George F. *Bulletin Boards.* New York: Reinhold, 1962.

Kemp, Jerrold E. *Planning and Producing Audiovisual Materials.* San Francisco: Chandler, 1968.

Margolin, Joseph B., and Misch, Marion R. *Computers in the Classroom.* New York: Spartan Books, 1970.

Margulies, Stuart, and Eigen, Lewis D. *Applied Programmed Instruction.* New York: John Wiley & Sons, 1962.

Minor, Ed, and Frye, Harvey R. *Techniques for Producing Visual Instructional Media.* 2nd ed. New York: McGraw-Hill, 1970.

Schramm, Wilbur, ed. *Quality in Instructional Television.* Honolulu: University Press of Hawaii, 1972.

Scuorzo, Herbert E. *The Practical Audiovisual Handbook for Teachers.* West Nyack, New York: Parker, 1967.

Smith, Karl U., and Smith, Margaret Foltz. *Cybernetic Principles of Learning and Educational Design.* New York: Holt, Rinehart & Winston, 1966.

Taber, Julian I.; Glaser, Robert; and Schaefer, Halmuth H. *Learning and Programmed Instruction.* Reading, Massachusetts: Addison-Wesley, 1965.

Weisberber, Robert A., ed. *Developmental Efforts in Individualized Learning.* Itasca, Illinois: F. E. Peacock, 1971.

Wittich, Walter Arno, and Schuller, Charles Francis. *Audiovisual Materials: Their Nature and Use.* 3rd ed. New York: Harper and Brothers, 1962.

Wyman, Raymond. *Mediaware: Selection, Operation and Maintenance.* Dubuque, Iowa: Wm. C. Brown, 1969.

Chapter 12
Accident Prevention and Safety

The Importance of Safety

From the time that industrial education was first introduced in schools, the possibility of accidents has weighed heavily on the conscientious teacher. In more recent years, the moral responsibility has been augmented by a degree of legal liability, coinciding with the increasing growth of claims for damage in connection with school accidents. Without attempting to discuss legal responsibilities, it might well be assumed that the safety of the student should, and generally is, the most immediate and constant concern of the teacher. While the rate of accidents is probably not unduly high in most schools, it can be further reduced.

Accident-Causing Conditions

All accidents in which the school or teacher may be at fault are divided into two general classes: (1) those caused by faulty conditions of the room and the equipment, and (2) those caused by insufficient instruction and management. An analysis of these general causes appears in the following:

Conditions of room and equipment which may cause accidents:
- Low ceilings.
- Poor light (natural and artificial).
- Badly located machines, causing interference between operators.
- Failure to mark safety zones around hazardous equipment.
- Unguarded belts, pulleys, gears, and cutters.
- Dull tools and machines, particularly in woodworking labs.
- Unguarded switches.
- Waste and scrap stock on the floor.
- Wrong type of clothing worn.
- Inadequately protected stairways and ladders leading to balconies and platforms.
- Poorly constructed stock racks.
- Lack of ventilation in finishing rooms where lacquer is used, and in rooms where forging, metal casting, or similar work is done.

Insufficiency in instruction which may cause accidents:
- Lack of teacher's knowledge of how to use tools and machines.
- Failure to give adequate preliminary instruction.
- Failure to follow up such instruction and to supervise the initial efforts of the students.
- Allowing students to play in the laboratory.
- Overtime work without supervision.
- Allowing guards to be removed.

TEACHING INDUSTRIAL EDUCATION

- Failure to provide goggles and insist upon their use.
- Allowing experimentation in the use of equipment.
- Failure to establish proper attitudes toward the problem of accidents.
- Failure to check the setup of each machine before allowing operation.
- Failure to provide for adequate ventilation.

Some of these conditions will be further explained in subsequent paragraphs.

Accident Prevention

If it may be assumed that this analysis is acceptable, proceeding to check the lab and one's teaching is clearly the next thing to do. The first group of causes cannot all be remedied at once, if they exist. Low ceilings, for instance, probably cannot be raised. Machines may have to stay where they are for the present. However, poor lighting conditions can be remedied by the installation of skylights and mirrors, and by the addition of proper artificial lighting fixtures. Lighting conditions have been found to have a close connection with accidents. The obtaining of proper guards for pulleys and gears and general guards for machines should be listed for immediate attention. If properly impressed, the administration will supply them without too much delay. Some guards can be made in the laboratory if no other means for obtaining them is available. The tendency to allow school machines and equipment to be more poorly guarded than those used in industrial plants should not be tolerated.

Laboratory Improvement

Dull cutter blades on machines, especially in woodworking laboratories, have probably caused as much difficulty as many other causes combined. Whoever has tried to put a piece of hardwood over a dull jointer or tried to rip on a badly filed or set ripsaw will realize the truth of this. In Chapter 8, stress was laid upon the necessity for conditioning the equipment before school begins. This is an essential step in helping to insure a year free from accidents. It is, however, only a first step. It must be followed by repeated attention to all phases of equipment maintenance, and especially to the matter of keeping all cutting tools sharp. What has been said about machines holds true also with reference to hand tools, although the consequences are usually less serious in case of accidents with the latter.

This brings up the problem of the teacher budgeting time to maintain the equipment. Many machines get into poor condition not because the instructor is careless but because he or she has not set aside time in the program for doing the necessary work. It has been suggested previously that some teachers expect the time actually spent in class instruction to constitute their entire working day. That cannot be if the laboratory is to be safe, and the equipment is to be in condition for efficient work. After all, it is probably much better to put in a little more overtime than to be in a constant state of anxiety regarding the condition of belts, switches, and other items, whose poor repair may cause accidents.

CHAPTER 12—ACCIDENT PREVENTION AND SAFETY

Everyone will agree that scraps and debris on the floor constitute a grave danger, particularly around machines. However, labs will be free of debris only when there is a special place for such material, and when there is full cooperation in depositing debris there. Few teachers are spending the energy necessary to solve this problem.

It is a good custom to mark the working space for each machine on the floor, and to allow only the operator within the marked area while the machine is in use. Mats made out of some nonslip material provide safe footing for the operator. In the absence of these, some paint or glue and fine sand may serve the same purpose. When mats are used it becomes necessary to secure all edges firmly.

The use of charts and signs calling attention to dangers in use of machines, or stating rules to be followed, appears to be of value only up to a certain point. If there are too many signs, they become commonplace and lose their value. They should not be depended upon, for after they have been in place for a while they are not noticed. Whatever subconscious effect they might have is probably of questionable value. To clutter the shop with large, unsightly signs probably does more harm than good.

Instructional Improvement

It is the instructor who is primarily responsible for establishing a safe work environment. The instructor bears the most criticism when accidents occur. Better teaching and better organization will prevent accidents. The most conscientious and able teachers have the fewest charges against them in this regard, barring those cases where students seem deliberately to have forced accidents upon themselves.

In giving instructions to high school students concerning the use of machines it is well to remember that they are accustomed to listening to many rules and regulations. This, however, does not mean that they are in the habit of being governed by all of them. On the contrary, they are likely to be fairly expert in evading rules and "getting by." For this reason it will be of little use to make a few general suggestions and expect perfect adherence to them. Students should have a thorough understanding of the purpose of the rules for their conduct in the use of machines and should see how they will profit by observing them.

It is absolutely necessary that the instructor get the full cooperation of the students, and that they feel the responsibility of the outcome of their own actions while at work on the machines. It is the attitude of mind that prompts students to violate rules and hope to "get by" that plays havoc with them when they get into the lab or out on the job.

Experience has proved the necessity of impressing students strongly with the fact that rules of safety in the shop are not arbitrary. Also, established methods of procedure carry within them the best safety rules.

An introductory presentation of rules of safety will insure the attentiveness of the class during demonstrations in the actual use of the machines.

TEACHING INDUSTRIAL EDUCATION

As soon as the students see that the rules exist to insure their safety and promote efficiency, the goal has been accomplished. The degree of success of the first lesson is a fair index of the job remaining for the teacher. It may, and probably will, take several lessons before the ideal situation is reached or even approached, but a beginning must be made at once.

It is possible that, while an instructor must make a strong impression on some in order to make them sufficiently cautious, there sometimes may be a few students who are overimpressed with the dangers and become inhibited in their actions. If this is the condition, such students must be reassured or their caution constitutes a danger. Skillful demonstrations by the teacher will help to overcome the difficulty. The best remedy is probably some quantity job on a machine. Ripping a large number of boards, or some similar piece of work, will make the person gain confidence in the fact that the machine in itself is not dangerous when properly handled. A sympathetic understanding between students and instructor is helpful at all times.

Student Hazards Adolescents often rebel against rules and regulations. They sometimes desire to disregard advice, to try out new schemes and methods, and to do a job differently from the way the teacher says it should be done. While these tendencies have value and should be recognized in some types of work, every means must be employed to discourage them when power machinery is being operated. There are probably not many better ways of putting a board through a ripsaw or hoisting an automobile than those which have been determined after much experience. Just how to make young students see this is the problem of the instructor. Very firm steps may need to be taken to prevent dangerous experimentation by students using power machinery.

In every laboratory where high interest in the work prevails, there are always requests for a chance to stay after regular class hours. Students who request such privileges are usually the more reliable ones. However, when the instructor has duties to perform outside of the room, the student workers are left alone.

There is danger in this practice. In the first place, such work is usually done at that time of the day when accidents are liable to occur. It has been found in industry that the larger number of accidents happen toward the close of the day. Also, there is a tendency for students to congregate in the lab after school hours whenever the lab is open, and particularly as soon as the instructor goes out. Even though such irregularities are not intentional, they contribute to a hazardous situation wherein student attention is likely to be diverted and accidents are more apt to occur.

Safety Precautions Even after all steps have been taken for accident prevention, it is still wise to think of the possibility of accidents, and to be prepared for them. The teacher, the student, and the school must all be considered. Even the teacher who has satisfied moral responsibility through efficient planning and teaching wishes to protect himself or herself and the school against legal responsibility. In this connection, the safeguarding of students, instructors, and school facilities might require some of the following procedures:

Provide insurance. Some boards of education have purchased blanket insurance covering all types of accidents that may occur while children are the legal charges of the school.

Obtain permission from parents. In many industrial education programs, it is the practice to request the parent or guardian to sign a permit that gives their permission for the student to use machines in the lab and also declares that they will not hold the school responsible for any accidents that may occur. While such a statement still may not legally release the board of education from responsibility, it may make the parent more hesitant to claim damages.

Have a first-aid kit. Every facility should be provided with adequate first-aid material. Antiseptics, bandages, and other simple preparations should always be available for taking care of smaller wounds and for caring for more severe cases until medical aid can be obtained.

Have students pass safety tests. It is recommended that written tests be given to students to test their comprehension of that instruction given regarding tool manipulation and the use of power equipment. In these tests the student writes out the safety rules covering each piece of equipment and writes out steps for completing operations on the various machines. These written test papers are then put in the files of the principal or the board of education. They are kept there until the student and the student's parents have, because of the time elapsed, forfeited their rights to bring lawsuits for injuries that might have been sustained in school. It is wise to remember, however, that passing a test will not guarantee safe use of a machine. A student's habits of safety can only be evaluated through observation, not by written answers.

Have knowledge of first aid. Every teacher owes it to himself and the students to know how to administer first aid to injured persons. With such knowledge, the teacher can safeguard students in severe cases of bleeding or shock. Most cities now offer courses in such work under the auspices of the Red Cross or some other agency. All instructors who lack the necessary knowledge and skill in this regard should acquire it without delay. Small wounds or scratches should always receive immediate treatment and be reported through regular channels provided for by the school administration. All serious accidents should be referred directly to the school nurse or physician for treatment.

Industrial Safety Education

It would seem reasonable to expect that every teacher in elementary and secondary schools should accept the responsibility of giving safety instruction and developing safety consciousness in students. In the industrial

TEACHING INDUSTRIAL EDUCATION

education laboratory, superior opportunities for such instruction present themselves because the program, due to its nature and the type of materials and equipment used, parallels more closely the environment of the home or of industry. It is in such environments that most accidents occur. While the amount of time that should be devoted exclusively to general safety instruction may be a debatable question, it still remains that in the laboratory setting, safety practices for the home and industry can best be stressed in connection with the use and handling of materials such as acid, and of inflammable substances such as paints and finishes. The proper use of electrical appliances might also be dealt with, along with measures for fire prevention. Attention should be called to the various conditions that might contribute to dangerous situations regarding the use of paints, chemicals, and electrical equipment.

The following additional suggestions to the instructor may be of value:

Know the state and federal laws. The instructor should be completely familiar with state laws covering eye safety and the guarding of machines. In addition, the teacher should be familiar with those ordinances that govern any other area of the program such as those included in the Occupational Safety and Health Act ("OSHA") standards. All rules included therein may not apply to schools, but it is well to have the school laboratories conform in full to all regulations that can be put into practice. Such procedure may eliminate embarrassing situations later. The instructor should not feel that he or she has gained if an OSHA inspector fails to visit the school. It is much better to call for the inspector, and to follow his or her recommendations.

Know safety instruction materials. Much printed material bearing upon safety in school activities has become available in recent years. State and national departments of education will either have material of this type for distribution, or will be in a position to refer the inquirer to suitable sources. Many school systems in larger cities have published extensive safety rules and suggestions for local use.

The teacher should be familiar not only with state and national laws covering safety practices, but should also obtain all available suggestions for training pupils in safety habits both in and out of school. Written material on safety should be available to students in the school. Published instructions will seem more factual and authoritative than oral instructions given by the teacher.

Check machines. Get in the habit of checking every new setup of all machines before granting permission for use. This will often be the means of preventing an accident.

Check unreliable students. Some students who may come to the industrial education laboratory are not capable of handling a machine intelligently. Through conversation, however, such students can often give a false impression of their ability.

CHAPTER 12—ACCIDENT PREVENTION AND SAFETY

Check up prerequisites. Although students may state that they have the ability to perform certain machine operations, the fulfillment of definite prerequisites should be insisted upon before any student may work with the machines. Students might be required to demonstrate their ability to the teacher before they are entrusted with the use of power equipment. Often, this is the only way to detect lack of experience. Such early detection will help to insure that the student does not get into difficulty later.

Practice constant supervision. It has been suggested previously that announcements regarding safety practices are not enough. Constant supervision is needed to be sure that exceptions to the rules do not occur. The use of a safety foreman or "engineer" in the class organization, as discussed elsewhere, is helpful in impressing students with good safety practices.

DISCUSSION QUESTIONS

1. Make a complete check of safety conditions in a school laboratory. Write a report that might be given to the administration.

2. Describe the most effective utilization of safety signs in the laboratory.

3. From further readings, make a list of the most common causes of accidents in industrial education.

4. What are some of the means by which the instructor can interest the school board in spending money for adequate safety appliances in the shop?

5. After reviewing OSHA standards, design a form for use in checking safety conditions in a school laboratory.

6. In what type of industrial facilities do most accidents occur?

7. In what type of school labs do most accidents occur?

8. What should be the instructor's attitude toward keeping the laboratory open after regular class hours?

9. Does the fact that the instructor has had extensive industrial experience always mean that he or she will be able to prevent accidents among the students? Explain your answer.

10. To what extent are the schools of your state responsible for students outside of the classroom?

11. Show how lack of a cooperative attitude on the student's part may be a cause for accidents.

12. Make out a form that you would send out for parents' signatures before students would be permitted to use machines.

13. If students are taken on observation trips to industrial plants, what is the teacher's responsibility for accidents that may occur?

14. Make up a list of safety rules for a laboratory of industrial education.

15. In what ways may an instructor protect himself or herself from legal liability in connection with accidents?

16. Has the number of accidents in the school increased or decreased during the past decade? Why?

17. What agency in your state enforces safety in industry? In schools?

ADDITIONAL READINGS

American National Red Cross. *Standard First Aid and Personal Safety.* Garden City, New York: Doubleday, 1973.

Baker, G. E. "Safety in the School Laboratory." *School Shop,* May 1967, pp. 38–40.

Best's Safety Directory: Safety—Industrial Hygiene—Security. 15th ed. Morristown, New Jersey: A. M. Best, 1975.

Doolin, Michael J. "Eye Safety in Schools." *Industrial Arts and Vocational Education,* October 1968, pp. 67–74.

Esposito, Gerard. "Teacher Liability for Accidents in the School Shop." *Industrial Arts and Vocational Education,* October 1968, pp. 63–65.

Kigin, Denis J. *Teacher Liability in School-Shop Accidents.* Ann Arbor: Prakken Publications, 1973.

National Safety Council. *Accident Prevention Manual for Industrial Operations.* 7th ed. Chicago: National Safety Council, 1974.

Peterson, Dan. *Techniques of Safety Management.* New York: McGraw-Hill, 1971.

Simonds, Rollin H. and Grimaldi, John V. *Safety Management—Accident Cost and Control.* Homewood, Illinois: Richard D. Irwin, 1963.

U.S. Department of Labor, Occupational Safety and Health Administration. *Construction—Safety and Health Regulations, Part 1926, OSHA #2207,* 1974.

U.S. Department of Labor, Occupational Safety and Health Administration. *General Industry—Safety and Health Regulations, Part 1910, OSHA #2206,* 1974.

U.S. Department of Labor, Occupational Safety and Health Administration. *Instructor's Manual: Employer/Employee Rights and Responsibilities under the Occupational Safety and Health Act of 1970, PL 91-596, OSHA #2096.*

U.S. Department of Labor, Occupational Safety and Health Administration. *The Principles and Techniques of Mechanical Guarding, OSHA #2057,* 1973.

U.S. Department of Labor, Occupational Safety and Health Administration. *Student Materials: Employer/Employee Rights and Responsibilities under the Occupational Safety and Health Act of 1970, PL 91-596, OSHA #2105.*

Webster, Richard G. "Modernize Your Instruction in Accident Prevention." *School Shop,* September 1968, pp. 80–82.

Williams, William A. *An Accident Prevention Program for School Shops and Laboratories.* Chicago: National Safety Council.

Chapter 13
Evaluation of Student Achievement

Measurement and Evaluation

Evaluation is a process of calculating, judging, or appraising value, quality, or ability in terms of relative or absolute measurement. This value is established in terms of less than, or more than, some concept of amount or goodness. Evaluation can be informal, in which values are assigned by judgment, or it can be formal. By formal, we imply a process of testing or measurement.

Achievement and performance can only be measured in relation to the student's fulfillment of the established course objectives. In order to determine the amount of fulfillment, however, the level of proficiency must be measured before and following instruction. Such instruments as pre-tests may establish a mastery of the material before instruction, thereby allowing the student to embark on an independent study problem or to assist the instructor with his or her fellow students.

Traditionally, teachers are expected to grade each student. Tests and judgments are made by the teacher in the process of evaluation. One might ask, why should teachers measure students' abilities and assign grades? Parents surely evaluate and even test their children in the process of helping them mature and become ethical adults. However, do they give grades? In an informal way, they do. The "grade," which may also serve as a reward, may be an opportunity to go to summer camp. It may be less dramatic, as is a mother's simple compliment to her daughter.

For the following reasons, formal education is made more effective as a result of evaluation and the assigning of grades.

Teaching Effectiveness. Teachers can determine how well they have succeeded by noting the achievement of students. Many factors are involved in determining the effectiveness of teaching via the accomplishment of students. Therefore, these factors should be reviewed with care. Capability of students is a case in point. Determining the effectiveness of teaching may be one of the most important justifications for evaluation.

Student Accomplishment. Objectives are established for a particular class. Every conscientious teacher hopes each student will fulfill objectives as well as he or she is able. An evaluation program will determine the degree of student achievement and may dictate greater effort on the part of both student and teacher.

Student Proficiency. One of the real reasons for an evaluation program is to inform the student of how well he or she has succeeded. Students should know if they possess outstanding, average, or inadequate abilities. This information may serve to inspire students to greater accomplishments. Students should be made aware of, or help determine, objectives for the course. They then can determine if the objectives have been achieved. They should be informed of the success they have attained in competition with their classmates. They will then be able to compare their success in industrial education class to their success in other classes. Because of the methods used and the nature of the instructional content, they feel that they are presented with a more equal opportunity to compete with their fellow students, and perhaps to surpass their accomplishments in other classes.

Parental Information. Grades gain prestige for both student and parent. Students receiving the best grades in a class definitely gain recognition. Parents likewise gain recognition, particularly if honor roll lists are published in the school newspaper or the local newspaper. An obvious reason for parental interest is that parents like to encourage their children to develop their abilities to their highest levels. Thus, grades provide a basis for discussion and motivation.

Student Motivation. Properly motivated students, because they want to know and be able to perform, will work and study to achieve the goals established for the course. This desire is predicated on socially acceptable, worthy objectives. Motivation of this type is the kind every conscientious teacher hopes to provide. Should a teacher fail to motivate students intrinsically in terms of desire and goals, grades sometimes help serve as a motivating force. Students respond to competition and will work hard for high grades. Of course, if a student is seeking only a grade, their accomplishments in class may not be affected by anything other than their desire to meet the objectives of the course.

Individual Differences. An evaluation program will determine the learning rate of students. Early in the semester, by tests and observation, a teacher may determine the limitations and capabilities of students. It is assumed that the good teacher will tailor a program to the ability of the student. The level of individual student accomplishment is dependent upon intellectual ability, levels of aspiration, previous experiences, and attitudes toward work and study. The level of accomplishment is also influenced by the physical facilities available and by the quality of instruction. The general health and social adjustment of the student are also important.

Testing may be used both for classifying students into homogeneous groups and for determining the kinds of problems to be investigated by an individual. If an evaluation program isolates differences, the teacher should take steps to recognize them. Evaluating a student both as *scholar* and *person* will enable the teacher to gain information that is of great value in guidance. Teachers of industrial education, because of both the informal evaluation and a testing program, can provide social, educational, moral, and occupational guidance.

Curriculum Improvement. Evaluation of students over more than one semester may indicate the need for a revision or restatement of objectives. Upgraded objectives should cause a student to excel, but if they are too difficult and never quite reached, they lose effectiveness.

Lack of success on the part of most students may necessitate a review of methods used. Similarly, methods may be changed because of the advanced capabilities of a class. Content, both in complexity and amount, can be ascertained by achievement as determined through evaluation.

Predictive Value. The success achieved by a student in school is an index of both ability and ambition. Colleges determine who shall be admitted by grades earned in class and by college aptitude tests. Industry in like manner decides whom to employ by referring to school grades. Teachers refer to grade records as they write recommendations for both higher education and employment, for they know that grades represent potential success in either field.

The process of evaluation can be used as a method of teaching. No student studies more diligently than the one preparing for an examination. Discussion of the test and the answers to the questions is a most effective method of reinforcing learning. The student who knows the right answer is provided additional experiences which will help him or her remember, and the student who misses a question will learn the correct answer and not likely forget it.

Evaluation Terminology

In addition to achievement tests, school systems give scholastic tests to determine intellectual ability. They also give tests to determine mechanical aptitude and other special abilities. These tests are usually administered by the guidance department of a school but the results are made available to the industrial education department. Industrial educators should seek information on these tests from the school guidance counselors. They might also refer to the books on tests and measurements listed in the bibliography at the end of this chapter.

We would be remiss, however, if a few common symbols and terms used in evaluation were not defined. Those symbols most used in an evaluation program are shown in Fig. 13-1.

The four criteria for judging a test instrument are:

- *Validity.* A test or test question is valid if it tests that which it purports to measure. If a test is written to determine the student's knowledge in a subject area but determines mostly the student's ability to read, the test is not valid.
- *Reliability.* A test must be so written that it will accurately and consistently test students for specific knowledge or manipulative ability. In other words, it must be accurate and trustworthy. Obviously, a test can be reliable and at

the same time be invalid. For example, a test on the principles of lathe operation would not validly test a student's knowledge of the techniques involved in the performance of wood-turning operations.

• *Objectivity.* Tests should be constructed so that several teachers or even students may arrive at the same score with the help of the key. A subjective interpretation of answers should not be necessary.

• *Standardization.* Refers to the fact that the test has been given to a well-defined group (for example, high school juniors in industrial education) and that records (norms) have been kept regarding the scores achieved by those students. In addition, standardization refers to the method used to compare individual performance with group performance.

The three measures of central tendency are:

• *Mean.* Teachers speak of averages, but the term "mean" is more commonly used in statistical analysis. It designates the number determined by dividing the total value of all raw scores on an examination by the number of students, as shown in Fig. 13-2. This score represents the score of the typical student in class and is represented by "$\bar{X}$."

• *Median.* Median is another term used to designate a typical score. It is the value or score which represents the middle of a spread. Half of the scores are above and half below.

• *Mode.* Mode is a term used to describe central tendency in student scores. It is the most frequently occurring score in the distribution of scores earned by any group of students on a test.

The measure of variability is:

• *Standard Deviation.* The standard deviation is a measure of variability or dispersion of a set of scores calculated around the mean. If the scores are tightly grouped around the mean the standard deviation will be small. Conversely, if the scores are widely scattered above and below the mean the standard deviation will be large. When used in conjunction with a measure of central tendency such as the mean, the standard deviation statistic can be used to provide the classroom teacher with meaningful information concerning raw scores. Using the same distribution of raw

Symbol	Meaning
Σ	The Greek capital letter "sigma," meaning to sum all scores.
σ	Symbol for population standard deviation.
$\bar{X}$	Mean, or average, of a group of scores.
X	Raw score.
N	The number of scores.
x	The deviation of a score from the mean of its distribution; generally $(X - \bar{X})$.

13-1. Symbols used in an evaluation program.

scores and mean from Fig. 13-2, the following two examples in Figs. 13-3 and 13-4 indicate typical methods of computing the standard deviation.

Teachers generally have not used standard deviation in their analysis of scores because of the apparent complexity of the calculations. However, this problem can be alleviated through the use of a relatively inexpensive electronic calculator. The use of a calculator will enable a classroom teacher to perform the necessary calculations quickly. When using an electronic calculator, it is recommended that the raw score method be used because of the ease of computation.

Refer to the section on "Marking Systems" and Fig. 13-7 for an explanation of how these original raw scores may be assigned grade values through a continuation of this exacting approach to measurement and evaluation.

Industrial education teachers evaluate students on three performance factors or bases for measurement. They are:

1. *Skill development*—grading of problems, projects, or operations completed in the laboratory during the semester.

2. *Knowledge acquisition*—determination of the content comprehension of each student.

3. *Personal behavior*—judgmental observations of attitudes, characteristics, and appreciations which students exhibit in the school environment.

Skill Development

Evaluation of the project has for years been one of the chief measuring devices in industrial education. The project will, whenever it exists, serve as tangible evidence of the student's ability to apply technical information to the solution of industrial problems. In evaluating projects, problems, and the performance of operations, four criteria should be considered:

Raw Score X	
90	
88	
86	$\bar{X} = \dfrac{\Sigma X}{N}$
83	
78	$\bar{X} = \dfrac{780}{10} = 78$
75	
72	
70	
70	
68	
$\Sigma X = 780$	

13-2. Computation of the mean.

TEACHING INDUSTRIAL EDUCATION

1. *Accuracy.* The activity should be performed according to plan, use, and intended design.

2. *Technique.* Of varying importance in different industrial education programs, craftsmanship is nevertheless desirable when considering the student's skill in the correct utilization of tools, machines, and materials.

3. *Appearance.* Order, neatness, finish, and cleanliness are necessary in most product-oriented industrial pursuits.

4. *Completion.* The size and difficulty of the activity should be judged in relation to the speed and adaptability of the student during the performance.

Projects, problems, and operational performance should be evaluated periodically throughout the course in order to promote continuous improvement. Accurate progress records should be kept. Rating scales will help to make judgments more accurate.

Performance tests, a method of evaluating student problem-solving ability, are discussed later in this chapter.

Knowledge Acquisition   Through the inclusion of textbooks and other reading materials in industrial education coursework, the class is provided with a common tool for learning subject-matter content. Also scheduled into the class time for each week are lectures, demonstrations, seminars, industrial visitors, field trips, films, and many other means of gaining information about the subject under study. From such a broad exposure, the student expands his or her knowledge of the technical discipline.

This acquisition of technical information is best evaluated through the use of oral and written tests. Most tests used by industrial educators are of the

Raw Score X	$(X - \bar{X})$ x	x^2	
90	12	144	
88	10	100	$\sigma = \sqrt{\dfrac{\Sigma x^2}{N}}$
86	8	64	
83	5	25	$\sigma = \sqrt{\dfrac{606}{10}}$
78	0	0	
75	−3	9	$\sigma = 7.78$
72	−6	36	
70	−8	64	
70	−8	64	
68	−10	100	
	$\Sigma x = 0$	$\Sigma x^2 = 606$	

13-3. *Standard deviation by the deviation score method.*

CHAPTER 13—EVALUATION OF STUDENT ACHIEVEMENT

standard subjective and objective types. The construction and utilization of these tests are discussed in detail later in this chapter.

Before constructing any tests, however, the instructor must be cognizant of the different ways in which the educated person uses information as a tool. The truly educated person is one who not only has remembered an abundance of information but also has a deep understanding of the material, and the ability to apply the knowledge to the solution of problem situations, and analyze its impact. He or she should also be able to draw conclusions based on the results, and evaluate the final outcomes of the informational application. Since the educational objectives for the course have been stated in these terms, it is imperative for the instructor to design evaluative instruments for measuring the student's fulfillment of those aims. Refer to Chapter 5 for the derivation of meaningful instructional objectives.

Personal Behavior

The informal and personal relationship existing between student and teacher in industrial education enables a teacher to form judgments of students that are amazingly definitive, particularly as they relate to an appraisal of ability and potential.

As said, the appraisal of industrial educators will be more accurate if a record is kept during the semester. Use the rating scale for evaluating students on factors such as initiative, cooperation, and citizenship. It is also advisable to write descriptions of individuals so as to achieve an extra analytical guide when grading. If objectives for a course include the formation of certain attitudes, habits, concepts, and ideals, it will be mandatory that the teacher make evaluative judgments of student behavior.

Raw Score X	X²
90	8100
88	7744
86	7396
83	6889
78	6084
75	5625
72	5184
70	4900
70	4900
68	4624
ΣX = 780	ΣX² = 61446

$$\sigma = \sqrt{\frac{\Sigma X^2 - \frac{(\Sigma X)^2}{N}}{N}}$$

$$\sigma = \sqrt{\frac{61446 - \frac{(780)^2}{10}}{10}}$$

$$\sigma = 7.78$$

13-4. Standard deviation by the raw score method.

Attitudes are best evaluated through observation of student behavior. The development of a good attitude is important, since a student possessing a positive outlook on life and work will experience greater job satisfaction. The industrial educator has only to talk to personnel managers in industry to discover that it is the absence of a good attitude in workers, and not their lack of technical competency, which often presents the greatest hindrance to efficient production.

In any educational environment, the student must be encouraged to participate as fully as possible in the learning experiences made available. As a consequence, he or she should develop an appreciation of the inherent values of objects, ideas, and attitudes. In industrial education, for instance, the student should develop an appreciation of the relative merits of the subject matter. The student should also be able to assess product quality. The students' participation in collective efforts should develop his or her ability to judge personalities and evaluate character traits. The student who has been presented with the opportunity to exercise leadership should better be able to determine his or her own personal preferences. The development of this ability might serve as the first step towards the student's pursuit of rewarding objectives.

Much student learning takes place through following the instructor's example in demonstrations. It is also of extreme importance that the teacher exhibit those attitudinal qualities and professional-personal characteristics that he or she expects the students to exemplify. Although industrial education has always been concerned with the promotion and evaluation of technical information and application, stress must also be directed toward the positive development of personal characteristics.

Evaluation of personal attributes must be based on the intended behaviors as stated in the course objectives. They are relatively difficult to measure, except through the utilization of a 5-point, 3-point, or pass-fail system of grading. Most grade reports sent home at the culmination of marking periods evaluate character traits such as those listed in Fig. 13-5.

Test Construction

Specific objectives exist for education, for industrial education, and for any particular class. Examinations are written with the aim of determining how well the informational objectives have been achieved. Examinations are selected by the teacher to best accomplish this end. In some instances, ready-made tests are provided with textbooks or workbooks. It is also possible to purchase tests. In most instances, teachers would rather prepare their own. However, some generalizations are noted here, as they apply to most examinations.

- *Use words the students understand.* If the questions use unfamiliar words, the test will determine students' reading ability rather than their comprehension of facts.

CHAPTER 13—EVALUATION OF STUDENT ACHIEVEMENT

PERSONAL EVALUATION

STUDENT: _____ Grade or subject _____ Date _____

For each of the following traits indicate your rating of the student.

	Poor	Fair	Average	Good	Excellent
WORK HABITS					
1. Industry					
2. Accuracy					
3. Promptness					
4. Concentration					
GROUP ATTITUDES					
1. Reliability					
2. Cooperation					
3. Leadership					
4. Sportsmanship					
5. Respect for others' rights					
PERSONAL CHARACTERISTICS					
1. Friendliness					
2. Courtesy					
3. Neatness					
a. in person					
b. in work					
4. Self-confidence					
5. Poise					
6. Self-control					

COMMENTS AND RECOMMENDATIONS:
(Use reverse side of additional space is required.)

_____

_____

_____

_____

Name of teacher: _____

Date: _____

13-5. Sample form for the evaluation of the personal behavior of students.

TEACHING INDUSTRIAL EDUCATION

- *Place answers in a random pattern.* Students quickly sense a pattern such as odd numbers true and even numbers false. Other patterns such as four correct and the fifth false are equally obvious to the students.
- *Do not quote the textbook.* Students who do not comprehend content may recognize a statement that they saw in print or heard earlier. The question would then test memory and not the understanding of a concept.
- *Avoid catch questions.* This type of question is answered correctly by the bright student, but asking it is often unfair to students with inferior verbal comprehension.
- *Avoid dependent questions.* Very little is accomplished if a test asks a student to name three types of pictorial drawings and later names them in asking another question.
- *Write questions that are as specific as possible.* Experienced teachers have learned that a class of twenty students can find answers in addition to the ones solicited. If questions are written in a general tone, many acceptable answers will be received. This robs the test of its objectivity. Time spent in checking questions with others and writing them correctly will be more than saved when correcting papers.
- *Avoid clues.* Certain words or phrases enable the intellectually capable to answer questions without knowing the concept that is being checked by the test. Specific determiners such as "all" and "never," used in true-false questions, are examples.
- *Make directions as simple and as short as possible.* It may be advisable in many instances to read directions to the students and ask if they have questions. A sample question should be answered for their benefit.
- *Group similar questions.* All true-false questions, for example, should be together. It is also advisable to group questions as they pertain to a unit of work or thought.
- *Draw sketches clearly and correctly.* Some teachers have been embarrassed to learn that their sketches are incorrectly drawn or incomplete. Seek professional help from the drafting instructor, if necessary.
- *Provide the student with plenty of room to write.* It is well to provide approximately the same space for all answers. Students may seek short or long words to match spaces.
- *Write answers to the tests.* If this is done, minor errors may be noted and the teacher will have a key for correcting student papers. It is particularly important that teachers write the answers for essay questions before giving or correcting the examination.
- *Write more questions than you anticipate using.* Rereading questions, particularly some time after writing them, will enable the teacher to select the best or eliminate the least effective.
- *Reproduce questions so that they can be easily read.* Poorly duplicated sheets may cause a student to misread a test question or use too much time trying to decipher what is being asked

- *Write tests so that they can be scored easily.* Some teachers use an overlay that enables them to determine at a glance if questions are answered correctly. Many other ingenious methods are being used by teachers in correcting papers. Many schools are purchasing machines that can score answer sheets for objective tests.
- *Construct tests so that they evaluate the entire class.* If most students write the correct answers to a question, it is of little value and should be eliminated. Similarly, if most students fail to answer a question correctly, it should be eliminated. Consequently, teachers usually tailor tests to enable most students to get more than fifty percent of the answers correct. See the section concerning "item analysis" later in the chapter.
- *Prepare questions at the time instruction takes place.* Memory sometimes fails the teacher who attempts to prepare questions weeks after teaching a lesson.
- *Test only that information or ability which is requested in the objectives of a course.* Tests which check insignificant items rather than the important ones are a waste of time.
- *Put yourself in the place of students as you write the examination.* If a teacher, when preparing an examination, can think of himself or herself as the student writing the test, there is no doubt the test will be a good one.
- *Study other tests.* Consult all possible sources to help achieve better testing.

Subjective Tests

Essay examinations are typical subjective tests. Industrial educators do not use this type as much as the objective test. One may argue that a measure of ability or accomplishment can be determined more accurately and in less time by true-false examinations or other objective tests. It is also true that the judgment of the scorer is involved in correcting essay examinations and that the human element allows error. Also, some teachers report that industrial education students may lack the ability to write out and organize their ideas clearly and concisely. *Decided values can be achieved via subjective examinations,* both in teaching and evaluating. These examinations make students recall information, organize facts and concepts, promulgate hypotheses and proposals, and develop their writing skills. Even the less academic student who achieves a measure of success in industrial education may later achieve some success—locally or more widely—writing about technical subjects.

Essay examinations are criticized because they test a kind of ability that is not typical of industrial education students. Let us not forget that we champion our discipline because it is practical. Writing about our work is a practical experience and helps industrial education achieve integration with other disciplines in the school.

Objective Tests

An objective test is one which, with the help of a key or master sheet, can be accurately scored by anyone. Thus, subjective judgment is required only in the creation of such a test, not in its correction. There is but one right answer for each problem. *Multiple-choice, true-false, completion* and *matching* are typical kinds of objective examinations. Objective examinations are popular, because they are easily corrected, and because their correction does not require that the teacher make immediate subjective judgments on every answer. Students can demonstrate ability in relation to a greater body of knowledge in less time in an objective examination than they can by writing an essay. Most teachers complain that even a limited testing program is time consuming and interferes with the learning that could take place through demonstrations, discussions, and laboratory activities. Students in industrial education do not usually like written tests. They prefer to let work in the laboratory measure their ability. Yet only written tests enable teachers to analyze and evaluate a student's understanding of certain concepts.

Multiple Choice   Multiple-choice tests are composed of questions or incomplete statements that are usually followed by four or more possible answers. Only one answer is correct. The others appear or sound correct, but they are wrong. Directions state that the correct answers be indicated by a check or line drawn under the correct statement. Most tests include a sample question with the correct answer indicated to help the student.

These tests are accepted as the most exacting of the objective examinations. Students must exercise judgment. They may also be required to interpret, select, and discriminate. Recall and recognition may not help the student to select the correct answers. One must admit that an element of guessing does exist, but it is proportional to the number of possible answers. Multiple-choice tests are familiar to most students. They are easily scored by personal scanning or by machine.

Teachers find that multiple-choice examinations are the most difficult to construct, particularly if such tests are designed to test application, judgment, and discrimination rather than just memory. One finds it challenging to create three or more possibilities that sound as if they could be correct but are definitely wrong. Very little is accomplished by inserting possibilities that the average student will isolate as not being feasible answers.

True-False   A true-false test is a statement or described situation that may be correct or incorrect. Students are asked to read the questions and indicate whether the statement is right or wrong. Some teachers request that the student write an "F" in a prescribed place if the statement is false and a "T" if it is true. A "yes" or "no" or "+" and "−" can also be used.

It is quite obvious that a true-false test permits an even chance at guessing the correct answer. Some tests attempt to penalize guessing either by subtracting the number wrong from the number right or by subtracting two points for every wrong answer. If guessing is to be penalized, the student should be so informed in the directions for reacting to the test. It is questioned whether much is gained by penalizing guessing. Students are tempted to guess even if admonished not to do so.

Some true-false tests have the advantage of necessitating written answers. For instance, students may be asked to explain in a few words why a statement is false, or they may be asked simply to change an underlined word.

Students are familiar with true-false tests and react favorably to them. These tests enable teachers, in relatively little time, to cover large areas of subject matter. Scoring can be done objectively and easily. Information can be reviewed by correcting a test with the class. Much interest can be motivated by the true-false test.

Another advantage of this type of test is that it is easy to construct. One should be mindful, however, of the challenge inherent in writing true-false tests so that they test judgment and reasoning ability as well as recall of facts and concepts.

Guessing becomes especially troublesome if students are able to determine answers to questions because of terminology, clues, or statements such as "always," "never," and "every," which label questions as false. In the true-false test, teachers are likely to cover insignificant points of information, rather than the more important points. They also find it difficult to write questions that are either completely true or completely false. True-false questions that cover controversial issues are decidedly difficult to write.

Complete directions written in simple language familiar to the student should precede the examination, and a sample question should be answered to help the student. The questions should be fairly equally divided between true and false. Of course, one should avoid a pattern such as making odd numbered questions false. It is not appropriate to use the same terminology as that used in a textbook or that used in lecturing to a class. Words and phrases unfamiliar to students should also be avoided. Avoid stating questions negatively, and attempt to make all questions approximately the same length.

Completion

Completion tests require the student to supply a missing word in a statement. Some questions require figures, dates, or sketches to be inserted. The statement, when properly completed, is always true.

Some authorities classify the completion test question as a recall question and think of it as a modified form of the essay question. Answers to some completion questions may require a complete sentence or paragraph. The answers to still others may necessitate a listing of sequential steps or dates, or the drawing of a sketch.

One of the major values of this type of test is that it requires students to recall information. It also may require them to use judgment and problem-solving ability. Mathematical problems can be stated. The test measures

TEACHING INDUSTRIAL EDUCATION

who, what, when, where, and why. For the most part, guessing is eliminated. The test can be objectively scored if it is properly written.

Writing a good completion examination is a definite challenge. They should be so written that only one answer is acceptable. Experience in writing completion tests will prevent possible errors. The fact that these tests seem easy to prepare has caused them to be used disproportionately in relation to other test forms. Remember that the instrument relies completely on recall. Students may know the fact expressed but may not at the moment be able to remember a particular word, on which the question depends.

Testing recall only may force students to stress the memorization of a fact over knowledge of its value and use. Also, a student with a high native intelligence may, because of a good memory and an exceptional verbal facility, succeed on a completion test, in spite of the fact that he or she has acquired none of the real values meant to be gained in a technical course.

Some of the things to remember when writing completion tests are:

- Words to be inserted in a statement should appear at the end or near the end of a sentence.
- Plenty of room should be provided in which to insert the required word, words, figure, or sketch.
- All blank spaces should be approximately the same length. Different sized blank spaces may suggest long or short words.
- If two words are required, two ruled blank spaces should be indicated.

Matching   Matching tests require students to match related words, statements, figures, dates, or sketches. Usually the examination is structured in two columns, with the one at the left representing the original statements. The items in the column at the right are to be matched with those at the left. To be effective, there should be more possibilities on the right than there are statements on the left. Too much student time is wasted by tests of this type that contain more than twelve items. Different forms of the test can be developed. The examination is much like the multiple-choice test but is much easier to construct. It is completely objective and can be scored quickly. Guessing is eliminated if the test is properly constructed. One weakness of the test is that it causes students to overemphasize the memorization of facts. To be effective, the test must be limited to homogeneous information. One should use sketches, if possible. Dates and figures should be tested for chronological order or for their value. The entire test, including directions, should be on one page.

Object Identification   Object identification tests evaluate student knowledge of tools, machines, raw materials, fasteners, and finishes. The actual item is displayed and the student is required to identify it by name or describe its use or operation.

CHAPTER 13—EVALUATION OF STUDENT ACHIEVEMENT

Many industrial educators believe students should know names of common tools and be able to identify them, as well as to spell their names. This can be achieved in a number of ways. One of the simplest is to place tools about the room with a number noted on a card next to or beneath the tool. Cards are consecutively numbered. It is advisable to use as many tools as there are students in the class. Teachers pass out to each student a piece of paper that has numbers on it from one to the number of students in the class. Students are instructed to take a position next to a tool, examine the tool, and write its name on the slip of paper next to the number that labels the tool. After a minute or two, the teacher signals and each student progresses to the next numbered tool.

Students enjoy this type of examination. It is easily administered and easily scored. Its greatest disadvantage is that students are forced to adhere to the time schedule dictated by the teacher. Slow students find it difficult to keep up. Yet unless the process moves rather rapidly, the fast students become bored. A simpler, though less effective, method is for the teacher to hold up a tool or item for the students to see. Each student then writes the name or description of the tool. Tools, processes, and supplies may also be identified on picture sheets.

Performance Tests

One of the objectives of industrial education is the teaching of manipulative skills. Skill or manipulative ability can be checked by a performance test that enables a teacher to determine quite objectively how much manipulative ability a student has achieved at the time the test is given. This test requires a student to make some simple object or do an exercise according to a plan. A teacher observes and scores the student on his or her performance.

The first responsibility when preparing a performance test is to determine what skills or operations are to be checked. Next, a detailed drawing is prepared for the student to follow in demonstrating the skills in question. Specific directions are prepared for the student and also for the person administering the test. Check sheets and rating scales must be prepared to achieve objective scoring of ability and effort.

A test of this type should provide information regarding the physical skill of the student, his or her knowledge of the operations and their sequence, and the time it takes to perform them. It should also indicate the quality of the student's workmanship.

Tools and materials should be placed in readiness for the test. (Ability to select tools and materials can be more efficiently tested by other devices.) Directions for the student should be presented on or with the drawing of the object to be made.

This is the only test of skill or manipulative ability. It is rather easy to prepare and can be made objective if proper preparations for scoring have been made. Experience in writing, giving, and scoring a manipulative performance test will cause the teacher to be much more effective in the everyday evaluation of students as well as in the appraisal of completed projects.

The big disadvantage of this type of test is that it takes excessive time both on the part of the instructor and students, although a team of two students could serve as the teacher and score the student taking the examination. Then, the experience would be of value to all involved. Another disadvantage of the test is that in most instances the item made or produced has no functional value. Therefore the activity is classified as an exercise. It is a challenging experience to construct scoring sheets for the test. Obviously, however, it takes much of the teacher's time. Students are subjected to a lot of pressure when taking the test. The test cannot be comprehensive, since available time will not permit it.

Item Analysis

Once the test has been administered, it is necessary to evaluate the strengths and weaknesses of the various objective questions. The item analysis procedure will provide the teacher with information regarding (a) the percentage of students who answered each question correctly (difficulty level), and (b) how many more high-scoring than low-scoring students answered it correctly (index of discrimination). Upon completion of the item analysis, the teacher can build a file of test items that prove to be effective, and eliminate those items that are too difficult, too easy, or nondiscriminating.

Before describing the mechanics of item analysis, it might be helpful to indicate the number of students necessary to produce stable data. Generally, the number taking the test should be in excess of 100. However, item analyses are often used for tests given to far fewer students with beneficial results. The test maker who uses small item analysis groups must be aware of the fact that his or her data will be somewhat unstable or that item characteristics may shift markedly from one group to the next.

First, all test papers are corrected and ranked according to total raw scores. The top and bottom thirds become the upper and lower groups. The middle third is eliminated from all computations. It is important that there be an equal number of papers in the upper and lower groups.

Next, the *difficulty level* indicates the percentage of students who answered each question correctly. To compute the level of difficulty, the teacher may use the formula:

$$P = \frac{N_c}{N_t}(100)$$

P = level of difficulty expressed as a percentage.
N_c = number of students who answer the item correctly.
N_t = total number of students who attempt the item.
Resulting values are entered on the form shown in Fig. 13-6.

CHAPTER 13—EVALUATION OF STUDENT ACHIEVEMENT

The *discrimination index* is determined by subtracting the number of correct responses obtained by the lower group from the number of correct responses obtained by the upper group and dividing the result by the number of subjects in either the upper or lower group. Computation of this index involves the formula:

$$D = \frac{N_u - N_l}{N}$$

D = discrimination index.
N_u = number of correct responses by the upper group.
N_l = number of correct responses by the lower group.
N = total number of subjects in either upper or lower group.

All of this data can be summarized in chart form. An example of such a form is illustrated in Fig. 13-6.

Generally speaking, items with levels of difficulty in the general vicinity of 25 to 80 percent are valuable and should be retained. Items with a discrimination index below +0.20 are usually eliminated or revised, while items above +0.40 are considered very good. Negative values indicate items which differentiate between students in the wrong direction (more low-scoring students answered correctly than high-scoring students), and are usually discarded.

Some writers suggest that traditional methods of item analysis are too laborious and time-consuming. Much of the compilation of data can easily be achieved by a show of hands in class. Final computations can be done quickly at a later time with an electronic calculator. This approach adds to

Name of Test _____ Class _____ Date _____
Number of papers in upper and lower groups __8__
Total number of tests __24__

Item No.	High	Low	Difficulty	Discrimination	Action
1.	7	4	69	0.37	OK
2.	4	1	31	0.37	OK
3.	5	1	37	0.50	OK
4.	8	8	100	0.00	revise
5.	6	2	50	0.50	OK
6.	7	8	94	−0.12	reject

13-6. *Item analysis work sheet.*

the students' understanding of the test and provides a more valid basis for the discussion of individual test items.

Determination of Grades

As previously discussed, the grade serves as an index of accomplishment. Colleges admit students on the basis of their grade reports, and industry examines the grades of the young people they employ.

Most teachers find grading one of their less enjoyable responsibilities. Knowing that standards must be maintained, teachers enjoy the success experienced by the best students but worry about assigning low or failing grades. Nevertheless, the requirements must be met.

Grades are assigned to students on the basis of how much they have learned and on the basis of what they can do. These accomplishments are considered in relationship to the objectives established for the course. In industrial education, objectives require that students develop good character as well as acquire knowledge and skill. Educating students to develop both high ideals and an awareness of the principles of responsible citizenship is not only the greatest challenge in teaching but is also that which it is most difficult to evaluate.

Teacher judgment must play a part in assigning grades. Only a personal relationship with and knowledge about the students will provide a basis for grading. It is questioned whether any industrial educator bases grades wholly on objective information.

Tests serve as a second basis for assigning grades. Final tests, if given, should count more than small quizzes. It is relatively simple to determine the accomplishments of students by means of a test.

Projects serve as the third basis for assigning grades. Projects should be graded at predetermined stages of completion or predetermined dates during the semester.

Written and oral reports may be required in industrial education, especially where the instructor has established a contemporary educational program promoting student involvement. Written reports of independent study provide a sound introduction to oral presentations and participation in student-directed seminars, discussions, and demonstrations.

Characteristics of Efficient Grading

One cannot overemphasize the necessity for planning a definitive marking system. Much time will be saved and embarrassment avoided if a teacher can produce evidence and explain to parents and students how marks are determined. An efficient marking system should possess the following characteristics.

Grading should require only a small amount of the teacher's time. Grading should require as little of the teacher's class time as possible. Any time that can be used before or after school, or during free periods, should be given to grading.

CHAPTER 13—EVALUATION OF STUDENT ACHIEVEMENT

Grades should be based upon as many factors as possible. Projects, tests, reports, and student behavior should be evaluated in determining a grade. The number of times a student has volunteered or participated in special activities should also be recognized.

Marking should be frequent. Teachers are not able to evaluate with the same objectivity each day. It is, therefore, necessary that grades be recorded frequently in an attempt to achieve greater fairness. Frequent entries also speak for conscientiousness, particularly when marks are reviewed by students, parents, or administration. Reliance on memory is not necessary if grades are recorded frequently.

Uniform standards should be maintained. Industrial education is in need of standards acceptable to most people in the profession. Teachers can secure help in determining a level of student accomplishment by conferring with other teachers and by reviewing books and magazines in education. Years of experience will enable teachers to establish their own standards.

Students should understand the system. Some industrial educators have achieved great success by asking students to participate in formulating the basis of the grading system. Students should be told how grades are determined and should be invited to keep a record of their own accomplishments. Teachers will not face embarrassment if they adhere to the system.

Students should have access to their grades. It appears that most students enjoy seeing their grades. Students with manipulative ability, in many instances, achieve their greatest success in industrial education and, therefore, are pleased with their own progress.

Students should participate in evaluation. The best way for students to experience the problems teachers face in grading is for them to help the instructor score the classwork. Students enjoy the experience. They are likely to be more severe than the teacher in scoring one another. Students demonstrate great ability and insight in grading projects. They remember details the teacher may have forgotten, and any unfair practices on the part of a student are known to classmates. Finally, ranking projects in the order of their worth is an interesting experience for both teacher and student.

Marking should be done as objectively as possible. Judgment is necessary in grading students, but the tabulation of grades can be objective. Teachers should attempt to be as fair as possible. They should guard against prejudice. Incidents of misbehavior, if corrected, should be forgotten. Aggressiveness on the part of students is sometimes misinterpreted by teachers. The use of rating scales will enable the teacher to be more objective.

Records must be permanent. Grades are valuable not only at the time they are reported but also years later when students seek employment or promotions. A quick look at a grade book usually refreshes a teacher's memory. Teachers should adopt a grading system for entry in permanent record books, which can be filed either in the school administrator's office or in the laboratory.

Marking Systems

Autonomy enjoyed by local school districts has caused the educational profession to use many types of marking systems. Some districts give letter grades, with "A" designating superior performance. Usually six letters are used, with "F" designating failure and "E" an incomplete. An obvious disadvantage in using the letter grade is that letters cannot be averaged. Knowing that most teachers convert letter grades to number grades, it might be advisable to use the number grade at the outset.

The most popular number grade system establishes 100 as perfect. The passing grade is usually established as 70 or 75.

A second numerical system is based on a "1–5" or "1–10" scale. Either end of the continuum can be accepted as high. The "1–5" system is used by many teachers instead of letter grades. For example, the number "5" functions as an "A," "4" as a "B." Averages are easily determined. Letter grades are placed on report cards and school records.

Another system used is that of rank order. It helps check the accuracy of the grading system if students are ranked.

Some schools require teachers to write a description of student accomplishment. Parental conferences are required, to discuss each student's rating and needs.

Many collegiate institutions and a number of secondary schools use either a "pass-fail" or a "superior-acceptable-deficient" (three-level) system of grading. In the pass-fail system, students who fulfill course objectives are allowed and encouraged to proceed to the next course unit. Failing in such a system simply requires the student to repeat the work until an acceptable level of performance is reached. The three-level system places the majority of any given class of students in the acceptable category. Only those students who excel would be awarded the superior grade for outstanding achievement. The work of those who under-achieve would be graded deficient. They would be required to continue work until they mastered the instructional material, or they would be required to take other recommended steps.

Since one of the most difficult and demanding tasks facing teachers is that of distributing grades on an examination, or at the end of a unit or course, an equitable system must be used. Whereas grading has often been somewhat haphazard or based on a 100 point scale, the use of the mean and standard deviation offers teachers a more scientific grade distribution plan. This method, shown in Fig. 13-7, measures the achievement of individual students in relation to the achievement of the class as a whole. The grade of each student depends upon his or her distance above or below this mean, or typical position.

CHAPTER 13—EVALUATION OF STUDENT ACHIEVEMENT

Recording Achievement

Grading systems used by teachers reflect individual taste. A system that works well for one teacher may be completely unacceptable to a second. Beginning teachers are encouraged to observe various systems and then perfect their own.

School districts usually provide a record book for grades. These books should be retained either by the teacher or the central office for future reference. Because of the nature of industrial education, record books issued by the district are often inadequate. Records should provide spaces in which to write test grades, project grades, and others that the teacher may wish to record. Records should also provide space for designating dates.

Many industrial educators prefer a progress chart. Students' names appear on the chart as well as the activities they are to perform. Projects may be listed, rather than activities. The chart may also include test grades. Refer to Fig. 13-8.

$A = \bar{X} + 1.5\sigma$ and above
$B = \bar{X} + 0.5\sigma$ to 1.5σ
$C = +0.5\sigma$ to -0.5σ
$D = \bar{X} - 0.5\sigma$ to -1.5σ
$F = \bar{X} - 1.5\sigma$ and below

$\bar{X}$ = Mean
σ = Standard deviation

Using the following raw scores, grades can be distributed using the mean and standard deviation method.

	Raw Score X	
A	90	
B	88, 86, 83	
C	78, 75	
D	72, 70, 70, 68	

$\bar{X} = 78$
$\sigma = 7.78$

$A = 78 + (1.5 \times 7.78) = 89.7$
$B = 78 + (0.5 \times 7.78) = 81.9$
$C = 78 - (0.5 \times 7.78) = 74.1$
$D = 78 - (1.5 \times 7.78) = 66.3$

13-7. Distribution of grades using the mean and standard deviation.

TEACHING INDUSTRIAL EDUCATION

Grading and the necessity for evaluating student progress are important in any educational program. One should never lose sight, however, of the primary objectives of education, teaching and learning.

PROGRESS CHART

Name	Using crosscut saw	Using ripsaw	Surface planing	Edge planing	Using try square	Using marking gauge	Using backsaw	Grinding plane iron	Whetting plane iron	Using brace and bit	Driving nails	Using woodscrews	Using miter box	Using wood file	Using spokeshave	FINAL
Adams, Edward																
Byzinski, Mary																
Caldero, Carmen																
Clary, Richard																
Demsey, Thomas																

13-8. Suggested progress chart for tool operations in woodworking technology.

DISCUSSION QUESTIONS

1. In what type of classes should effort be given special consideration?
2. In what ways would you determine whether a student is acquiring and applying the necessary "items of knowledge"?
3. To what extent, if any, should the student's personality be taken into consideration when grades are assigned?
4. Name a number of specific situations in which the "attitude" of students would be tested.
5. Give your reasons for thinking that "pass" or "fail" is or is not an adequate marking system.
6. Other factors being equal, do you think that a student who has stayed after school to finish a project should receive a grade higher or lower

than that received by those students who finished the project within the required time?

7. What would be the best scheme for grading a production job in the school laboratory?

8. List favorable and unfavorable points with reference to the daily grading system.

9. Do you think that a grade distribution based upon the mean and standard deviation should be compulsory for teachers? Why?

10. Make out a form for a record card that can go with the student from school to school.

11. To what extent do you think that an open grading system would discourage less able students?

12. Is there, in your opinion, danger that students may be so interested in grades that they may fail to benefit otherwise from the instruction?

13. What are the advantages and disadvantages in having students participate in grading their own work?

14. Do you think that students in general are inclined to grade their own work higher or lower than its actual worth?

15. To what extent do you agree or disagree with the five-point grading system suggested in this chapter?

16. Do you consider that uniform standards of attainment for the study of woodwork or electricity in junior high schools should be set up and adhered to?

17. In your opinion is the present tendency toward uniformity of teaching content or away from it?

18. Upon what would you base a set of standards for attainment in industrial education?

19. What means would a teacher have for checking the validity of a true-false test before giving it to the class?

20. Choose a technical subject of your choice. Make up a test on it containing twenty-five multiple choice questions and twenty-five true-false questions. Administer the test and run an item analysis on the results.

21. Do you consider available achievement tests in industrial education to be as valuable as similar tests in mathematics and English?

22. Set up a list of raw scores for a test administered to a class of eighteen students. Compute the mean and standard deviation. Assign letter grades according to the results of your computations.

ADDITIONAL READINGS

Baird, Ronald J. *Contemporary Industrial Teaching.* South Holland, Illinois: Goodheart-Willcox, 1972.

Cenci, Louis, and Weaver, Gilbert G. *Teaching Occupational Skills.* 2nd ed. New York: Pitman, 1968.

Friese, John F., and Williams, William A. *Course Making in Industrial Education.* Peoria, Illinois: Chas. A. Bennett, 1966.

Helmstadter, G. C. *Principles of Psychological Measurement.* New York: Appleton-Century-Crofts, 1964.

Lien, Arnold J. *Measurement and Evaluation of Learning.* 2nd ed., Dubuque, Iowa: Wm. C. Brown Co., 1967.

Littrell, Joseph J. *Guide to Industrial Teaching.* Peoria, Illinois: Chas. A. Bennett, 1970.

Lueck, William R., et. al. *Effective Secondary Education.* Minneapolis: Burgess, 1966.

Mager, Robert F., and Pipe, Peter. *Analyzing Performance Problems.* Belmont, California: Fearon, 1970.

Pautler, Albert J. *Teaching Shop and Laboratory Subjects.* Columbus, Ohio: Charles E. Merrill, 1971.

Storey, Arthur G. *The Measurement of Classroom Learning.* Chicago: Science Research Associates, Inc., 1970.

Terwilliger, James S. *Assigning Grades to Students.* Glenview, Illinois: Scott, Foresman, 1971.

Chapter 14

Closing the School Year

Maintaining Organization

The closing days of a course or a school year are important, but often they are sadly neglected. While many are enthusiastic in starting something, not as many will maintain their enthusiasm to the end of a project. This applies to teachers as well as to students. However, teachers who have kept a fair degree of organization during most of the course have patterned student behavior by their example. Relaxation of discipline and procedures during the last week of class sometimes undoes many of the good things that have been accomplished throughout the year. Although there is probably more danger of such an occurrence at the close of the year with vacation time coming, a change of semesters or classes often presents similar, although less serious, problems.

Many reasons can be recognized for the tendency of class organization to weaken during this period:

- Regular demonstrations and other instruction may appear to be finished, or may have to be set aside in order that students utilize remaining laboratory time for constructive activities. This may occur either because students were too ambitious in project selection, or failed to use their time to good advantage.
- Students are rushed for time in completing work, and feel that the year is about over, so tools and materials are not cared for as they previously had been.
- Tools are borrowed by other departments, and by groups arranging exhibits, entertainments, and other special features.
- Senior classes, or individual seniors in classes, feel that they should have a certain amount of freedom, and are often excused from regular attendance by the central office.
- The instructor may not be scheduled to return. He or she may carry a grievance, which may affect professional pride and judgment. Also, the teacher may no longer feel a sense of responsibility.

As a consequence of some of these and other factors, many school labs are in utter chaos during the closing days of the year. Conditions may sometimes be so aggravated that students who are already behind in their work may find it impossible to finish. Tools are out of the places where they have been kept throughout the year. The glue is hard, the clamps are gone, the files are broken, belts are slipping, and many of the tools are dull or out of adjustment. The well-meaning teacher who assumes that

TEACHING INDUSTRIAL EDUCATION

all tools will be accounted for at the close of classes will alter that assumption when the rush is over.

At this time, the loafer in the lab is one of the greatest problems. This is the student who in many cases has done the best work. This student has worked quickly and well, and for that reason he or she is now idle. Each student will continue work if given a job. There will be plenty of work, if the instructor can find time and resourcefulness to recognize and organize it. If the instructor would take time to list those items that should receive attention before the school year ends, or before he or she can meet the next class, the teacher can select from the list those jobs that students might be able to do. In this way, the teacher will find enough work to keep everyone busy until the last minute. In all cases, the special jobs should be rotated so that every student will be able to broaden his or her experience.

Laboratory Maintenance

Hand tools of all kinds are likely to rust during the vacation months unless given special attention. Oily waste for general cleaning, and fine emery cloth soaked in oil for rusty or discolored spots, will serve well. The cleaning of tools is a necessary task in all laboratories, and doing a thorough job will engage a number of students for a considerable length of time. The tool clerks might also undertake this activity, if there is spare time in their schedule.

In all labs, but particularly in woodworking labs, there is need for putting tools in condition for the next term. Grinding edged tools is a large task in itself, and if the teacher leaves it for himself or his successor to do, much time will have to be spent in routine work, which makes a good training job for students at this time. If such work is assigned, however, it must be supervised very closely, for poor grinding of edged-tools is worse than no grinding. It takes as long to grind a tool again as to do the job right in the first place. No apology needs to be made for asking students to assist in reconditioning tools that they have worked with during the year.

Some teachers are inclined to feel that students of high school age are not reliable enough to complete such operations as grinding knives for woodworking machines, yet these students may be grinding the valves of automobiles, timing the spark, and even completely overhauling engines, either at home or in school. If the teaching has been up to expectations during the year, the attitude of students at this time should be such that they will gladly tackle any job assigned and welcome the responsibility that goes with it.

Finishing rooms, whether connected with woodworking or metals-processing laboratories, need special attention. If there are teachers who, because of their own habits of neatness and order, are inclined to feel that this suggestion is unnecessary, it is recommended that they visit other school laboratories to obtain more information. Even a limited visit of that kind will convince anyone that more needs to be said on this subject. In

CHAPTER 14—CLOSING THE SCHOOL YEAR

general, cleaning the room and its furnishings, storing brushes and spray equipment, sealing unused finishing materials, and discarding empty cans and sample pieces will go far toward creating a good learning environment for the next group of students.

Equipment Inventory

The students can be of help in taking the required inventory of the equipment. This inventory should be of the type acceptable in a business concern. It should not be an inventory of the type so often taken in the laboratory, that is, an inventory that has no definite value beyond keeping the students busy.

If this work is properly supervised, it will furnish training as fine as any that the students have had during the course. When the teacher has the results of the inventory he or she should be able to tell the number of tools of each kind on hand, their locations, the condition of each tool, and the parts needed for repairs. As the inventories are taken, the tools should be moved into certain locations so that no item is counted twice.

In order to have this type of work produce definite results, it is necessary to have some kind of blank that calls for specific data, and supervise the students closely to see that no guessing is done in filling in these forms. The exact arrangement of the blank is not of great importance, provided the necessary items are included. As a check, inventories of the previous year should be consulted. If this is not done, some tools may be overlooked.

Supplies Inventory

No place in the laboratory is more likely to need attention than the stockrooms and supply cabinets. This is true whether the laboratory activities are concerned with metals processing, power mechanics, electronics, woodworking, graphic arts, or technical drawing. Even with the best system and teaching, it is difficult to keep supplies in perfect order, particularly toward the end of the year.

In order properly to control supplies, it will be necessary to straighten stock and take a complete inventory of all material on hand. In handling some types of material it may be best to do these jobs simultaneously. In other cases (such as a lumber inventory), the inventory can be taken after the material is arranged according to kinds and sizes. A typical form for this purpose is shown in connection with the discussion of inventories in Chapter 7.

Requisitions

Requests for new equipment, and complete requisitions for necessary supplies, should be furnished before vacation begins. This is a good practice, even though the instructor may be available during vacation. It frequently occurs that the decisions on the acquisition of major items and the budgeting of their expenses are often made quite early. What was said regarding recommendations in general applies here, namely, that it is important to be positive in one's statements and reasonable in requests for expenditures. Clear justification should be offered for each item requested. A method of arriving at supply figures was discussed briefly in Chapter 8. The instructor who has experience will be able to make more accurate estimates of supply and equipment needs. If the instructor has been careful in keeping exact records of the materials used, little time or effort should be consumed in preparing requisitions for those courses that will be repeated in the future.

Planning is essential in order to provide the industrial education program with the supplies necessary to future instruction. When the board of education requests, as it often will, complete requisitions from six months to a year in advance, there is a temptation to treat the problem hastily and in a casual manner, rather than to take the time to analyze the situation. It might also be suggested that an instructor have the requisitions ready at the requested time, for such promptness indicates efficiency. Efficient planning makes it just as possible to be a day ahead of schedule as a day behind.

Reports Some teachers chafe under the practice of having to make semester or annual reports. However, the more farsighted teachers of industrial education will welcome the opportunity to do so. Even though no report is asked for, the instructor should take the opportunity to put some of the phases of the program for the semester or school year in writing. The instructor can determine from circumstances just where such a written report should be sent. In systems where there is no supervisor of industrial education, the report may be sent to the principal or directly to the superintendent. Through the annual or semiannual report, the teacher has the opportunity to place a number of facts before the administration, including at least the following items:

- The number of students served by the program.
- The types of study and activity covered or taught.
- The number of class hours utilized in instruction.
- New courses initiated during the semester or year.
- Special projects or problems engaged in for the school, community, or charitable organizations.
- Instructor's recommendations regarding the personnel and the program for the coming year.

There is publicity value in reporting the results of your instructional and professional activity. Such a report may well be accompanied by a few photographs of work accomplished, or of classes in action, since it is possible that the photographs may be shown to others who are interested, including members of the board of education. The report should be brief and to the point, with the material tabulated when possible. Even though the report may be well-written, supervisors or superintendents do not wish to read lengthy statements. The more that can be said in a small amount of space, the more attention the material will probably receive.

Recommendations for changes in the program and expansions of the facility might also be included in reports of this type. Conditions causing serious drawbacks to the work can be mentioned, and remedies can be suggested.

Whatever recommendations are made should be logical and proposed with the idea that action will be taken. Requests should be courteous, but firm. Without a conviction that the instructor knows what he or she is talking about, the superintendent will not seriously consider any recommendations. Some teachers are in the habit of asking for much more than they expect. This is bad practice, for it displays insincerity on the teacher's part, and destroys the confidence of the administration in the teacher.

Permanent Records

The keeping of student records has been discussed at length in previous chapters. Here it remains only to say that a teacher with professional pride will be scrupulous in the task of completing all possible records for students. These records may become more useful in the future, and keeping them should be considered a moral obligation of the teacher.

An Orderly Finish

Many advantages of doing the work in an orderly way are apparent, among which are the following:

- Students receive additional knowledge and experience and acquire valuable habits.
- Students who leave the lab and do not return carry with them a respect for the work and for the teacher.
- Students who return will be in a better frame of mind to start in the right way, and will reap the profit of their work done at the close of the previous year.
- Prospective students and visitors (of whom there are many during the closing days) will form a positive opinion of the conditions maintained in the industrial education facilities.
- The teacher is largely relieved of the work he or she otherwise would be obliged to do before the beginning of a new school year.
- It will be easier to start work properly and promptly when the new classes come into the laboratory.

At this time of the year, a review of equipment and procedures will provide more direction toward the constructive utilization of time during the closing days of the school year.

DISCUSSION QUESTIONS

1. What are some advantages of having the students take the inventory of equipment and supplies?

2. How should a laboratory teacher manage the problem of lending tools to other departments?

3. Why is it good practice for the teacher to keep a permanent record of the work of all students who study and work under his or her guidance?

TEACHING INDUSTRIAL EDUCATION

4. Write a report to a superintendent covering the work of your students in industrial education. Assume such a range of activity as you would expect to have in operation.

5. Draft a set of rules for the finishing room that will largely eliminate the problem of special attention during the closing days of the school year.

6. Outline, on paper, an interesting and practical scheme for organizing the lab at the end of the year.

7. Upon what conditions, if any, should students be allowed to borrow tools for home use?

8. What can the teacher do with unfinished projects or other articles at the end of the school year?

9. Make out a requisition for materials needed by a class of twenty students for one semester in the industrial education area of your choice. Describe your methods for arriving at quantities.

10. List jobs, other than those described in this chapter, that students might perform during the closing days of the school year.

11. Make a written presentation to a superintendent proposing the introduction of a new course for the coming school year. State the assumed conditions warranting such a proposal.

ADDITIONAL READINGS

Baird, Ronald J. *Contemporary Industrial Teaching*. South Holland, Illinois: Goodheart-Willcox, 1972.

Cenci, Louis, and Weaver, Gilbert G. *Teaching Occupational Skills*. 2nd ed. New York: Pitman, 1968.

Littrell, Joseph J. *Guide to Industrial Teaching*. Peoria, Illinois: Chas. A. Bennett, 1970.

Pautler, Albert J. *Teaching Shop and Laboratory Subjects*. Columbus, Ohio: Charles E. Merrill, 1971.

Silvius, G. Harold, and Curry, Estell H. *Managing Multiple Activities in Industrial Education*. 2nd ed. Bloomington, Illinois: McKnight & McKnight, 1971.

Silvius, G. Harold, and Curry, Estell H. *Teaching Successfully in Industrial Education*. 2nd ed. Bloomington, Illinois: McKnight & McKnight, 1967.

Chapter 15
Professional Development

Occupational Opportunities

Persons who plan on teaching industrial education, and those who are preparing themselves for work in this field, have a right to be concerned about the scope and limitations of their future opportunities. Limited listing of the types of opportunities which may come to those who have prepared themselves to teach may be of help in regard to this question.

A broad variety of situations may be found within the field of industrial education. The extent to which a teacher can adjust to any or all of these will depend upon his or her training and experience as well as upon temperament and personal choice.

Single-unit labs in junior high schools. Such labs have increased in number very rapidly in city school systems. The person who expects to be successful in this type of facility must have a thorough knowledge of and skill in the specific subject involved. He or she must, in addition, have an interest in the problems of early adolescence and a sympathy for the student of that age.

General-unit laboratory in junior high schools. The organization of this type of lab has been discussed in Chapter 7. To be successful in the general-unit laboratory, the teacher must possess the same attitudes and basic knowledge as the teacher in the unit laboratory. However, since a broader scope of mechanical work is covered in the general-unit laboratory, the teacher must possess a variety of skills, instead of being skilled in only certain types of operations.

Industry and technology in elementary schools. Opportunities are numerous for service in the smaller elementary schools. In many cases such appointments involve teaching in several schools as part of the instructor's weekly program; and sometimes, in addition to lab work, the teaching of other subjects becomes a part of the task.

The smaller high schools and union high schools. In these schools it is often necessary to teach two or more distinct types of industrial education. Requests for service coming from these schools indicate that almost any combination of activities may present itself. The general-unit lab in all its variations is found in these types of high schools.

Nonvocational work in city high schools. In this connection the single-unit lab is the most common, but in many city high schools, particularly where the ninth grade is included, the general-unit lab is in use. To teach unit courses in any high school, the teacher must possess a definite degree of skill in the subject that he or she attempts to teach, in addition to having the required knowledge of the objectives, principles, and methods pertaining to the special type of work, and to the program of the school in general. The program may be general in nature, or more strictly technical as a preparation for engineering courses.

Vocational work in the high school. Mastery of the trade, both from the standpoint of methods and skills is the first prerequisite for teaching vocational classes. Methods of teaching, knowledge of objectives, and understanding of youth are of equal importance.

Special schools and classes. For teachers interested in those special students who find it difficult to profit from the regular school program, there are special opportunities for service. The public-school systems often segregate such students for special attention. The industrial educator will become popular and valuable if he or she will learn to understand the problems involved and prepare to solve them. Opportunities exist in working with mentally retarded and physically handicapped students of all ages.

The "industrial" schools. Persons with understanding and mechanical skill are needed in the special schools for youths who have been placed in institutions of correction. To restore such individuals to society is a service worthy of the attempts of the most skillful of teachers.

Part-time classes. The part-time educational program which has become a part of all larger school systems offers opportunities for teachers of industrial education in all principal types of laboratory activity.

Adult classes. Through night-school programs, teachers of industry and technology often have opportunity to extend their services and earn additional salary. This field is rich in possibilities for the industrial educator.

Technical institutes. Throughout the nation, an increasing number of vocational-technical institutes and junior colleges are being built to offer instruction in specialized programs leading to associate degrees. Instructors in these situations are usually selected on the basis of their technical knowledge, occupational experience, and academic degrees.

Colleges and universities. Requiring at least a master's degree, and usually requiring an advanced study certificate or doctorate, collegiate teaching positions are open to the industrial educator. Instructional openings are possible in industrial-teacher education as well as in engineering.

Guidance and counseling. While occupational study and guidance do not fall exclusively within the realm of industry and technology, it may be mentioned that experience in industry and business forms a splendid background for rendering service in this field. Thus it happens that teachers of industrial education often become interested in a certain group of students for whom the school has done very little, and through this interest they are welcomed as counselors for larger groups. The practical outlook upon life possessed by the teacher of technical subjects is the outlook needed by a large majority of high school students.

CHAPTER 15—PROFESSIONAL DEVELOPMENT

Supervision and administration. While a supervisory position in industrial education is not a natural and logical ultimate attainment for all ambitious industrial educators, such supervisors usually come from the ranks of those with considerable teaching experience within the field to be supervised.

The fact might be stressed, however, that there must of necessity be many teachers for each supervisor. It may also be of value to point out that many persons who are doing outstanding work as instructors do not become equally successful as supervisors. To be a teacher of boys and girls is a noble occupation for which some are eminently fitted, and in which they are happily engaged. The supervisor's job, although different, is not easier. For a limited number of outstanding teachers it is worthwhile to obtain the necessary additional preparation for service as a supervisor.

The positions of counselor, vice-principal, principal, and superintendent are logical goals of industrial educators who wish to go into administrative work. As a matter of fact, teachers whose backgrounds have brought them in contact with industry and technology have an advantage in dealing with many aspects of school administration. The profound effect of invention and industry upon the pattern of modern living necessitates an understanding and appreciation by those administrators who are in positions to affect the social and educational development of youth. The teacher in industrial education should be in an excellent position to exercise such responsibilities.

Staff Organization

In relatively small intermediate and secondary schools, usually only one or two industrial educators are employed. In order to cover the offerings of the entire discipline, each one instructs in two or three subject areas.

Larger schools have the advantage of allowing each teacher the opportunity to instruct in a particular subject specialty. All teachers within a discipline are conveniently grouped within a department or division. One of the members is often designated "chairperson" or "department head," with varying degrees of authority and responsibility. Depending on the school system, the department faculty may elect the most experienced or respected teacher to this position; or the administration may select the chairperson, choosing that individual who is most capable of coordinating the department's business. As alternatives to this traditional departmental structure, team teaching and differentiated staffing patterns have been developed.

Team teaching. Although struggling to find the right formula, team teaching has gained momentum in recent years as a means of solving scheduling problems and utilizing space, equipment, and the services of professional staff more efficiently. Of the many variations possible, the most basic—and the most popular—is *the single-subject plan.* Here, two or more teachers in the same department join together for coordination and instructional implementation of the material to be presented to the students.

For example, two drafting teachers might plan a machine design course together. Each might prefer to prepare those sections of the course with which he or she is most familiar. Presentation and evaluation would also become a joint endeavor. In this way, students receive instruction on every individual subject contained in a course from that teacher who is most informed on the subject.

The interdisciplinary approach to team teaching becomes an organizational nightmare if tried within the confines of the traditional school system. However, if the faculty has previously decided to restructure the departmental organization, the interdisciplinary approach offers students and faculty an exciting opportunity in educational relevance. A thematic approach to teaching and learning is made possible by coordinating many subjects. For instance, a team comprised of a social studies teacher, an art teacher, science teachers, a home economics teacher, and an industrial educator could collaborate in the planning and presentation of many educational activities formed around the central theme of "environment" or "ecology," so relevant in people's attitudes toward the interface of society and technology.

Differentiated staffing. As a further refinement of the team organization, staff responsibilities can be assigned according to aptitude, interest, experience, and personality traits. Teachers are also selected on the basis of the rapport they are able to establish with students. The team leader, or master teacher, so named because of the individual's education and experience, is in the position of greatest authority and responsibility. In some school systems, team coordinators are on a status equal to that of the principal or superintendent, and often achieve equal financial rewards for their efforts. Through such a plan, effective teachers can stay in the classroom and need not become administrators in order to make high salaries.

Tutoring of individuals and the instruction of small groups is done by the various levels of staff teachers, while the presentations to large groups are made by the team leader. Local citizens, other teachers and students, and community leaders are also significant members of the team, for it is through their experiences that the outside world becomes better integrated with the classroom and laboratory.

Student teachers may form another level of the teaching team, providing youthful vigor and another viewpoint on the instructional strategies, while taking part in an educational activity for their own benefit and enrichment, as a part of their teacher-education curriculum.

Finally, teacher aides complete the team. Such duties as duplication of materials, operation of media centers, and test correction usually become their responsibilities, especially where little or no professional preparation is necessary. In the future, though, teacher aides with associate degrees may become a great force by making many specialized contributions in the field of education.

CHAPTER 15—PROFESSIONAL DEVELOPMENT

In industrial education, staff differentiation offers many possibilities for faculty utilization. Many practitioners prefer to provide students with information in the classroom, while others feel programs should revolve around laboratory activities. Each faculty member would have the choice as to the type of instruction on which he or she would like to concentrate. For those with outstanding verbal skills, the presentation of lectures and the conducting of discussions, seminars, and tours might be most appropriate. Those with outstanding craft skills may find more success in presenting demonstrations and organizing laboratory activities.

The staff organization of the school of the future will probably be structured like that of many other professional institutions. Just as a hospital has its technicians, aides, nurses, doctors, and specialists, so too will the school employ a multileveled personnel organization, with the inherent capability of providing continuing intellectual stimulation. Within this framework, an individual's professional growth will be governed more by desire, management expertise, and skills than by college major, degree, seniority, or tenure.

Measuring Instructional Effectiveness

The conscientious teacher is always eager to learn to what extent his or her instruction is effective. Those who work directly under a supervisor may receive suggestions and personal information from time to time indicating the degree of success of their work. However, too often the teacher goes along for the major part of the school year without being evaluated. In general, there are three available procedures for measuring the effectiveness of instruction: self-evaluation, evaluation by the administration, and evaluation by the students.

Self-Evaluation

Being rated by others is valuable insofar as the rating is specific, detailed, and expert. But in the absence of such rating, and even in connection with it, it is of great importance that the instructor devise a scheme for rating his or her own effectiveness and employ such a scheme conscientiously. To this end it is suggested that the instructor review the following questions.

Is enough time being spent on the work for which the salary is received? There is a tendency for some teachers to get into the habit of feeling that they are sacrificing themselves to the cause, when in reality, a time card kept faithfully for a month might show some interesting facts. It is possible to use much time in begrudging the service instead of using the time to accomplish the job.

Some teachers allow themselves to become engrossed in private enterprises. These tasks, innocently undertaken, and in some cases almost a necessity, may gradually demand so much time that they seriously impede teaching efficiency.

Is the working time correctly apportioned among the various teaching activities? Some instructors spend much time building equipment or designing projects, rather than instructing the students who come to be taught. Although the teacher must devote time to professional development and to establishing outside contacts, such activities should not be undertaken at the expense of the instruction of the students.

Is the work being carried out according to a definite, previously prepared plan? Are regular demonstrations and other methods of teaching continued systematically, or is the statement, "Go to work where you left off yesterday," becoming more common? How often does the instructor have to apologize for lack of preparation in his teaching? Is the course of study being followed, or has the teacher decided that it was too demanding, with the result that classes are poorly organized?

Is the teacher skilled in mechanical work? The degree of efficiency that can be reached depends upon the answer to the question. The best summer occupation for some teachers would be employment in a trade. Standards of workmanship and methods of procedure practiced by the students cannot be expected to surpass those demonstrated by the instructor.

Is the teacher's first interest in industrial education? Teachers who are making their work a temporary "stepping-stone" have no right to stand in the way of educational progress. Academically minded industrial educators can get beyond the use of the laboratory for a certain type of experimentation, but practical methods of problem-solving should be emphasized.

What results are being accomplished? Is work being finished in an orderly way, or is there an indication that the semester or year will close with the storerooms full of unfinished articles. Such a situation indicates inefficiency and poor management.

In what condition is the equipment? If the equipment was in good shape at the beginning of the course, is it still in that condition through constant care? Or is attention to it becoming irregular, and are methods of handling it gradually becoming lax? Poorly kept tools hinder teaching efficiency and put the teacher on the defensive.

Are new ideas invited and put into practice? Will this year's work be exactly like that of last year and the year before, in spite of the new ideas that have been offered by members of the profession, and the changes that have taken place in industry? Are new wood finishes, automobile accessories, drafting-room practices, and the like being investigated, evaluated, and incorporated into the curriculum?

Is the teacher making himself or herself acquainted with new means for evaluating student work? Is the teacher familiar with the attempts made to standardize phases of teaching through objective tests? Such tests may still be imperfect, but the teacher who would be efficient will hasten to make all possible use of them and to assist in perfecting them.

Is the school library being used? It is one thing to have a library. It is quite another to encourage industrial education students to use it. Is the "reading habit" being developed through the use of these books?

CHAPTER 15—PROFESSIONAL DEVELOPMENT

Is related and technical information being applied? The giving of related and technical information to students is important to the industrial education program. There are teachers who start out bravely with a program for regular presentation of such material. But often, for a number of reasons, the interest of both the teacher and the students diminishes. Presenting relevant information in an interesting manner can help to prevent this. No longer can instruction in a few manipulative processes be considered the most outstanding characteristic of efficient teaching.

Are personal contacts being made? Some teachers teach for a lifetime without really knowing a single student. An awareness of the problems of the students is a characteristic of effective teaching. Contacts with parents should also be sought.

In what condition are departmental records? The keeping of accurate records is essential to efficient teaching. At the end of the year can parents or prospective employers receive an intelligent statement of all activities of a certain student? If another teacher comes on the job next year, will he or she find intelligible and adequate information regarding materials used, grades, courses of study, numbers enrolled, and the like? Or must the new teacher start from the beginning?

Is the teacher's health being considered? The instructor is responsible for his or her own health. Supervisors and administrators may not stress the importance of good health until the time comes for the rating of a teacher's physical fitness. Then, the teacher who has failed to care for his or her health is at a disadvantage.

What is the teacher's relationship with fellow workers? The teacher's attitude toward other teachers in the department, and toward those in other departments, tells a forceful story. The instructor who fails to make friends with associates, or who has a low opinion of them, can hardly attain maximum success either in his or her professional work or in out-of-school contacts.

What is the teacher's relationship with the administration? By administration is meant supervisor, principal, superintendent, purchasing agent, or any other person in position to judge the usefulness and value of the service of the teacher. Is there a feeling of warm friendship mingled with wholesome respect for the principal or supervisor? Or is there simply a cool acceptance of orders, with an attitude of avoiding contacts as far as possible? The latter condition is not always caused by a feeling of insubordination on the part of the teacher. Often, it may result because the teacher feels that he or she should attend to his or her own business. Not infrequently, aloofness is caused by sheer timidity. Whatever the cause may be, not being acquainted with the administration is a disadvantage at the time of the annual rating.

What professional growth is being experienced? A teacher's life is complex. The school looks for things in addition to the number of hours spent in the laboratory. Among these is the teacher's knowledge of modern

TEACHING INDUSTRIAL EDUCATION

educational policies, practices, aims, and objectives. The teacher can obtain such knowledge by reading professional journals and books, by attending summer schools, and by speaking with teachers at institutes and other meetings.

Supervisory Evaluation   Many kinds of rating forms have evolved for determining the degree of efficiency demonstrated by teachers. These forms are of varying complexity and are used with varying degrees of thoroughness, depending upon administrative zeal and available supervisory personnel. The following listing of items has been made up from teacher-rating scales and will indicate a fairly comprehensive sampling of points commonly used in rating industrial educators.

  I. *Personal qualities:*
   1. Appearance—dress, alertness, cleanliness, evidence of good health.
   2. Speech—voice quality, diction, vocal variety.
   3. Emotional stability—poise, calmness, reserve, tact.
   4. Reliability—punctuality, integrity, sincerity.
   5. Interest—enthusiasm, initiative.
   6. Loyalty—to administration, to fellow teachers.
   7. Ethical standards—personal, professional.
   8. Attitude toward work—enthusiasm, initiative.

  II. *Professional preparation:*
   1. Manipulative skill—tool processes, chalkboard sketching, designing.
   2. Knowledge of subject matter.
   3. Practical experience in craftwork.
   4. Verbal communication skills.
   5. Knowledge of adolescent psychology.
   6. Ability to analyze and organize subject matter.
   7. Knowledge of related and technical material.

  III. *Teaching technique:*
   1. Arousing and maintaining interest.
   2. Clearness in presentation of teaching material.
   3. Class organization.
   4. Class participation.
   5. Skill in use of teaching aids.
   6. Originality.
   7. Following courses of study.
   8. Coordination and integration of work with other subjects.
   9. Evidence of pupil growth.
   10. Variety in instructional techniques.
   11. Testing for results.
   12. Results accomplished.

IV. *Managerial ability:*
   1. Discipline.
   2. Student participation in management.
   3. Routing of work in laboratory.
   4. Variety of projects.
   5. Condition of equipment.
   6. Use of exhibits.
   7. System of tool keeping.
   8. Making supplies available.
   9. Turning in reports.

The teacher's observance of these points and of others that may be used is usually rated according to a numerical scale. A scoring system of this type will indicate individual marks for each item and section, and the total of all points will indicate an overall score. The items listed may, of course, be added to and amplified in detail. This is done in some school systems, resulting in extended listings of qualities necessary for success. However, the items presented here will suffice as a checklist for the teacher who wishes to be informed of those qualities that supervisors and administrators are likely to consider as marks of successful teaching.

Similar points of evaluation are used in rating intern teachers under supervision in teacher-training institutions. There appears to be a tendency, however, to simplify teacher-rating scales for this purpose, and attempts are often made to group items into larger areas of success factors. Such practice should generally be welcomed both by the personnel who will do the rating and the student-teacher being rated. Simplified rating forms are also favored by many administrators in public schools. See Fig. 10–1 for a sample rating sheet.

Student Evaluation

It is important to evaluate one's own performance in order to direct self-improvement. And while it is important to receive constructive guidance from supervisory personnel, the instructor can obtain another valid indication of his teaching effectiveness from his students. An evaluation of student test results and student construction projects will help a teacher to determine the effectiveness of his or her instruction. An instructor may also evaluate personal and professional qualities by ascertaining student reaction through conversation or rating sheets.

The fundamental reason for the teacher's presence in the classroom is to facilitate learning. Since most students achieve best in a positive, constructive learning environment, it is imperative that the teacher provide such an atmosphere. When a majority of students in a given class fail to fulfill the course objectives at an acceptable level, the teacher must review his or her methods in order to establish improved ways of instructional communication. The level of quality of instruction is best evaluated through a review of the instruction which preceded the learning. The curriculum should be adjusted if a majority of students often fail to meet the requirements of the course.

Students who experience success tend to develop a positive attitude toward school and education in general, and establish a pattern of continued success. The industrial education program provides learning opportunities for many talented, active students who find it difficult to achieve in a rigid, sedentary academic atmosphere. Therefore, it is all the more necessary that industrial educators exhibit a sensitive teaching personality to make learning more enjoyable, and success more possible.

This leads directly into the second method of teacher evaluation by students. Often, teachers sense that they lack the respect of their students. The instructor must respect his or her students before he or she can expect to gain respect from them. Some teachers feel they must remain aloof in order to retain the respect of the class. Others may develop an authoritarian manner and rule by fear. Some decide that decisions must be made democratically, which sometimes diminishes the teacher's control of the class and may produce classroom anarchy.

To some extent, all teachers provide, in their classrooms and laboratories, a learning environment which is unique. Each student reacts in his or her own way to a particular learning environment. The teacher will find it quite interesting and informative to seek out student attitudes toward revising or retaining the structure of the learning program, and the rules and behaviors required by that program. Some students are open enough in conversation to provide direct, valid reactions. Others, because of lack of interest, inability to express themselves, or fear of the classmates' criticism, may feel more comfortable in anonymously completing a check sheet or rating scale. Whichever method or combination of methods the teacher uses, he or she will find the students quite perceptive when it comes to evaluation of the instructor. After all, these students have dealt daily with numerous teachers. The teacher should allow criticism, but should not submit to ridicule. The entire process should be considered in a positive, constructive manner by students and teachers, since it is one step toward improving the quality of instruction.

The Professional Educator

In order to be an effective member of a teaching staff, a teacher must possess more than an ability to instruct students in a particular subject. In some respects the most severe tests of the instructor's integrity and value come outside of teaching hours. The following suggestions may be of value at this point.

Be loyal. Loyalty to supervisor, principal, and superintendent is of utmost importance. One may differ with present policies and practices and still be loyal. The teacher who cannot sympathize with the work of the school and with those who are responsible for its management, and cannot suffer in silence, should use all available channels to effect desirable alterations and

CHAPTER 15—PROFESSIONAL DEVELOPMENT

innovations. There may be teachers who feel that they should be the supervisor or department head—sometimes justly so—but since they are not, they should try to be good instructors and not undermine the work of others in the school.

Be cooperative. Many teachers are good workers, but not good teamworkers. Cooperation is looked for in any school program, and particularly in industrial education, where the activities touch more directly upon the practical and technical aspects of life. Cooperation with the principal, the co-workers in the department, and with other departments of the school is absolutely necessary for the ultimate success of one's own work and that of the entire school. Lack of cooperation is caused by an improper or overly biased viewpoint. A suspicion of the motives of others, a feeling of insecurity in one's own position, a narrow outlook, and an unnatural concern for one's own dignity are all harmful to a spirit of cooperation. However, an optimistic attitude, a belief in the integrity of others, and a willingness to offer assistance will help to develop cooperation and professionalism.

Be appreciative of the work of others. Lack of appreciation of the values of academic subjects is sometimes shown by industrial educators. Such an attitude displays shortsightedness and lack of understanding. To speak disparagingly of the subject matter and teachers in other departments of the school is to show ignorance and lack of vision. No good teacher will attempt to build up his or her own work through the process of tearing down that of others.

Become involved. There is also danger that teachers of industrial education may fail to see notices on bulletin boards or otherwise miss various announcements. This is often due to the fact that bulletin boards sometimes are not located in prominent places. This means that such instructors need to be doubly alert with reference to announcements and general requirements. It is a deplorable fact that in some schools, "shop" teachers have proved disappointing in their attendance to special duties. The professional teacher will be eager to attend all meetings to which he or she has been called, and participate in discussions of all activities pertaining to the entire school.

Faculty meetings are likely to be looked upon as an unnecessary evil. Sometimes they deserve to be so considered. Where such meetings are scheduled and carried out as a perfunctory performance, with no definite plan or program, they may not be inviting after the day's work is finished. When preceded by purposeful planning of program and procedure, faculty meetings can contribute not only to the efficiency of instruction and administration, but also to the professional improvement of the teachers.

Whether the meetings are of special interest or not, it is the duty of a teacher to attend. The sooner he achieves this attitude of mind, the better it will be for everyone concerned. Many plausible reasons may be given why the industrial educator does not go to these meetings, and every other teacher can probably furnish similar ones. The industrial educator may need to give attention to certain tools or other pieces of equipment. He or she may have to attend to materials which have not been properly stored. There is probably some tendency on the part of administrators to overlook absences on account of these special duties. Nevertheless, the efficient teacher plans his work so that he can attend scheduled meetings for which he has received due notification.

Check personal appearance. Personal appearance and neatness of dress are important to the teacher of industrial education. In the laboratory, the teacher should be dressed for work. The dignity of the teacher's position demands that the teacher watch his or her appearance carefully both in and out of the laboratory. This diligence in watching personal appearance tends to subside with time. The teacher who is not alert to the situation may find himself or herself failing to apply the energy needed in this connection. There is no reason for being ashamed to get one's hands into grease and dirt in the laboratory; neither is there any reason for carrying that dirt outside the laboratory.

The custom of confining "manual training" to the basement, or to the most unattractive room, has left with many teachers an apologetic attitude toward the subject and its teaching. Although industrial education has been recognized as one of the major and most essential subjects in the curriculum, many industrial education teachers still feel that their subject is inferior to others. They hesitate to accept what both school administrations and the public have come to take for granted, that industrial education is one of the most valuable aspects of the school program.

Develop a professional library. No instructor can expect to achieve the greatest success without gradually acquiring a personal library. Just how extensive this can be will depend somewhat upon the type of work engaged in, and the interests of the individual. The amount of material will probably also be governed by the length of time the teacher has been in service. The material that can be gathered for help in teaching may be classified into separate categories.

- *Professional magazines.* Their purpose is to inform teachers of the latest ideas and the most mature judgments with regard to principles and practices within the field. Thus, they help teachers to be innovative in their teaching practices.
- *Trade journals.* These journals help to keep a teacher aware of developments in those industries related to the field. It is essential that the industrial education teacher examine trade journals. If the teacher fails to do so, he or she may find that methods used in the trade ten years ago may not be used now. One way to keep up with modern industry is through the journals of the trade. Some mechanical operations taught in school change more rapidly than others, but all are constantly changing.

CHAPTER 15—PROFESSIONAL DEVELOPMENT

- *Technical magazines.* Magazines of this type cover popular phases of science and craftsmanship. Thus, they contain many suggestions for the instructor. They often contain articles of interest and value to both students and adults, and material pertaining to related and occupational information.
- *Professional books.* Collecting and reading books pertaining to one's professional work may not guarantee efficiency in teaching, but they are indications of such efficiency. If in doubt, make a survey of those who have progressed and assumed leadership. Not that all parts of all books are directly useful, but they provide the reader with a background, a foundation upon which to base his or her own actions. Without becoming acquainted with those principles and teaching methods organized and presented by others, the instructor cannot expect to reach maximum efficiency in his own work. Teachers are usually eager to obtain books containing plans for projects and things to be made. They should be similarly eager to discover the best possible methods of instructing their students, and of transmitting values more lasting than those associated with the learning of a few tool operations and the acquiring of a little skill.

Establish relationships with industry. A person who expects to maintain and increase his or her effectiveness as a professional educator will not fail to establish and maintain contacts with individuals in business and industry. To one whose time is largely spent in the schoolroom dealing with maturing personalities, the opportunities to mingle with businesspeople should be cherished. Luncheon clubs, service groups, and others, are open for memberships. By participating in these organizations, the teacher may widen his or her vision and also gain practical outlooks on problems.

Time should be set aside for regular contacts with those who manage and operate industries. It is also important to keep in close touch with trade methods in craftsmanship and production, for these methods change from time to time.

Participate in the community. An instructor can probably confine his or her activities to the school and school plant, and still be considered a good teacher. By common agreement the teacher would be a better teacher if he or she participated in community activities. Any community offers many opportunities for worthwhile contributions to the common good. The nature of these activities and just how much time should be spent on them will naturally be determined by each individual. Charitable, civic, and church-affiliated organizations are often in need of contributions to their educational and recreational programs.

Educators are also becoming associated with political organizations in the community. Since they are educated professionals, as are doctors and lawyers, it is important for teachers to participate in the administration and operation of municipal enterprises. Many teachers hold elective offices in their communities. No attempt is made here to define duties in connection with these opportunities; it is sufficient merely to say that the leadership society expects and is entitled to from the teaching profession should extend outside the schoolroom.

Attend conventions and institutes. Some teachers faithfully attend conventions and institutes while others stay at home. Both receive the same salary. What is one gaining that the other is not? Those who go, if their attendance is voluntary, have answered this question in their own minds. But those who stay home, or who wish that they could stay home, have difficulty in finding sufficient values to justify them in spending time and limited resources in order to attend.

Receiving a first-hand knowledge of methods and organizations in schools and school systems where the most effective work is done is another advantage which may be gained. Programs of merit are reviewed by persons who have devoted considerable time to their study. The teacher attending the convention may find that many of these programs and ideas may be useful in his or her own classroom.

Leaders in the field may be found at conventions. To meet them personally, to become inspired by their personalities, and to learn something of their secrets for success should be worthwhile to every person in the profession.

The general inspiration that comes from hearing speakers of power and vision, and the renewed confidence in the value of the work, are matters worthy of consideration. "Without vision the people perish," is especially true in the teaching profession. The best of teachers will become discouraged when struggling along. A convention is a source of inspiration without which no progressive teacher should plan the year's work.

To participate in working out unsolved problems, of which there are many in the field of industrial education, to assist in clarifying aims and objectives and in formulating policies for this increasingly important phase of education should be the ambition of every teacher. Some will contribute little, others much. In contributing, if only by his or her interest and presence, the teacher assists in giving stability and permanence to the program. Thus, the program will have the capacity to provide the teacher with more opportunities for better service.

One test of a teacher's effectiveness is whether he or she is open to new ideas and suggestions. The spirit of experimentation keeps the instructor enthusiastic. Too many teachers are looking back instead of forward, and doing their work this year as they did last year. Their work loses its freshness for them and their pupils. Meanwhile, there are other teachers who discover and organize new methods, new products, new approaches. Creating new approaches, looking for innovative ideas in magazines and books, and seeking such ideas from those in industry is a duty of all teachers.

CHAPTER 15—PROFESSIONAL DEVELOPMENT

Many teachers who are doing outstanding and unique work go to their graves with their "trade secrets." It should be an accepted duty to communicate to others those problems and procedures that have originality and that have been found to be of special value. Such contributions can be made in magazine articles or in speeches at conventions.

Career Advancement

In the various divisions of industrial education, the teacher's task has grown with amazing rapidity. In some cases, the teacher may not be equal to the task. At one time, instructing students in only woodworking and drawing was considered sufficient for the smaller schools. Such a narrow program of instruction is no longer considered sufficient—except by those teachers who have not learned of the progress that has taken place.

There is a tendency on the part of some industrial educators to rebel against suggestions and requirements that, while upgrading the course, involve general training rather than instruction in specialized technical skills.

Teachers today are confronted with the question of professional advancement. The pressure brought to bear is variously interpreted. Some feel that the scheme is the result of the whims of the superintendent. Others feel that it is to increase the average scholarship rating for the teachers in order that they and the school might gain in reputation. Not all can see that they will be better teachers after having completed further study.

There are several important reasons why teachers of industrial education can profitably participate in programs that serve to advance their professional standing.

- *Teachers are rated largely upon the basis of academic attainment.* Industrial educators are in a professional-academic world, not the occupationally oriented world of industry. Teachers are therefore judged by the courses they have taken and the degrees they have obtained from accredited institutions of higher learning.
- *New teachers are more fully prepared.* Qualifications governing the entrance into the profession are gradually being raised. Persons already in the field with less than those qualifications will find more serious competition, and usually wish to consider the problem of attaining a higher rating through acquiring advanced academic credits.
- *The laboratory teacher should be on a par with other teachers.* This includes educational refinement, use of language, appreciation of general values of educational procedure, understanding of the entire curriculum, and other essential qualifications. Such qualities come from the proper attitude in regard to the general aspects of the program, and from interest in and study of the program's various subjects.
- *Personal contacts with instructors of other subjects are a valuable asset.* To mingle only with teachers in one's own field narrows the teacher's

TEACHING INDUSTRIAL EDUCATION

vision. Study and discussion of basic problems, and even of special problems in fields other than one's own, will broaden the teacher's vision and abilities.

The teacher who began teaching some decades ago, and who does his or her work this year as last year and the year before, is not as effective as he or she might be. Such teachers have failed to catch the spirit of progress through the various means within their reach. The demands upon youth are changing, and so are their interests and ambitions. If a teacher looks back upon past accomplishments, instead of forward to new possibilities, his or her material and instruction may become commonplace. Looking forward will result in research, anticipation, further preparation, and better service to youth, industrial education, and the teaching profession.

DISCUSSION QUESTIONS

1. Is teaching in industrial education sometimes used as a stepping-stone to other occupations? Make a list of reasons why persons quit teaching and go into other types of work.

2. As an instructor in a high school, what contributions could you make to the programs for faculty meetings?

3. Make out a schedule for the school year showing activities through which an industrial educator may consciously grow in the profession.

4. In what respects, if any, are teachers expected to be superior to other persons in personal conduct?

5. What means have been established by boards of education to encourage and assure that teachers engage in further study?

6. List ten professional books, with their authors and publishers, that you would wish an industrial educator to possess in his or her personal library and use regularly as reference materials.

7. Compose a list of trade journals and popular magazines that would be valuable in helping to keep industrial educators informed of new developments in industry.

8. Name the national associations and activities of interest to industrial educators.

9. Compose a study of six nationally known teachers or administrators in industrial education. Determine the influence of their educational and industrial backgrounds on their success in attaining their present positions.

10. In what way may an industrial educator compare his or her work with that of his or her colleagues?

11. Through what procedures may a teacher learn how he or she is rated by fellow teachers?

12. Design a sample rating sheet for student evaluation of your teaching in industrial education.

13. What teacher's organizations exist in your state for promoting industrial education?

14. Because of the inherent hierarchy in the differentiated staff, is it

CHAPTER 15—PROFESSIONAL DEVELOPMENT

possible, especially with an inexperienced staff, for negative feelings to develop? What can be done to balance the overall instructional load?

15. Establish a set of personal-professional goals as career development guidelines. How and when do you feel you can attain them?

ADDITIONAL READINGS

Allen, Dwight W., and Seifman, Eli. eds. *The Teacher's Handbook.* Glenview Illinois: Scott, Foresman, 1971.

Baird, Ronald J. *Contemporary Industrial Teaching.* South Holland, Illinois: Goodheart-Willcox, 1972.

Bakamis, William A. *Improving Instruction in Industrial Arts.* Milwaukee, Wisconsin: Bruce, 1966.

Cenci, Louis, and Weaver, Gilbert G. *Teaching Occupational Skills.* 2nd ed. New York: Pitman, 1968.

Larson, Milton E. *Teaching Related Subjects in Trade, Industrial and Technical Education.* Columbus, Ohio: Charles E. Merrill, 1972.

Leighbody, Gerald B., and Kidd, Donald M. *Methods of Teaching Shop and Technical Subjects.* Albany, New York: Delmar, 1966.

Littrell, Joseph J. *Guide to Industrial Teaching.* Peoria, Illinois: Chas. A. Bennett, 1970.

Pautler, Albert J. *Teaching Shop and Laboratory Subjects.* Columbus, Ohio: Charles E. Merrill, 1971.

Silvius, G. Harold, and Curry, Estell H. *Managing Multiple Activities in Industrial Education.* 2nd ed. Bloomington, Illinois: McKnight & McKnight, 1971.

Silvius, G. Harold, and Curry, Estell H. *Teaching Successfully in Industrial Education.* 2nd ed. Bloomington, Illinois: McKnight & McKnight, 1967.

Index

A

"A & M" colleges. *See* Morrill Act.
Accident prevention, 199–205
Accountability, 19, 70
Achtmuty, Richard T., 31
American Industrial Arts Association, 33, 37
American Industry Project, 39, 40
Annoyances in classroom, 163, 164
Audio-visual materials, use in programs, 91, 186–195

B

Bacon, Francis, 25, 49
Beginning the school year, 121–137
Behavior modification, 78
Behavioral objectives
   student, 67, 70, 78, 179
   teacher, 19
Bennett, Charles A., 31
Bonser, Frederick G., 32, 33, 37
Bookmaking arts, 31
Boyle, Robert, 26
Branched program format, 177, 180

C

Career education, 46–50
Certification of teachers, 14, 15
Charts. *See* Tables.
Check list for lab planning, 100, 101
Clary, Joe R., 44
Class records, 125, 126
Closing the school year, 231–235
Clothing, as course subject, 63
Clusters (occupational), 44–49
Coeducational programs, 92, 93

Comenius, John, 25, 49
Communication, as course subject, 64
Comprehensive laboratory, 99
Continuing education, 14
Correlated Curriculum Project, 45
Correlated lab activities, 93, 94
Counseling skills, 14, 17
Course of study
   defined, 57
   format, 66, 67
   selection of, 60
   sources for, 58–60
Craftmanship development, 83
Culinary arts, 31
Curriculum
   conceptual approach, 39–42, 46, 47
   project method, 33, 38, 41
   for technology, 50–52
   unit method, 38, 42, 43
Cygnaeus, Uno, 29

D

Data communication, 53
Della Vos, Victor, 28
Demonstration method, 133, 134, 151–155
Deviation score method, 212
DeVore, Paul, 51
Dewey, John, 30, 49
Dictionary of Occupational Titles, 47, 48
Discipline, 140–149
Discovery method, 158, 159
Display media, 183–186
Domestic industries, 28
Douglas Commission Report, 31
Dreves, Fred J. Jr., 50
Drill projects, 83
Duffy, Joseph, 51
Duplication processes, 180–183

254

INDEX

E

Educational imperatives, 72
Elementary school programs, 49, 50
Energy and power, 53
Enterprise program, 51
Environment, effect on discipline, 145–147
Equipment, 106–108, 111, 127, 233
Ericson, Emanuel E., 33
Evaluation and measurement, 207–227
Evaluation
   of instruction, 165, 166
   of student, 245, 246
   of teacher, 241–245
Extracurricular involvement, 18

F

Face, Wesley, 40
Facility design, 100
Fellenberg, Philip von, 27
Fitchburg-Dracut thematic approach, 42, 43
Flug, Eugene, 40
Folk schools, 29
Foods, as course subject, 63
Friese, John F., 33
Froebel, Friedrich, 27, 49
Functions of industry, 39, 40

G

Galaxy Plan, 46
General-unit laboratory, 98
George-Barden Act, 32
George-Ellzey and George-Dean Acts, 32
George-Reed Act, 32
Goal fulfillment, 88
Grades, determination of, 224–228
Graphic arts, 31
Griffith, Ira S., 30
Group production. *See* Team production.

H

Hammond, James J., 38, 39
Honor system, 115
Hunt, Elizabeth, 50

I

Industrial arts, defined, 30, 32, 33, 34
Industrial Arts Curriculum Project, 41, 42
Industrial education
   characteristics of teachers in, 12
   distinguished from vocational-industrial education, 33, 34
   financing of, 118
   goals of, 70–80
   historical programs, 33, 37–53
   philosophy of, 25
   teaching opportunities in, 237, 239
Industriology concept, 41, 42
Industry classification, 41, 42
Instruction
   evaluation, 14
   sheets, 172, 173
Integrated curricula, 95
Interdisciplinary cooperation, 93
Inventories, 110, 126, 233, 234
Item analysis work sheet, 223

K

Kirby, Jack, 42

L

Laboratories, school, 98–106
Laboratory
   maintenance, 232–234
   planning, 100–106
   safety practice in, 199–205
   sanitation, 114

INDEX

Learning activity packets, 177–180
Learning process, 70, 71, 168
Lecture, 155–157
Legislation, 29–32, 44
Lesson plan, 161–163
Library, professional, 248, 249
Linear program format, 175, 176
Locke, John, 26
Lux, Donald, 41

M

Magnuson Bill, 194
Maine State Plan, 39
Maintenance
  of equipment, 111
  of laboratory, 232–234
Maley, Donald E., 38, 39, 43
Management of class
  by teacher, 140–142
  student participation in, 142–144
Manpower Development Training Act, 44
Manual arts, 30
Manual skills training, 25–31
Manual Training School of St. Louis, 30
Marland, Sydney P., 46
Maryland Plan, 38, 39, 42, 43
Massachusetts Institute of Technology, 30
Materials and supplies, 108–111
Mean computation, 211
Mechanic arts, 31
Mechanic arts movement, 28
Media, use of, 169–195
Micheels, William J., 33
Mitchell, John, 39
Mobile laboratory, 99, 100
Morrill Act, 29
Motivation of student, 87, 88, 208

N

National Defense Education Act (NDEA), 32

New York Trade School, 31
Newspapers and schools, 20, 21
Newton, Isaac, 26

O

Occupational information, 67, 89, 92, 237–239
Occupational training, 44–46
Occupational, Vocational, and Technical program, 45
Olsen, Delmar, 37, 39
Olson, Jerry C., 45
Orchestrated systems, 39–41
Outline for the study of an occupation, 92

P

Performance
  objectives, 78, 79
  tests, 221, 222
Pestalozzi, Johann Heinrich, 26, 49
Philadelphia Centennial Exposition, 28, 30
Planning for instruction, 159–163
Plastic arts, 31
Power, as course subject, 63, 64
Printed media, 170–172
Problems in curriculum development, 42
Production
  processes, 53
  projects, 83
Program
  balance, 95, 96
  development, 81
Programmed materials, 174–177
Progress chart, 228
Project *ABLE*, 45
Project
  as learning method, 33, 38, 42, 45, 82–87
  selection, 61, 83–86
  to solve problem, 86, 87
Public relations, 20–22

INDEX

R

Ray, Willis, 41
Raw score method, 213
Recording grades, 227, 228
Reports to administration, 234, 235
Richards, Charles R., 30
Rousseau, Jean Jacques, 26, 49
Runkle, John D., 30
Russian Exhibit of Mechanic Arts. *See* Philadelphia Centennial Exposition.

S

Safety, 199–205
Salomon, Otto, 29
"Self-activity" education, 27
Self-evaluation, 241–244
Selvidge, Robert W., 31
Seminars and discussions, 157
Shelter, as course of study, 63
Silvius, G. Harold, 33
Single-unit laboratory, 98
Skill development, 211, 212
Sloyd, 28, 29, 83
Smith-Hughes Act, 31
Special student, 134–136
Stadt, Ronald W., 51
Staff organization, 239–241
Stern, Jacob
Student
    evaluation for teaching effectiveness, 245, 246
    exploitation, 115–117
    interest factor, 61
    motivation, 87, 88
    needs, 72
    safety precautions, 202
Subject matter
    in elementary schools, 62, 63
    in intermediate grades, 64, 65
    in secondary schools, 65, 66
    sources for, 58–60

Sullivan, James A., 51
Supervisory evaluation, 244, 245
Supplies, 101, 111, 127, 233
Symbols used in evaluation, 210
Systems Network Analysis Process ("snap maps"), 40, 41

T

Tables
    branched program sample, 178
    computation of the mean, 211
    distribution of grades using mean and standard deviation, 227
    evaluation of instruction, 166
    form for permanent record or inventory of equipment, 111
    item analysis work sheet, 223
    linear program format, 175
    linear program sample, 176
    personal evaluation, 215
    progress chart, 228
    record of purchase of supplies, 112
    requisition for materials, 113
    standard deviation by the deviation score method, 212
    standard deviation by the raw score method, 213
    symbols used in evaluation program, 210
Teacher
    as professional educator, 246–251
    behavioral objectives for, 19
    career advancement of, 251, 252
    certification of, 14, 15, 122
    changes in program by, 136, 137
    community involvement of, 249–251
    disciplinary role of, 144, 145
    education, 238
    evaluation, 241–245
    first meeting of, with class, 129–134
    preparation, 13, 237–252
    readiness guidelines, 128, 129
    role in learning, 168

INDEX

Teacher—(continued)
  role in safety practice, 199–205
Teaching
  accountability, 19, 70
  evaluation, 207
  loads and efficiency, 15–17
  methods, 38, 39, 151, 155–163
  rewards in, 10
  steps in learning, 11
  success, 121
  team, 94, 95
Team production, 84–86
Technology curriculum, 50–52
Technology for Children Project, 50
Technology programs, 88, 89
Terminology, in evaluation, 209–211
Test analysis, 222–224
Test construction, 214–222
Testing. See Evaluation.
Textbooks, 30, 171
Textile arts, 31
Tool processes, 61, 62, 81, 82
Tool storage, 102–106
Towers, Edward, 41
Transportation, as course subject, 64
Turnquist, Carl H., 46

U

Unit method, 87, 88
Unitary teaching, 38, 39, 42
Units in courses, 62

V

VEA. See Vocational Education Act.
Vocational education, 31, 44
Vocational Education Act, 32
Vocational industrial education, defined, 34
Vocational programs, 44–46

W

Warner, William E., 33, 37, 39
Wilber, Gordon O., 33, 37
Woodward, Calvin, 29, 30
"Working schools," 26

Y

Yoho, Lewis, 40